Ex Libris

About these two books . . .

We live in a time when all institutions in our society are being challenged, but none is under heavier siege than the home. Because the family is unquestionably the most basic and integral unit of our culture, great attention—secular and spiritual—has been focused on the problem. Guideposts, through the pages of its magazine, has presented many articles showing how husbands and wives, parents and children, brothers and sisters have coped with difficult relationships.

Now, we have selected two books which speak to some of these needs. The first, *A New Joy*, is by Colleen Townsend Evans, a former actress, now the wife of a distinguished minister and mother of four teen-agers. Mrs. Evans has written about family relationships with much sensitivity in Guideposts before, but this is her first book-length manuscript and we are impressed with her perceptiveness, her incisive way of writing to the heart of commonplace family dilemmas. Structuring her book on the Beatitudes, Mrs. Evans shares anecdotes and experiences about herself and her family openly and honestly. She shows how the merciful, the generous, the righteous, the peacemakers can be effective Christians today. The result is a book full of compassion, insight and practical guidance.

The second half of this 2-in-1 selection is Larry Christenson's much discussed *The Christian Family*. In its pages, Mr. Christenson, a Lutheran pastor, attempts to sort out the roles for each member of the family as he interprets them from Scripture. His categories include God's order for mates, for wives, for children, for parents, for husbands. Bucking some current liberal thinking and confronting situations which many family counselors avoid, Mr. Christenson sets guidelines for molding a spiritually healthy, happy family. Spelled out are specific procedures and principles for handling difficult situations all parents, husbands and wives must face. As a father himself, he believes in well defined standards and structure for children and consistent discipline when failure occurs. Guideposts feels confident both of these books will challenge all who read them. We also believe they will help many readers deal more effectively with the day-to-day family problems we all face.

The Editors

A New Joy

The Christian Family

A New Joy

Colleen Townsend Evans

GUIDEPOSTS ASSOCIATES, INC.
Carmel, New York

TO Louie

Gratefully. . . .

A moment ago I decided to write my acknowledgments — which may be a mistake at this time. You see, we are "packed" into our favorite spot in the high Sierra . . . the experience of being here as a family and the outrageous beauty that surrounds us make me feel grateful to everyone and everything. The Sierra are heady wine for me, and as a result these acknowledgments may be much longer than they would have been had I written them in the city. But here goes. . . .

First, my family. . . . I once heard of a man who dedicated a book to "my family, without whose help this would have been done in half the time." Ah, yes — but on the other hand, without my family's encouragement, interest, and inspiration I never would have begun writing this book. A casual "Hey, Mom — how're you doing on your thing?" from one of the boys . . . or a daughter who was not only willing to listen, but was always genuinely interested, meant more to me than they will ever know.

Then, my friends . . . those who prayed . . . those who urged me on and listened to what I read them. You know who you are, and how much I appreciate your help.

Then, the people and the books (other than the Scriptures) that have shaped my thinking on the Beatitudes. . . . My husband's commentaries were always so helpful to me in my study . . . Dr. Ralph Sockman's *The Higher Happiness* was filled with his deep insights . . . so often I found my own thoughts and feelings paralleling his. . . . Dr. J. B. Phillips's paraphrase of the Sermon on the Mount, my favorite translation and the one used in this book.

And then, the women in that first study group in the Bel Air church . . . sharing so much of themselves as we paraphrased and applied to

5

our own lives these powerful words of Jesus. What a fellowship we had as we studied, labored, and loved together. Thank you, gals!

And now you, Phyllis . . . surely, this book would never have been completed without your persistence and your gifts. Though we have only been together three times, you are a "soul sister." We "feel" together, and in the deepest sense it has been a joy to work with you. You have taken my little scraps of paper, my bundles of pages written in longhand fifty pages at a time, and with your editorial skills brought order out of chaos. I don't know how to thank you, Phyllis, but as you always seem to know how I feel—please know now.

Now, one final acknowledgment. (I warned you this would be long!) There are many who have taught me and nurtured me in my faith since I started on the Way. To them I am continually grateful. But there are those who were my friends *before* I started on the Way —and they stuck by me even though my ready answers and do-it-yourself faith must have been discouraging to them. They never pushed or preached—they simply shared their new faith in Christ with me in such a winsome way that—well, what else could I do? And so, to them—to that contagiously joyful group of young people —now not so young, but still spreading and keeping the faith in their own way . . . at Synanon House in California, in a classroom at Princeton University, in a psychologist's office, in homes, and in pulpits across the land—to them, a Thank You that leaps from my heart.

One of that group not only helped to start me on the Way . . . in God's grace he chose to walk it with me. I too chose him—and I choose him now. And so this book is dedicated . . .

Contents

Preface 11

1 The Humble Women 17

2 The Sorrowing Women 28

3 The Gentle Women 43

4 The Fulfilled Women 54

5 The Generous Women 64

6 The Sincere Women 78

7 The Peacemaking Women 93

8 The Suffering Women 105

9 The Salty Christians 117

Preface

I have just come in from a walk along the beach. It was cold today, so my nose is red and my body tingles. What a wonderful, beautiful feeling!

Walking the beach is something I love, but that isn't all. I need it. It isn't something I do every day for exercise. No, I save the beach for days when I need the sea's ministry. For there are times when I need the wind—like the wind of the Spirit—to blow the cobwebs from my mind and let me think more clearly. And there are times when the vastness of the sea reminds me of the vastness of God's love, and the tide's ebb and flow of His dependability.

One night I walked the beach until dawn seeking the strength I needed to face surgery—for some reason a thing I found particularly difficult at that time. Why? I asked myself. Then the words of my doctor-friend came to my mind, giving me a clue: "I think we'll find everything in good order, Coke, but we can't be sure."

It was fear, not of surgery but of the unknown, that tormented me. Over and over I told myself it was a common enough fear, but it numbed me. Release came only when I allowed myself to remember that God can even be—can *especially* be—trusted with the unknowns of our lives.

How many times my husband Lou and I have been drawn to the sea when we needed guidance on specific issues in our church or in our own lives. We realize that God is everywhere and always within our reach, so that we don't have to go to a particular place to talk to Him. It's just that we can get away from life's distractions when we walk the quiet beach where nothing interrupts our conversation. It isn't God who needs the silence—*we* do.

So it has gone—walks, too many to count, during these past several years when we have had the privilege of living alongside the sea. And so it was today. I needed to think, to sort things out in my mind, for I had been asked a question I didn't know how to answer.

When a person writes a book, he usually includes a preface explaining the purpose of the book. Well, I had written a book, and now Fleming H. Revell Company, my publishers, asked me for a preface. In other words, my readers would be asking me, "Why did you write this book?" The question was simple enough. Not so the answer.

I suppose I could say I wrote the book because I was asked to. A few years ago I wrote an article for *Guideposts* entitled "Express Your True Feelings." It was based on the Beatitude "Happy are the utterly sincere, for they will see God" (Matthew 5:8). Revell suggested that I write a book about all the Beatitudes, and I liked the idea. But that isn't the whole story, and the book didn't really begin there.

It began many years ago and certainly not as a book. It was a study, a simple, feeling-level study, that grew out of my own life. In those days I was a young wife and the mother of four little children. Although I had been a Christian only a few years, my life had been very glowing and exciting—up to that time. But with the responsibilities and work of a family comes fatigue, and one morning I woke up wondering where the glow had gone.

I began to think back a few years, searching for an answer. Yes, it was there all right—at first I could see it dimly, but gradually the visibility improved.

For several years before I married Louie I had worked in

the motion picture industry. I thoroughly enjoyed my career
and especially the people with whom I worked. During those
years I also became a very enthusiastic believer in Jesus Christ.
To me it didn't seem unusual that a spiritual rebirth should
happen to someone in my profession—I have known, and
still know, many dedicated Christians in the motion picture
industry. But to many people the combination of my belief
and my profession had a special attraction. Because of that I
was often asked to speak to various groups, telling them how
Christ came into my life. Even after I left my motion picture
work for my "other career," the one I wanted more, the
speaking invitations continued.

Because I have always been eager to share my faith, I said
yes to as many requests as I could, although speaking was not
then (and is not now) a thing I leap toward with joy. Eventually the pressure became uncomfortable because I allowed
myself to be influenced by a few people who felt that it was
not only my opportunity but my duty to speak about Jesus
publicly.

Yes, I could see where the glow had gone. It had retreated
to deep inside me. I was beginning to feel like an "up front"
Christian and obviously I was resisting the celebrity bit. It is
one thing to talk about being a Christian in front of groups,
but quite another to be a Christian in your home and in your
community. I longed to be more deeply Christian where it
really counted, but I needed help.

God has a marvelous sense of timing. At the very moment
when I really needed it, I decided to join a women's Bible-
study group in the new church we were starting in Bel Air,
California. I did it simply to learn more about the Bible,
never expecting that it would offer me anything more.

Our group met once a week, exploring several different
methods of studying the Bible. Then, after dealing with the
historical and theological background of a passage, we were
asked to rewrite it in our own words, forgetting everything
but what the passage meant to each of us, personally. As I did

that, the Scriptures suddenly became very real. I'll never forget the excitement I felt when I began to see that the Bible could be applied to life today—and especially to *my* life.

But why a book about the Beatitudes? I chose them because in these words Jesus was speaking to believers like me—they weren't very pious and they were far from perfect, but they had decided *for* Jesus. Now they needed His help in trying to live the life to which He had called them.

Help is exactly what you will find in the Beatitudes, for here is where Jesus spells out His gospel of love. He tells us what love is, how it feels, and what it does. Instead of listing laws and commandments, He explains how our inner motivations and heart responses can either help us express love or get in its way. Specifically, practically, and in such a down-to-earth manner, Jesus gets to the core of the Christian life.

That was what I needed several years ago, and so my study of the Beatitudes began. I wanted to find out what these beautiful words meant when Jesus spoke them almost two thousand years ago—and what they might mean to me, a woman living in our complicated modern world.

I immersed myself in Matthew 5, eventually becoming familiar with the Sermon on the Mount in every translation I could find. Gradually I could feel what it must have been like to be in that crowd of believers at Jesus' feet. I could see myself among them as I wrote a paraphrase of what I thought Jesus might have said to me had I been alone with Him that day. Finally, and perhaps more important than anything else, I prayed that the *attitudes* Jesus described might become a part of me, from the inside out.

Because it helps me to write down my thoughts and feelings, I began to record the practical applications of the Beatitudes as they came to me. Sometimes they would come during moments of meditation and prayer, but more often they came unexpectedly as I was rushing from place to place doing my thing for the day. And so, this book has been written on scraps of paper as I waited for the car pool to take my children to school or as I took my turn as driver and waited outside the school, on the program for a play, or on the back of a church bulletin when I was struck with an idea in church. (Forgive me, Louie!) My children are now teen-agers and therefore the jottings shared here cover the musings and feelings of years.

But—back to the question I considered as I walked the beach this morning. Why did I write this book at all? By now you know, just as I do. I wrote it out of my own need. I wrote it because I have found the Bible—and here, specifically, the Beatitudes—to be real and vital to me, a woman living today. I am sharing in this way because during the past few years I have learned that sharing our needs, our struggles, our joys, our affirmations, our love—in short, sharing ourselves—can be one of life's richest experiences. And so I am receiving perhaps more than my share.

If, through this book, I can help one woman discover that Jesus Christ is real, and that His Word is something she can use in her everyday life, I shall be forever grateful.

These pages are not about talking the talk, but about walking the walk. And now, I'll shake the sand from my shoes and get on with it.

COLLEEN TOWNSEND EVANS

I

Happy are the humble-minded, for the kingdom
of Heaven is theirs!

Matthew 5:3 PHILLIPS

Blessed are the poor in spirit: for theirs is the
kingdom of heaven.

Matthew 5:3 KJV

The Humble Women

Poor . . . I can't imagine anyone *wanting* to be poor . . . to be
totally destitute, in need, anxious, hopeless, frightened. . . .
Surely our loving Lord doesn't want this for us?

And yet, Jesus says that only if we are poor will we be
happy. . . . "Blessed are the poor in spirit: for theirs is the
kingdom of heaven."

There were many poor people sitting at Jesus' feet when He
spoke these words, and He wasn't telling them that they
never had it so good. No—Jesus had great compassion for
human need, and the sight of the suffering poor grieved Him.
Obviously He was talking about something beyond physical
need.

All right . . . suppose I were in the crowd that came to hear

17

Him speak—and suppose I were poor. . . . I wouldn't have come to get food—He had none. I wouldn't have come for money—He had none. But perhaps I would have come because I needed something else, something that only Jesus could give me.

Yes—now there seems to be new meaning in the word *poor.* I was thinking of it in terms of the kind of poverty we're trying to eliminate from our world . . . starvation, disease, ignorance. But there is another kind of poverty—one that is much worse and not as visible. There is a poverty of the spirit. And that's what Jesus is talking about in the first Beatitude.

"Blessed are the poor in spirit. . . ." This seems to be the center from which the other Beatitudes radiate. For unless we know how poor we are without Christ, we'll never reach out for Him. If we feel we can take care of ourselves, why ask for help—even from God?

Come to think of it, the happiest people I know are those who have tried and failed—even hit bottom—and then reached out for help. Realizing their spiritual bankruptcy, they asked Jesus to take over their lives. They entered the kingdom through the door of their own need, and they were met by God's grace.

They're not only the happiest but the freest people I've known . . . free to be, to love, and to let God work through them. They enjoy each moment, with no regrets for yesterday and no worries about tomorrow. They don't have to prove anything—they work because they *want* to, not because the world *expects* it of them. To me, these people are very rich—not necessarily in material things, but in the things of the spirit. They possess the peace and joy that come from walking close to God. And yet, this route to the kingdom begins with the painful admission that we are poor and needy.

For me it began during my mid-teens when, without actually seeking it, I had an experience that was both mystical and profound. One evening when I was alone, I went to my room—and found myself in the presence of a blinding white light. It was all around me . . . overwhelming, consuming. I was part of it and it was part of me. At the core of my being—in my spirit—I felt free and peaceful. I was aware of my oneness with all things, all people—and especially with God.

Ever since that moment I have never doubted the reality of God or His presence in our human lives. Although that experience wasn't repeated, I still have the strength and assurance it gave me. That was the beginning of my conscious spiritual journey.

For many years I didn't mention that evening to anyone except my mother. In fact, even now I wonder about sharing such an intensely personal incident, for I think we are in trouble when we base our faith upon experience or feeling alone. And yet, what we have seen and heard and touched is a valid part of ourselves. For me, that moment was where my pilgrimage began.

In the years that followed I held fast to my faith in God, allowing Him to influence my life but not to guide it. . . . I could do that myself. Then, during my college years, I began to feel a gnawing hunger—there *had* to be more to life than what I saw on the surface. We *had* to do more than go through the motions. There *had* to be meaning, warmth, closeness, love. I was hungry for more of God in my life . . . but I didn't know where to find Him.

Up to that point my relationship with established religion had been casual . . . I had wandered in and out of church. Now I looked to the church to show me the way to God. I joined, I worked, I tithed, I tried—and I found only frustration and weariness. The route of "churchianity" was not for me.

By that time I had gone from college to Hollywood where I was put under contract to a motion picture studio and

promised a creative career. I thoroughly enjoyed my work . . .
it was fun, exciting, and lucrative—and I loved the people!
Materially, my background had been very simple, and for
the first time in my life I had some of the things I always
thought I wanted . . . plus glamorous surroundings, stimulating work, and talented people. Yet underneath the surface of
my being—deep down in my spirit—my possessions added up
to zero. I had more of everything, but "everything" was not
enough. The gnawing hunger was still there.

I felt poor—and in a way that had nothing to do with anything external. My poverty was on the inside. True, I had
been aware of my spiritual needs for months, but now the
needs were greater. Before, there was always something I
could do about them—work harder, try harder, search further. Not anymore . . . I had run out of things to do . . . I
had done them all and I was exhausted. And what good were
all my efforts? Where did they get me? Spiritually I was
bankrupt. Let someone else try.

Someone did. At that most needful time in my life I met a
group of young new Christians. They were such warm, real
people, and I felt myself being drawn toward their loving
concern for me. They became my friends, and I began to
hear what they were saying about God.

My friends told me that God was real . . . but I already
knew that. They said there is a God-sized vacuum in each of
us, and until it is filled with God we will never have true
peace . . . I was beginning to know that. But then they told
me something I had never known—they told me how to find
God!

They said I wouldn't find Him by doing good or by working harder.

They said I wouldn't find Him through any efforts of my
own.

They said I would find Him through a Person . . . through

a Person so much like myself that He would understand my needs, yet Someone so thoroughly *God* that He could feed my hungry spirit.

At last I understood. At last I had been shown the Way. My friends urged me to follow it . . . to give Jesus my impoverished life and let Him make something useful out of it. And so I did. It was quiet . . . and simple . . . and very, very real. I said yes to Jesus Christ . . . and the God I had known to be real—but far away—came into my life.

What a difference there is between a vague sort of faith and a personal relationship with a living Christ! He has given me direction and a goal—and nothing has ever been quite the same for me. If I had to describe in a few words how my life has been changed by becoming a Christian, I would borrow these words from Jesus: "The man who wants to save his life will lose it; but the man who loses his life for my sake will find it" (Matthew 16:25).

Left to ourselves, we find this world a lonely place. No matter how many friends we have, or how big the family, we feel cut off from a warmth and love we can't describe. . . . It's always "out there somewhere"—until we open our hearts and let the Holy Spirit "in here." He is a part of God Himself, and He will keep us company as long as we live on this earth.

In our kingdom-walk we are receivers—doers, too, but receivers first. Yet not all of us accept God's gifts. Some people, because of their pride, cannot reach out and take them. They resent God—and they are never happy.

Pride lives a very narrow life. It must have all the answers and insists on having its own way. It talks too much. It has trouble getting along with people . . . it is prejudiced . . . its ego is so big, you can't help bumping into it. Pride wants too much and offers too little.

Humility is just the opposite . . . its life is full and active.

Humility is smart enough to know we can't know everything. It listens, and looks at life through the eyes of others. Humility has many friends because it has time and space in its life for more than itself . . . the door to its heart is never locked. Humility is thankful for all it has, and because it has received so much, it gives unendingly.

Humility opens the way to God and happiness. Pride stands back, hands at its sides, and says, "No, thanks, I can do it myself." Humility is free to admit its need for God and others and comes with hands outstretched.

Thinking about humility reminds me of two wonderful people we met in Edinburgh many years ago. Louie and I had gone to Scotland so that he could complete his graduate studies at New College. We had spent summers in work camps overseas, but this time we were to be away from our country and our family for two years — and we were expecting our first child.

Louie's advisor and New Testament teacher was Professor James Stewart, a man well known as a New Testament scholar and a powerful preacher. We went to hear him preach at St. George's West on our first Sunday in Edinburgh, and after the service we stayed in our seats for a long time, savoring the inspiration his words had given us. He was a man small in stature and gigantic in spirit—a man of natural talents, a disciplined mind, and the power uniquely born of the Holy Spirit in a life. We were so grateful that Louie was to learn from this man for the next two years.

As great as he was in the pulpit, Professor Stewart was even more impressive as a human being . . . and in the gentlest, most humane way. We might have felt homesick those first months had it not been for the many kindnesses he and his lovely wife, Rosamund, sent our way.

They came to see me in the hospital when our son Dan was born six weeks earlier than expected. They invited us to spend

Christmas with them and their family, realizing that this was the first time we were away from home for the holidays. And then there were the evenings we and our fellow students spent at their house, drinking Ros's good tea and asking questions of Professor Stewart late into the night. . . . And Ros pedaling over to our flat on her bicycle with flowers picked from her garden, arriving just in time for a "wee visit" while I nursed the "bairn." (We had a baby a year in Scotland, so there was always a bairn.)

The "gift" that meant the most to us came when little Dan was six weeks old. By that time Louie was filling the pulpit in a little country church in Penicuik every Sunday, and we wanted to have our son baptized there. Louie, as Dan's father, couldn't perform the service—and of course you can guess who we *wanted* to do it. But we just didn't have the nerve to ask.

Getting to Penicuik wasn't easy. It meant a forty-five-minute ride through the Pentland hills—in the middle of winter. A car in postwar Britain was a luxury few of us could afford, and so we took a long, bumpy ride on a bus. It was too much to ask . . . warm and generous as Professor Stewart was, he was still a very busy man. A friend of ours offered to do the service and we gratefully accepted.

On the morning of Dan's baptism, I dressed him in his warmest and best, and the four of us took the long bus ride to Penicuik. It was cold and the roads were icy, so the ride was longer than usual. When we arrived at the church I was taken to the vestry. Then, at the appropriate moment in the service, I was led down the aisle, holding Dan in my arms. Out of the corner of my eye I thought I recognized a man sitting in the rear of the church. After the sacrament, I turned to walk back down the aisle and this time I got a better look. I had been right the first time—it *was* Professor Stewart! Hearing one of our friends mention that Dan was going to be baptized, he had come all the way out on the bus by himself to be there. After the service he slipped away as quietly as he came. *But he had been there.* In that act, and in countless others like it, he and Ros taught me more about the Christian life and attitude than all his sermons put together. Truly they are two who walk humbly with their Lord.

To be poor in spirit is to be in touch with our own need. It's uncomfortable . . . that's why our own spiritual need must be filled before we can touch the needs of others. Before we can appreciate the worth of another human being, we must feel that we ourselves are of value. And many of us don't.

It's a funny thing about pride . . . often it's a cover-up for a low opinion of the self. It's a way of saying, "All right, world, I know nobody can love me—so I'll look after myself!" It doesn't even give God a chance.

I have a friend, a very lovely person, who only a few years ago had so little feeling of self-worth that she almost called it quits. She was so desperately in need of self-respect that she was completely unable to give to others. Margot even found it difficult to function as wife and mother, but she covered up her sense of deficiency with a layer of pride. None of us realized how empty she felt inside.

One day Margot felt a mysterious stirring within her. Gently, but persistently, it pushed against her pride until it cracked . . . without quite understanding what she was doing, Margot reached out for help. She began coming to church for counseling, and when her minister realized how deep her feelings of unworthiness were, he persuaded her to see a sensitive, caring psychiatrist.

It's wonderful how God uses time and people. For many long, tiring months the minister and the psychiatrist worked with Margot and through them God was able to bring about a healing in her life.

Margot was driving home from the psychiatrist's office one day after a session that had been a breakthrough . . . a moment when the light of understanding broke through to her darkened spirit. As she drove through the park she began to feel warmed by that inner light and suddenly she found herself saying, "Margot, you're a precious person . . . you're special." Over and over she said it until she began to cry. She pulled over, stopped the car and sat basking in a wonderful new awareness of God's love for her.

When Margot started the car to drive home, she did something significant. She reached down and fastened her seat belt. She had never done that before. She had never cared enough about herself before. Now, in one simple action, she was saying, "God cares for me . . . and *I* care."

Margot was beginning a whole new life that was totally different from anything she had known. Love—God's love— transformed her into a generous and thoughtful person. Being able to receive made her able to give . . . and as she looked around she saw how much she was needed. At last she could look beyond herself to others.

A Christian walks humbly with his Lord, or he doesn't walk the Way. Humility itself can become proud—proud of being loved, proud of serving, proud of achieving. That's when Jesus reminds us of our poverty . . . to keep us humble, He takes us through one of life's many Valleys of Humiliation.

I don't know how to avoid these valleys—there are no detours along the Way. And I don't like what I just wrote—but I believe it.

Many years ago Louie and I wanted to go to Africa. Louie had been there earlier and he had lost his heart to it. I liked what he told me about the country, and especially about the people. In America we have so many external things that our hands do not easily reach out to receive what God offers. But in the Third World, where people have had to struggle and

suffer through disease, famine, and poverty, there seems to be
a willingness—even an eagerness—to reach out and accept
God's grace. The reports we've recently received from friends
in these areas thrill us as we hear that Christ is becoming
Lord to millions. And even back then, that was where we
wanted to work!

Hopefully, we offered ourselves—once in the beginning of
our ministry and again several years later. Each time the door
closed gently but firmly, and finally we got the message—
"Keep serving where you are."

And where were we? Right smack in the middle of affluent
America!

Don't get me wrong—it's not that I feel a person has to be
economically poor to be humble. Some of the most humble
people I know are in our present congregation—and they
would be considered affluent. But material wealth *can* blind
us to the needs of the deprived . . . exclusive, gracious living
can make us forget those who know of the gracious life only
from movies and TV . . . built-in security *can* make us in-
sensitive to those who have to worry about how they will pay
their bills all their lives. Worst of all, more than enough *can*
make us forget that we always need Christ.

Gradually we began to understand the meaning in the door
that closed . . . we have come to see the areas we serve as
bursting with potential for God. We are grateful for the challenge, and truly humbled by it. But make no mistake about it
—there are many Valleys of Humiliation in the City of
Affluence. We've been through some of them.

I especially remember being installed into the ministry of
one of our churches. Our friend, the Reverend James Jones,
was giving the charge to Louie when he pointed a finger at us
and said, "I have a feeling that in this place you will have to
decrease so that Christ can increase."

They were hard words for us to hear, but Jim was right. In

fact, he was prophetic. Through the years Christ *has* increased . . . and there *have* been valleys for us, many of them. But there has also been joy, joy in the fulfilling of the promise that "Every valley shall be exalted . . ." (Isaiah 40:4 KJV). It has often been painful for us to be put in touch with our own spiritual need, but it has brought us—and kept us—close to God. And believe me, that *is* happiness!

Yes, I'm ready now to go on to the other Beatitudes, Jesus. I need Your gifts so very much, and so I'm going with my hands open and outstretched. I want to learn what it means to be a Christian in the deepest sense. I want to become the kind of person You can use.

Happy is the woman who knows that without God she is nothing . . . but that with God working through her, she has the strength and power of His love. This woman will be quick to sense longing in the human spirit, and where there is need she will nourish it. Her humility will come from the very center of her being, and it will never allow her to look down on anyone—not even on people who look down on people. . . . And because her humility is real, she will know a bit of heaven right here on earth.

2

Happy are those who know what sorrow means,
for they will be given courage and comfort!

Matthew 5:4 PHILLIPS

Blessed are they that mourn: for they shall be
comforted.

Matthew 5:4 KJV

The Sorrowing Women

It's hard for me to think about mourning, Jesus. Mourning
is so painful, I just can't see how any kind of happiness can
come of it.

And yet You say it will. . . . You're telling us—*urging* us—
to mourn, to sorrow, so there must be something good in it
for us, something beyond the pain. Then I must look further . . . until I understand this Beatitude. It's important.

To mourn . . . what does it mean? To give way? to bend? to
break? Webster says simply, "To feel or express sorrow."
That helps a little, and it makes sense. To mourn is to *feel*
pain, to allow it to penetrate us, not to brace ourselves
against it. It means we can't pick and choose only the parts of

28

life that we like and reject the rest. No, if we are to experience life truly, deeply, and realistically, we must be vulnerable to all of life . . . not only its joys, but its sorrows as well.

But there's more, much more, to mourning. Even Webster suggests that the feeling of sorrow is not enough. We must express it, let it pass through us. And do we? How often I have heard people say, "Share your joys, but keep your sorrows to yourself." I think I know what they mean—no one likes to be around a person who wallows in self-pity, using sorrow as a means of attracting attention. But that's sickness, not mourning.

The heart was never meant to be a prison for pain. When we stifle an honest expression of real sorrow, we're denying part of our humanity. And if we are Jesus followers, we're denying His promise: "Happy are those who know what sorrow means, for they will be given courage and comfort."

The words of this Beatitude are simple, but their implication is deep and sound. It means that there *can* be comfort for our sorrows, but only if we face loss, fear, and anxiety squarely. When we allow ourselves to feel the pain of mourning, then we can be healed.

Somehow many of us Christians have come to believe just the opposite. We think that if we become truly spiritual the blows of life will not reach us; and that if they do, we will have the power to rise above them instantly. Is this really true? Does Christianity offer some kind of holy immunity against grief and pain? And does "living victoriously" mean living beyond fear, discouragement, loneliness, and desolation? I wonder . . . I really wonder. If it's true, then the Beatitude is false—and we know it is not.

Jesus is telling us to feel everything. To be spiritually alive is not to be dead to hurt and pain, but to be free to experience them, trusting God to bring us through them safely.

We need the dark nights, sleepless and agonizing as they are. We need the hurts that keep us tender and the unexplained sorrows that stretch our faith and trust. Living through them will make us different people—and the difference can be good!

Many years ago I spent a summer working as a volunteer, helping to build a refugee camp on the outskirts of Paris. I worked side by side with men and women who had been victims of a war, and as we came to know each other as friends their stories gradually tumbled out. They had lived through unbelievable terror and persecution, and although their dark night had passed, the fact that they had suffered would always be a part of their lives. Clearly they were different from the rest of us—sorrow had taught them what was really important in life. It had made them extremely sensitive to other people's needs. They gave instead of asking, they comforted when others complained. They were some of the most understanding, expressive human beings I have ever met. And through them I learned how God works through our dark nights, using them to deepen the shallow areas of our lives.

Then it's right for Christians to mourn, isn't it, Jesus? Is that what You're telling us in this Beatitude? Are You saying that, as Christians, we should feel *more* of life, not less? Yes, I think I understand. Unless we open ourselves up to pain and hurt and loss, You cannot heal us . . . for by shutting out the sorrow, we shut You out, too.

You knew the dark nights . . . many of them. And when You felt something, You didn't try to hide it. When Your friend Lazarus died, You cried, just the way I cry when a good friend is gone. It's not that I think I won't see my friend again—for I believe in Your heaven—but I will miss her here on earth.

In our church, which is quite large, we are in touch with death thirty or forty times a year. Still I find it hard to accept its frequency and finality. Part of me rejoices, knowing that death opens a door to an existence far more beautiful than I can comprehend. But another part of me — the here-and-now, earthy part — finds it hard to accept the physical separation and the sense of loss. Having known and loved the person, I mourn.

And when I mourn I am filled with pain that seems unbearable at first. But only at first. It doesn't go away quickly — in fact, it doesn't go away at all. It changes . . . as it pushes back the walls of my resistance to death, the pain itself is softened. Sometimes it turns to tears, and sometimes to quiet moments of reflection. It doesn't matter which. The important thing is that I am made vulnerable, receptive — to more pain? Perhaps, but certainly to God's healing love. And Jesus, who knew the human longing for a departed friend, makes the pain bearable and the loss understandable.

But sorrow can be a hardening experience as well. I have a friend who lost someone very close to her, and while many of us tried to comfort her, she wasn't open to a helping hand, human or divine. Somewhere in her childhood she had been taught to hide her feelings, especially the sad ones, and today, more than a year after her tragic loss, she is still unreachable. The pain inside her has grown in upon itself and become a kind of spiritual malignancy. The iron will that locks it in, locks the healing out.

Recently I learned that my friend is in the hospital and I'm concerned about her. If only she could unlock her heart and let the hurt, the loneliness, and the bitterness out into the open where Jesus could apply His healing light. Then perhaps she could share her grief with a friend — for God uses people in His healing process, too, and there are many who

care. I pray she will—oh, how I pray she will! But the decision is hers. The lock on the door of my friend's heart is on
the inside, and only she can open it.

How different the experience of mourning has been in the
life of another good friend. Mary and Joel Stein were two of
the most beautiful people I've ever known. They met and
married a little later than most couples and were blessed with
an immense capacity to enjoy each other. I knew them
through my work when I was a single career girl, and I don't
think they ever realized how much inspiration I found just
being in their home. Joel was quite a powerful man in our
field, but he was even more successful as a human being . . .
so warm, open, communicative, and real. His wife Mary was
a vivacious, outgoing woman who deserved him in every way.
In an industry not known for happy marriages, theirs was an
uncommonly good one.

For many years the Steins were childless. Then Mary gave
birth to a son who brought new meaning and joy to their
very happy home. And suddenly it was over. There wasn't
even a warning. One day Joel had a heart attack and a few
hours later he was gone. Everybody who knew and loved him
was shocked, but Mary's loss seemed unbearable. She was a
strong-minded person who always seemed able to face anything in life . . . but could she face death?

I was with Mary soon after Joel died, and I'll never forget
what she said: "Oh, Colleen, life will never be the same without him." I wondered whether she would be able to go on
with life at all. . . . How I longed to share her suffering, to
bring some rest to the tired, sleepless eyes. But I could only
wait . . . and pray . . . and hope.

I couldn't help asking myself whether Joel's death would
have been more bearable if Mary had been prepared for it . . .
perhaps a lingering illness softens the final blow? But as I and
Mary's other friends watched her go through her dark night,

we realized that death—whenever it comes, however it comes—is a stunning, rending loss.

Death will come to all of us, and to all we know and love. Yet it's only a word, never real, until it strikes close to us. There is nothing we can do beforehand to lessen its pain. It will pass through us or remain forever outside us waiting to get in. It will not go away.

Is mourning cruel? Yes, terribly. But God doesn't bring it upon us as a punishment or a toughening process. Mourning is part of our human condition. Because we can love—and because we need love—we must get close to other human beings. Our lives touch and mingle . . . we add to each other . . . and when a loved one is torn away, our love bleeds. That is mourning.

If there were some preventive spiritual medicine we could take ahead of time to lessen the pain and shorten the long days and weeks and months of sorrow—what then? Mourning would be simply an event that occurred, an obstacle along our way, but nothing that left its mark upon us. No happiness could possibly come of it, for we would never reach the second part of the Beatitude—God's refining, deepening, life-changing comfort.

I understood that when I watched Mary struggle with her pain. Gradually the confusion began to sort itself out and she felt some of her former strength returning. She had been right—life *wouldn't* be the same for her without Joel. Not ever. But God, working through the love and warmth of Mary's friends, helped her to see that life was still good. That appreciation was something she wanted to pass on to her son. And she did. Because she left herself open to sorrow—yet never indulged herself in it—she found Someone to share it with her. Then, when she was strong enough, she was able to lift the burden of grief from her child.

Fern, another very special friend of mine, was a different

kind of woman. Quiet, soft-spoken, vulnerable, her whole existence revolved around her young doctor-husband. They were happy, they had much to look forward to . . . and then Tom was gone and there was nothing left. Or so it seemed to Fern. Later she told me about those terrible days.

At first there was shock, a refusal to believe that Tom was dead. Then there was contempt for the life that lay ahead of her, a life she didn't want to live. For besides Fern's loneliness, there were practical problems to face . . . two children to support, her husband's aging mother to care for, very little money, no job, and no training for one.

Even worse was the call from the tomb, the visits to the graveside again and again. "I was like the women who went to Christ's tomb, weeping and carrying spices, expecting to minister to His body," Fern said. "But you remember how the angel met them at the tomb and told them that Jesus wasn't there? In a way, that's what happened to me. One day I began to cry, and that was the beginning of my letting go of sorrow. I could feel God standing close to me and I knew that my tears were part of His therapy. He came to me through them, because then He could get at my pain."

Fern realized that she had to make a decision. If she truly believed in God's promise of comfort, she had to trust Him completely. She had to depend on Him to give her the courage to face life again. Of course she couldn't do it herself . . . and that's why the future had looked so impossibly difficult to her. She never could have found her way alone in such darkness. But she didn't have to . . . there was a Light. . . . And oh, what an eager receiver she was! She not only accepted the Light, she absorbed it . . . it became part of her.

"God brings us comfort in so many ways," Fern said. "I could see Him reaching out to heal me through other people . . . in a handshake, in a smile, or a single word. And then one day, after another sleepless night, I saw Him in the sunrise—and I realized then that I had forgotten that the sun *does* rise every day. I had been looking only at the sunsets.

"At last I could commit Tom to God and stop being a tomb-looker. I knew that eventually I would be able to feel joy because my husband was in the presence of the Risen Lord. It was as if the stone of sorrow, like the stone closing Christ's tomb, had been rolled aside and I could see that God was there."

It was time for Fern to go on in life. We all knew it because we could feel God working through us to help her. First there was a job—a job she could handle and one that gave her room to grow. Then there were friends and family to help care for the children and Tom's mother, giving Fern time to adjust to the demands of a home and a job.

Finally there was joy—joy in her memories of a wonderful life with Tom . . . recalling the happy times they shared, the struggles that brought them closer and deepened their love . . . anticipation of the reunion they would have someday.

Fern never pitied herself, never became morbid on holidays or on the anniversary of Tom's death. "God wants us to celebrate life," she said. "And Tom isn't dead."

Neither is Fern. There is a lot of life for her to live. And she has become strong enough for others to lean on in their time of grief. In fact, she has become a great blessing in our congregation by helping many to turn away from the tomb. How often I have heard that Fern has helped someone turn the corner . . . going with that person to the graveside, helping to pray these simple, sorrow-touched words:

Oh, God, let this sorrow that has come upon me be to Your glory,
and reveal Yourself to others through it. . . .
I accept it, Lord. . . . Let Your name be glorified through it.

Fern came through her dark night because she opened herself up to its pain. She mourned—more deeply than anyone I have ever known—and she was comforted by a loving

God. She has truly lived this Beatitude, and I have seen happiness—hers and others'—come out of sorrow. I believe.

Death is not the only human experience that ushers mourning into our lives. In the summer, when our family goes traveling, we often contact old friends—some from college or seminary days, some from previous pastorates, and some I worked with years ago. It's wonderful to see them, and within a few short hours we always manage to catch up on the years of living. That's the way it is with good friends.

We're happy when we find our friends growing, stretching, and enjoying God's good life, and we celebrate with them. But sometimes we come upon friends in mourning, and it's not always death that lays them low. One friend may mourn a marriage broken after twenty-five years. Another mourns for an adult daughter stubbornly pursuing a course of life that will ultimately hurt her and others. Another is recovering from the loss of a breast in a mastectomy, and realistically facing what this means to a woman . . . she mourns over the physical, emotional, and psychological shock to her very feminine being.

As our friends honestly expose their pain to us and to God, as they open up and become vulnerable to Him, His light and love begin to do what only they can do . . . they heal. We have seen it happen, even in the midst of pain. As one friend said, "It hurts like crazy, but I'm beginning to feel this unexplainable peace—it has to be from God." And of course it is.

Very often there is nothing we can do beyond mourning. Like Jesus weeping over Lazarus' death, we must wait for comfort and the strength to go on. But there are other times when mourning is only the beginning of something that must be done.

I'm thinking of You, Jesus, when You mourned for the city of Jerusalem. You wept as You opened Yourself up to its agony . . . and then You went into the city to teach, to preach, and to heal. You did something about the causes of suffering.

Why do I find this kind of mourning so difficult, Lord? I'm learning to give myself up to a personal loss or tragedy, but this is something else. It's not always enough for me to feel someone else's pain, is it? And I can't express it simply in words or the touch of a hand. Much more is needed. In fact, this kind of mourning is very expensive—it means I must act. I must go to Jerusalem.

Perhaps, sensing the cost, I unconsciously try to shield myself. I turn away from this "Jerusalem" kind of mourning. Yes, a lot of us do. But You understand, Jesus . . . and You find ways to jolt us out of our apathy and bring us up close to our suffering, hurting, fellow human beings.

I'm remembering when our family first moved to La Jolla and we became interested in a project our church was involved in just across the border in Mexico. Along with several other churches and civic groups, we were helping to maintain a day school and maternity clinic in an impoverished area. Louie and I wanted to see how the project was coming along, so we asked the young minister in charge of it if our family could tag along on his next trip across the border. He agreed, and one beautiful, sunny Saturday morning the six of us piled into our car and followed our friend south for forty-five minutes. We were in another world.

We drove around a town bustling with tourists and shoppers and made our way to the hills and canyons. There, surrounded by hundreds of tiny shacks made of packing crates, scraps of tin, and cardboard boxes, was the *Casa*—day school, maternity clinic, and chapel, all in one small area.

I had spent summers in work camps, I had seen the aftermath of war . . . I was no stranger to deprivation at home and overseas. But I was not prepared for what I saw in those grim hills. This was *poverty*—and I will never use the word casually again.

I hope I'll always remember that day in my life. It's hard to believe that hope can rise from such depression, yet it did. Hope came in the form of the people who kept the *Casa* going . . . the lovely old Mexican lady who first saw the need for help many years ago and whose very presence is an inspiration to the staff . . . the Mexican teacher who runs the school . . . the American doctor who works there one day a week on her own time . . . and the volunteers who prepare and serve the children the only food most of them will eat all day. Truly, they are doers of the Word.

Children are quick to make friends, and as our four played with the *Casa* schoolchildren we talked as well as we could with the staff. There was a language barrier because none of us spoke fluent Spanish and the Mexicans spoke very little English, but we found that our hands and eyes could say a lot for us.

It was a long quiet drive home that evening. No one—not even Jamie, our youngest and liveliest—had much to say. When we arrived at our home (which suddenly looked very grand) we each went our own way, lost in our private thoughts. There was little sleep for any of us that night. We were in mourning.

We woke up feeling restless. We had wept for Jerusalem and now we wanted to do something—personally—about the misery we had seen there. But what?

Dan, our oldest son, was about eleven when we took our first trip to the *Casa*. Thoughtful, frugal with words, he didn't say much about how he felt. But at Christmastime that year, something he did told us very clearly. The students in his school decided not to exchange gifts with each other. Instead they sent food and toys to the *Casa*. The idea was Dan's, as we learned later from his principal. As head of the student council he had suggested the plan at a meeting, and when it was approved he helped organize it. Our son went to Jerusalem.

A few years later, during Easter vacation, Dan visited the *Casa* again. This time he went with a lot of his friends from church and they spent their vacation painting and repairing the school. It was a rewarding time for all of them.

Dan's ability to mourn, to feel another person's sorrow, has become an important part of his life. More and more we see it shaping him, leading him in ways that are right for him. Last summer he was part of an interracial team of American college students who went overseas to share Christian ways and means of meeting problems in depressed areas. It was more than an opportunity for them to serve — it was a meeting of minds, an exchange of ideas among young people from totally different backgrounds.

We're not all like Dan. Some of us take different roads to Jerusalem. And some of us turn back. It all depends upon our ability to sense sorrow and injustice, and our will to do something about them.

For some reason it helps me to experience sorrow directly or to know someone personally who is being mistreated — then I am stirred into action. It's just the way I am . . . the road I have to take.

One day several years ago I had a call from the mother of one of Jamie's classmates. Her name was Amy. She told me that the third grade, an unusually large class, was desperate for a room mother. Amy had been asked to help out and she said she would if another mother would share the load. I knew what was coming — would I be that other mother?

Well, I had just decided that my basket was full enough for the coming year. So I took a deep breath and explained how busy I was with children going to different schools, my church work and a few community activities. I saved the clincher for last: "You see, we have *four* children."

"Yes, I know," she said. "We have seven."

Well, I became Amy's helper for the year. We gave class parties and organized the usual activities during the holidays . . . and it was fun! We were a good team, and I made a wonderful new friend. Amy was a warm, open, considerate woman with a delightful sense of humor. We understood each other and could share the way we felt about our faith, our families, and the plain joy of being alive. It was a treat for us to be together. One night we even succeeded in getting our busy husbands to take us to a football game.

A few months ago something happened to change my relationship with Amy—and my life as well. I had a dream one night, and I, who can rarely remember my dreams, can still *feel* this one. In my dream I became Amy, and her children were mine. We were living in tiny rooms so crowded and cluttered that I felt I was losing my sense of dignity as a human being.

I woke up the next morning, a Sunday, feeling uneasy, angry, almost ill. I knew I had to find Amy, and when I went to church she was there, looking for me. For the first time since I had known her, the smile was gone from her face and her eyes were filled with tears. Would we be home that afternoon? She needed to talk.

We talked. And that afternoon Louie and I discovered another woman beneath Amy's cheerful, bouncy exterior. For Amy is black, and that day she told us what her life was really like—overworked, underpaid, she and her husband and children jammed into a four-room apartment because that was all they could afford.

This is important—Amy wasn't bitter. She didn't feel sorry

for herself. She didn't think the world owed her anything. But she was a woman, a wife, a mother, and she was hurting for her family. Oh, how she was hurting!

Knowing Amy, loving her as a friend, we hurt with her. We mourned . . . and we desperately wanted to help. How?

Somewhere in my memory something was calling for attention. What was it? A project—something our church mission commission was doing a few years ago . . . something that had caught my mind and interest, but not my heart.

I remembered! As I listened to Amy that Sunday and saw the pain in her eyes, I remembered that our mission commission had talked about sponsoring a low-income housing project for minority groups. A study had convinced them that this was our community's most urgent need. I knew the project was still in the works, but my passive support had not been enough to keep me informed of where it was at the moment.

Now it was different. I had a personal stake in that housing development because I was learning what it was like to live without it. And I knew what it would mean to someone I loved. Multiply that feeling by the number of families who could live in those new houses and you have a project that finally gets under way. Somehow two churches got together. Somehow two official boards joined forces under a determined and dedicated black pastor and our minister of missions. Somehow our congregations began to feel what I had felt . . . *human need*—not somebody else's need, but our own, for we were all one. A few weeks ago I looked at an architect's drawing of the project. Here and there in the split-level buildings the architect had sketched little stick figures representing men and women. But that wasn't what I really saw. No. I saw my friend Amy and her wonderful family comfortably settled in one of the larger apartments. And through seeing them, I saw their neighbors . . . *my* neighbors.

Thank You, Lord, for Amy . . . and for all the other Amys You will put in my life. I need them so. I want to be able to mourn, not only for myself but for others, just as You did. I want to be able to sense human need, and with Your help to find a way to meet that need. But first I must be free . . . free to feel sorrow. I'm not afraid of it anymore, for I too have seen the sun rise after the dark night. And it always will.

Happy is the woman who honestly faces her loss and opens herself up to sorrow . . . in her life and in her world. Because she trusts God to come to her and heal her wounded spirit, she finds a new and deeper meaning in His presence. She knows that she will never be the same woman again, but she also knows that she is not alone. He is there in the loving gestures of the friends who walk close beside her. . . . He is there to guide her through life's darkest times. Her own strength is not enough to sustain her, but she knows now that she can lean on Him.

3

Happy are those who claim nothing, for the whole earth will belong to them!

Matthew 5:5 PHILLIPS

Blessed are the meek: for they shall inherit the earth.

Matthew 5:5 KJV

The Gentle Women

I have a problem with this Beatitude. Frankly, I've never cared for it. Usually I pass over it quickly and try to ignore it.

The word *meekness* bothers me . . . when I think of someone meek, I see a mousey, "Caspar Milquetoast" type of person, and I react. In fact, I react so strongly that when I come to the words "Gentle Jesus, meek and mild," I want to stop singing the hymn. That isn't the way I see Jesus . . . I see Him strong—gentle, yes, but certainly not meek.

Still, I can't accept all the other Beatitudes, with their revolutionary effects on my life, and pretend this one isn't there. Jesus apparently thought it was important . . . He included it among the most practical guidelines Christians have ever been given. I must find out why . . . obviously I have misunderstood it.

Perhaps the word *meekness* meant something different when Jesus used it. I've never taken the time to learn the original languages in which the Bible was written. I'll have to read what scholars have to say. They can help me understand the historical background . . . I need to sense the setting in which the word was used. As I ask the Holy Spirit to teach me, He often leads me to the work of a scholar—a scholar whose gift opens up a whole new area of meaning to me.

I also look in the dictionary, but this time it doesn't help. It appears we have no single word to describe what *meekness* means in the biblical sense. And so I go to my Bible. As I search its pages, some new meaning begins to appear. In the Bible *meek* is used to describe two men—Moses and Jesus—which says a lot in itself . . . neither of them could possibly be considered *weak*. So what about meekness? What does it mean? Ah, here it comes . . . a meek person doesn't fight or argue with God. He doesn't defy His ways. No—just the opposite. A meek person submits his will to God. . . . He trusts God to shape his will into a force for goodness . . . into something God can use.

As I pondered this deeper meaning, mumbling to myself, my husband's curiosity was aroused. He pulled his Greek New Testament from the shelf and read Matthew 5 aloud. Then he checked it against his lexicon . . . and suddenly we both became excited about the new ideas that became apparent.

The Greek word for meek is *praos*. When used to describe sound, it means "soft and gentle." When used to describe an animal, it means "a wild animal that has been tamed" . . . one no less strong, but one whose strength has been channeled and made usable.

And when *praos* is used to describe a human being, it refers to a person who has been gentled, quieted, particularly after anger. This is not a weak person. This is a strong, spirited individual who has been tamed — molded — by God. He no longer flies off in all directions — he has a Way to go. Neither is his spirit broken . . . with God working through it, it is stronger than ever.

Meekness, then, means "strength" . . . but not raw power that may strike out and destroy. Meekness is gentle power . . . it builds, it lifts up, it restores.

The combination of gentleness with strength reminds me of two men we know who have similar qualities but use them in totally different ways. They both have talent, strong egos, and fascinating personalities, but that's where the similarity ends. One man lives for himself, driven by an ambition that can't seem to be satisfied. It isn't that he is cruel to his family, or that he doesn't care about them. I think he cares very much. It's just that he seems to be so driven — in his business as head of a large corporation, as well as in his social life among the VIP's who are always arriving, departing, overlapping. This man is also driven in his personal life . . . I get the feeling that he never wants to be alone, that perhaps he's afraid of solitude. But periodically his doctor puts him in the hospital for a few weeks, with a strictly enforced NO VISITORS sign on his door. And he is alone . . . but not by choice.

I don't know what drives our friend. It could be his desire for money, power, and position — or it could be some missing link in the chain of his life that makes him feel he has to prove something to be accepted by himself and the world. At any rate, I don't have to know why, because there is Someone who knows everything, absolutely everything, about our friend. He is the One — the only One — who can change his life patterns.

Louie and I love our friend very much . . . and in his way he tells us he loves us. We pray for him often . . . we pray that one day he will submit his life, with all its drivenness, to the One who knows and cares and can do something to help. We don't often put time limits on the Lord, but in this case, we pray that the miracle will happen before our friend's family is left bruised by the wayside . . . and before he is driven to destroy his own life.

The other man, equally aggressive and magnetic, has submitted his life to Christ . . . and what a difference that has made! Now, instead of using people, he allows God to use him as a blessing to so many lives.

He wasn't always that way. Louie and I met him before he knew Christ, and while he was an attractive person there was something reckless, almost destructive about him.

We met him at a party, one of the few that Louie and I have time to attend. I guess it's because I love people that I enjoy a good party. It's an adventure! There's always someone new to meet, someone whose life may be meant to touch mine, someone to be used by God to teach me something . . . and hopefully it works the other way around. That's why, before I go to a party, I always pray that I will be drawn toward the person God wants. And it has happened—many times.

It happened the night we met Hal. Just before we all sat down to dinner, there was a commotion at the door. It was a late and very noisy guest arriving. It was Hal. Obviously this wasn't his first party of the evening. Or perhaps he had had one all by himself before leaving home. Still, he was ready for conversation . . · in fact, he dominated it.

It was amazing how this man's presence seemed to fill the room. No doubt about it—here was a compelling, powerful personality. On the surface he was rough and loud, but as we were seated next to him for the rest of the evening, we began to see that the real man—the man underneath the scratchy surface—had great warmth, love, and sensitivity. We couldn't help thinking of the wonderful things God could do through such a man, if only . . . but Hal wasn't a Christian. He didn't seem to believe in anything but himself. Much as we coveted him for the Lord, we could only pray and wait.

Then, one Sunday a few weeks later, Hal and his whole family came to church—for the first time! I'm not sure why—perhaps out of curiosity . . . maybe a feeling of need. Anyway, it was just the beginning. In the months that followed, Hal stopped running his own life and turned it over to Christ.

Of course, I'm oversimplifying—it didn't happen that quickly. Nor did Hal give in easily. He struggled against submitting that powerful will to God—and at times he still struggles. From friends who knew him during his pre-Christian days, we learned that he was a man given to extremes. Some of this tendency remains—we see it cropping up every now and then—when he used to try to manipulate people into experiencing their faith in "the right way" (*his* way) . . . when he tried to link faith in Christ with a narrow political position. But always, because he is sincere in his commitment to Christ and puts Him before his own interests, he has abandoned these tactics. He has allowed himself to be led to where Christ is central to everything else in life. It's almost as if God had whispered to him, "You may be extreme in your love for Me, and in your love for your brothers and sisters in life, but nowhere else!"

Yes, Hal still struggles—but Jesus is a better, stronger, more persistent fighter! Now the real Hal has come to the surface where everyone can see him. He's a wonderful worker—not only in the church, but out in the community where his dynamic talents can do so much good. There seems to be no end to the things he can accomplish—but there is a difference in the way he uses his abilities. His strength—as great as ever—has been tamed. He uses it to lift up rather than to crush. Hal has gentle power.

Perhaps we must be strong before we can be gentle. It's

a matter of learning how to use our muscles, spiritual as well as physical . . . the hand that strikes learning to shield . . . the tongue that wounds learning words of comfort . . . seeking out a person's needs so that we may help instead of attack. . . .

Yes, I'm beginning to like this word *meekness*. And I wonder if it stretches the meaning too far to think of a meek person as someone bendable, adaptable to God and to life. Yes, I think it fits . . . and I think I need more meekness in my own life. So many things are changing today . . . our way of life, our values, our children, our institutions. I want to be able to shift gears easily . . . to understand and appreciate what is going on around me . . . to help wherever possible. So I can't be rigid. I must be bendable . . . strong enough on the inside to adapt on the outside. In other words, I must be meek in order to meet tomorrow.

Adaptable . . . that's a word I really like. *Happy are the adaptable* . . . it makes a lot of sense in our world. The unhappy people are the ones who feel threatened by the changes going on around them . . . they have little inner strength and so they look to traditions and institutions to give them a sense of security. Newness frightens them . . . they become rigid, and in their presence there is no peace.

But there are others who haven't hardened. Feeling the flow of life, they move in rhythm with it. Their trust in Christ is so real, and the security He gives them is so strong, that they cannot be threatened by change. They realize that newness is inherent in life . . . that if they themselves are going to expand and grow, they too must change. But they aren't dominated by change—they are free to evaluate it, to reject or accept it, according to its merits. These are the meek people of the world, and when I am with them I sense peace. With God's help, I want to be more like them.

Meek people don't make a lot of noise about their rights.

They will work for the rights of others, and in doing so they secure rights for all. As Dr. Ralph Sockman stressed in *The Higher Happiness*, the meek are more concerned with their responsibilities . . . instead of grabbing, they offer. While others fight their way through life, the meek walk quietly with God.

Yes, these are the people who will inherit the earth . . . and not by seizing it with force. The earth will come to them as a gift, because they are the true children of God.

I certainly need to be adaptable. It's not only my world that is changing . . . my home is, too—constantly. The only sure thing about my schedule for any given day is that it will change.

How many times I've started a day thinking, Ah, a quiet one, at last!—only to end up with unexpected guests for lunch or dinner, or a church group of fifty for a dessert meeting I forgot to put on my calendar. At those times it helps to be able to shift gears easily and noiselessly. (It also helps to have a freezer full of goodies—especially when your teen-agers keep the food situation in a constant state of emergency!)

Adaptability is something I've had to learn over the years, and I think God has used the circumstances of my life to make me more flexible. It wasn't easy for me during the early years of our marriage. I wanted so much to please, but it was hard for me to adjust to unexpected guests and interrupted plans for the day. I was used to an ordered, methodical way of life and suddenly my days were crowded with spontaneous activity. What a good thing it is that God created us with a built-in ability to change.

When I married Louie, one of my friends said that I married into a family that crowds more into a week than most families do in a year. And she was right . . . it was like jumping onto a fast-moving train! It was fun, and how I loved my

new family—but sometimes I had to hold on for dear life!
The truth is, they had a lot to teach me about being adaptable—especially my mother-in-law, who to me will always be
the Queen of Adaptability.

Even during our student years, we didn't just go to school
—we also traveled for the seminary and worked with young
people. Later, studying in Scotland, we served a country
church part time. Now I can look back with gratitude for the
experience.

I remember when we took our first church full time and
found ourselves deeply involved in the lives of many people
. . . it was a whole new world of sharing, giving, and caring,
and I had never known such happiness. I had also never
known such busyness, either . . . the last shreds of my ordered, methodical existence were fraying rapidly. I could feel
myself becoming rigid, resisting the changes going on in
my life. Then I realized that *I* would also have to change. I
would be rigid and sink, or become flexible and learn to swim.
I couldn't change overnight—we human beings aren't made
that way. But I knew, too, that God would help me to adapt,
little by little. And of course He did.

Now interruptions are so much a part of my life that I can
hardly believe I ever resented them. Surprisingly, I have
found "swimming" stimulating and pleasant—so long as I
have a little raft in the sun where I can climb aboard and be
totally alone. I'm talking about the few moments I set aside
for myself every day, no matter how hectic life may be. This
is *my* time—my time for prayer, for books, for quietness, or
simply goofing off. It is the one ordered part of my life, and
when my own inner needs have been met, I find that I am
much more adaptable to the needs of the people around me.
It seems that in taming us, God makes us useful to the others
in our lives.

Meekness . . . it's beginning to sound better, stronger, now that I know more about it. And meekness is something I need every day . . . for I must be adaptable to far more than the changes that occur in my world. I must develop an attitude of meekness—of adaptability—to the people around me, especially my family.

Lately I've been thinking a lot about our children and about the way our relationship to each other will change more quickly in the years ahead. All four of them are teen-agers now, which means they are in a period of enormous growth and development. Their beings are emerging, taking shape . . . and I can see how totally different they are from one another. Each one is a unique person, and I must adapt to their individuality.

A little while ago I realized—quite suddenly—that our children were no longer children. We were on a long vacation in Barbados—actually it was a study sabbatical for my husband. We were staying in a house our good friends loaned to us . . . a wonderful old mill house on a remote part of the island. Life was quiet and simple . . . no radio and, of course, no TV . . . the nearest city was many miles away and we had no car to take us there. Nothing invaded our world except the sun, the sea, the wind, and the simple things we had to do to live. We had our books and each other . . . and we discovered that we were very rich.

And there, in the midst of such blessings, God opened my eyes and I saw my children in a new way. Louie saw it, too. It dawned on both of us one night after we all lingered a long time at the dinner table. The food (fish speared by our sons) had been good and the candles were burning low . . . but still we talked on and on . . . discussing, reminiscing, laughing. It was delightful, enjoying each other so much—and then I realized that our children were growing up. They weren't just "our children" . . . they were people, people I genuinely liked. I enjoyed their company, their humor, their way of thinking. They were my friends.

That means I must be sensitive to their uniqueness . . . aware of their changing needs. They'll be meeting new situations in life, new people . . . they will change. And so must I.

Now that our boys tower over me, now that our daughter borrows any of my clothes that happen to be up-to-date, I find myself asking, "What can I do for them?" When they were little they needed me in so many tangible, obvious ways —and how that fulfilled my need to be needed! Now they will need me less . . . and in different, more subtle ways. As Dr. Haim Ginott puts it, "Their need is to have you *not* need them." This will require meekness from me. As they need me less, I must find other areas of life where I am needed more.

Then, too, like most other mothers of the world, I've done my share of dreaming about the future of our four children. And yet, even though I keep my dreams to myself, I'm not sure it's good for parents to form specific ambitions for their children. That's forcing a goal on them in words they may not hear but will nevertheless sense—and they should have goals of their own.

I can't help but think of another mother who, like me, "treasured all these things in her heart" and no doubt had glorious dreams for her Son. Was meekness hard for her, too? Did she struggle when it was time for her to give up her dreams so that God's plans for her Son could be fulfilled? And did she finally realize—as I must—that being a parent means molding children into *themselves,* not into what we may need for ourselves? I think she did . . . and I pray that I will, too.

What can I *do* for my children? The answer is obvious and I must accept it. . . . I must be like a mother bird sitting quietly, patiently, on the branch of a tree, watching as her young ones try their own wings. No longer does she hover

over the nest, offering the fluttering protection of her wings. That time is past. Now she preens her feathers with motherly pride when the little ones take flight . . . perhaps she hurts when they fall, yet she remains on the branch until they try again, refusing to interfere with the process that will eventually make them strong and free. If there is real danger, she is ready to go to them in an instant . . . and as there is always one whose need is greater than the others, she is ready to answer when he calls. But she is also ready to sit . . . and watch . . . and wait.

Dear Jesus, I'm not as patient as the mother bird, but it helps me to think of her—her quiet strength, her respect for her young, her meekness. That's what I need more of, Lord . . . this meekness, this inner strength . . . this bending to Your will. Then I'll be able to let my children learn to fly.

I can no longer ignore this Beatitude, Jesus. In fact, now that I understand what meekness really is, I like it . . . and I'm asking You to put more of it in my life. You know how much I can use it.

Happy is the woman who allows God to use her strength for His own good purposes. This woman has gentle power . . . she claims nothing for herself, but gives her life away in service to her family, to her friends, to her community, and to all those whom God has placed "in her basket." For by serving them, she is serving Christ. Like her Master, she is truly meek—not weak—and as He served others with no thought of anything in return, so does she. Yet love, respect, an honored place in the world, a feeling of worth and usefulness—everything a woman craves—will be hers. What more could a woman want from this world?

4

Happy are those who are hungry and thirsty for goodness, for they will be fully satisfied!

Matthew 5:6 PHILLIPS

Blessed are they which do hunger and thirst after righteousness: for they shall be filled.

Matthew 5:6 KJV

The Fulfilled Women

I have to dig deep into this Beatitude . . . at first it seems obvious. . . . Don't we all want to be good? And don't we feel much better when we do the right thing?

But there's more to these words than I see on the surface. I've been influenced by my world and its conveniences. . . . If I'm thirsty, I drink . . . if I'm hungry, I eat. Frankly, I don't give these needs much thought, because they can be satisfied so easily.

Suppose, though, that I lived in a desert land where water was scarce and one crop failure could mean starvation? Ah, yes, what about hunger and thirst under those conditions? Now I begin to see a difference . . . hunger and thirst become driving, powerful, urgent needs. They motivate my life and everything I do. I no longer simply *want* food and drink — *I must have them!* Without them I can't survive. And underneath all our modern conveniences, this is still true.

It is true of the spirit, too — and that's really what Jesus is telling us in this Beatitude. He's saying that it's not enough simply to *want* goodness . . . we must *crave* it. This world is our soul's desert . . . and unless our soul receives the quenching, nourishing qualities of goodness, it will perish.

There are right things and wrong things in life, and most of the time we can tell the difference between them. But just doing the right things because we think we should leaves us with an empty feeling. There's something wrong and we get no satisfaction out of it.

Jesus promises that satisfaction will come to those who seek the good things of God. He says that they will be filled — not with the material goods of this world, not with an easy way of life, not with something of limited value that can be taken away from them . . . but with the joy and contentment that come from doing God's will. The filled people are the truly happy people in life.

I think our young people understand this . . . if that seems like too much of a generalization, let's say that the young people I'm close to understand it. They sense what it takes to make life rich and full — they know it has little to do with money, possessions, and power, and much to do with giving, serving, and just plain enjoying. I admire their values. Our four children, for instance, would rather spend a vacation backpacking in the Sierra Nevada — which we've been doing ever since they were old enough to weather the trip — than at a fancy resort. (Which is fortunate for us, because we can't afford a resort, anyway!)

If there is such a thing as a generation gap today, it's certainly being widened by a difference in values. So many of our young people are disillusioned by their parents' obses-

sion with the things money can buy. While there are some
families who seem to grow closer together with the years,
there are others who are torn apart by what they seek. . . . Rebellious, disappointed children trying to pull down the expensive roof their parents put over their heads . . . parents
giving their children everything—except themselves.

I'm reminded of Pam, a lovely girl and the only child of
parents who gave her every physical blessing they could buy.
The only thing Pam didn't have was a warm, loving relationship at home—and she needed that above all else. But closeness takes time, and Pam's parents were too busy making
money to give her time. Closeness means a commitment, too,
but that had already been given to a corporation. We saw
what was happening, but there was no way to communicate
our concern . . . where there is a difference in values, there is
also a difference in language. So it was no surprise when our
phone rang late one night and we learned that Pam had run
away.

I wish there could be a happy ending to this story, but there
just isn't. Pam's parents know where she is, but they still can't
reach her "where she lives." Fortunately for Pam, she's young,
so we can still hope that she'll find happiness in her life   ,
but I don't think she'll go looking for it among "things."

Lord, I'm so glad You didn't say, "Happy are those who
are good. . . ." Who could possibly claim that! Not I! But You
said, *Happy are those who hunger and thirst* after *goodness*
. . . . Quite a different thing!

There have been times when I have hungered and thirsted
for more of You in my life, Jesus . . . and as I look back over
the years I can see that these have been the best moments.
But there have been other times when I've been caught up in
silly things . . . things that had no real meaning . . . and they
left me with an empty heart. And so the practical truth of

this Beatitude is becoming very clear to me. . . . Our happiest moments *are* those spent in seeking You and following Your Way in life.

But how do we do that, Lord? We're such material beings, and we live in a world that is built to serve our material desires. And yet it's only when we live the life of the spirit that we can find peace.

I guess we've got our work cut out for us . . . we have to turn our attention away from goods and toward goodness. I suppose we can begin in our minds . . . by thinking of goodness. . . . That's fine—but You know how imaginations are . . . the world is full of distractions, and our imaginations can run wild, leaving all our intentions far behind.

No . . . I'm sure there's a better way. . . . In Romans 12 it says, "Don't let the world around you squeeze you into its own mold, but let God remold your minds from within. . . ." Yes, God can do the job so much better than we can. If we let Him into our minds He can transform our imaginations. Then we can think in His terms.

We do have spiritual desires, just as we have material ones, but they need cultivation . . . deep inside us they hunger and thirst for the food they need to keep our inner beings alive. We have to bring these desires to the surface of our lives where they can influence what we do. And gradually our appetites will change. . . . "Taste and see that the Lord is good . . ." (Psalms 34:8 KJV). Yes, He is *very* good, and once we have tasted the kind of satisfaction that comes from following Him, we'll want more.

It seems to me that what we seek has a lot to do with who we really are. In other words, we become *like* the things we want most in life. And if it's money we want, we'll find a way to get it . . . but it will also get us.

That happened to a friend of mine. From the time we were

teen-agers, she knew exactly what she wanted out of life—
money and security—and plenty of both. Because she was a
girl of high moral standards, I knew she wouldn't com-
promise them to reach her goal. But she was also very determined and I never doubted that she would get what she
wanted. Yes, she did . she made it to the top on her own
and on her enormous talent Then she married a very wealthy
man. She had everything she wanted . . . or so it seemed. But
strange things began to happen to her life. . . . It was no
longer her own. Her days were crowded with meetings,
managers, contracts, and endless red tape. Boards were
formed to handle her money.

Our friend was a warm, caring woman who loved her
family, but she found less and less time for it. She belonged
to her possessions and she was becoming like one of them.
When she finally realized it, she began to fight for her freedom. With the honesty that was typical of her she began to
search her spirit, listening for the voice of need. And the
voice was very faint, because her spirit had gone unfed for a
long time

My friend made changes in her life . . . it took time and it
took courage . . . most of all it took faith—faith in the
promise that she could have a filled, satisfied life. First of all,
she began saying *no* to the things in her life . . . she didn't
have to spend all her time making money   . she didn't *have*
to worry about security . . . she even considered the worst
things that might happen if she lost everything. *Everything?*
Well, she found she could live without the things she owned,
but not without the people she loved. As long as she had her
husband and children, she was rich . . . none of her possessions had any real value . . . and once she was willing to let
go of them, they had no hold on her.

Jesus' promise was kept, as it always is. As my friend's
appetites changed (and appetite is what this Beatitude is all

about), her life began to fill with happiness. Her days were spent with the people she loved and her greatest joy came from the things they did together. She's still a very rich woman, but she has learned, as Christians should, to wear her possessions loosely. She uses them to bless others, as she has been blessed. Amazingly, they have blessed her, too—they have brought her close to human need, and this is what she hungers and thirsts to ease. Yes, in many, many ways my friend is deeply satisfied . . . at last.

I had another friend who sought fame. Somehow she felt that if she could make it big in her field she would have everything she could ever want. She was so lovely, so talented, so filled with potential as a human being . . . and she traded it all for a promise that never came true. She made it to the top, all right, and she had more fame than she could handle . . . but her spirit went hungry. At the peak of her career she was a lonely, dejected, disillusioned woman trying to find warmth in a cold, materialistic world. . . . And so she kept climbing higher, reaching out—but for what? She never seemed to know, and neither did any of us who loved her. We were aware of her loneliness, her spiritual and very human need, and we tried in our fumbling ways to help, but she always seemed just beyond our reach. If only she had been able to put her inner needs first . . . but her life ended, much too soon. I know it may seem odd to say that she died from a kind of starvation of the spirit—but I honestly believe she did.

There are some things in life we cannot understand, and this is one of them for me. I simply have to give it to God and go on. But whenever I remember my friend—and I often do—I pray that God will use me in the lives of the women I know. I'm not clever or witty or full of special wisdom . . . but one thing I know, both from my own experience and from those who are close to me: Happiness doesn't come from money or fame or achievement . . . it comes from God. And the closer we get to Him, the greater our joy will be

Today we hear a lot about the importance of being fulfilled as a woman. I couldn't agree more . . . and this Beatitude shows us the way — *Happy are the women who hunger and thirst after goodness . . . they shall be filled.*

Perhaps we may have different ideas about what fulfillment is . . . some of us want to put special talents to work . . . some want to right wrongs . . . some want to call attention to injustices . . . some want to add beauty to the world . . . some want to preserve it. There are so many worthy causes calling out to us.

I'm all for the gals who can do these things, but not all of us can be protestors . . . or crusaders . . . or teachers . . . or artists. Not all of us can juggle a home and a career without fumbling. Many of us will seek fulfillment right where we are . . . and that's usually at home.

When I think of being fulfilled as a woman, I think of being needed . . . the two, at least to me, are inseparable. Years ago, when we were studying in Scotland and our children were small, our life was simple. We shared an old, large house with another student family (later our very good friends), and we each paid twenty-seven dollars rent a month. Our basement kitchen had no modern conveniences. No refrigerator — but in Scotland, who needs one! No fancy stove — but a reliable old one we picked up at an auction. No central heating — but wonderful fireplaces. No washing machines — and with two babies in diapers, I could have used one, even in Scotland! There was lots of work, lots of joy, and lots of feeling very needed Yes, I was fulfilled every minute of every day, and it was deeply satisfying.

Later, back home in the States, I had all the helpful gadgets, and the work load was different. But I still felt needed. Our children's needs were more intangible, but just as real. . . .

Sometimes, as mothers, we begin to feel left out and a little obsolete when our children are no longer physically dependent upon us. . . . Perhaps this is when we should let our hearts feel out their needs . . . the need for us to be there when they come home from school . . . to listen when they're hurting . . . to hold them (if they're still small enough) . . . to rub a back when they're down and don't know why. This feeling, listening, scratching, rubbing—just being there—may be the world's most intangible ministry, but it's certainly the most filling. And its fullness will last us a lifetime.

It's a funny thing about seeking God's good things for yourself and your family . . . you find that you want them for others, too.

I remember that when I was a new Christian, I was eager to share my faith with everyone . . . the new life I had found was just too wonderful to keep to myself—and I certainly didn't . . . it overflowed onto everyone I met. As I look back I can see that I had more enthusiasm than tact. I remember one evening when I was having dinner with an actor friend and telling him about all the good things God had done for me—for everyone—for *him*. I'm afraid I never even stopped for breath. Finally, in desperation, he interrupted me and said, "Hold it—I believe! I believe!"

For a long time I had hungered and thirsted after God and His Way . . . and when He came into my life I felt such joy, such love and peace, such an awareness of life . . . it was so beautiful that I wanted everyone to know Jesus, my Liberator. I still do. . . .

But seeking after God and His goodness isn't limited to our spiritual lives. There are things to be done on earth . . . in our world. If I seek a good life and social justice for myself and my family, I must see that others have it, too. I must be-

come involved in the world outside my door. How much involvement depends upon the other demands on my time.
. . . One year I may work with a group that is trying to lift
the level of life in the ghetto . . . another year I may work
toward the passage of a bill that I feel is needed in a neglected area of our society. . . . In other years I hope to do
more.

There is work to be done close to home, among our friends
and neighbors, as we share life together. Last year, two of
our teen-agers wanted to go to a Young Life Summer Camp.
These camps are not only the most fun, but the most effective ones we know for high-schoolers, so Louie and I were
glad to eke the money out of our budget. Then we discovered
that two of our boys' friends wanted to go, and one of them
clearly couldn't afford it. As I was thinking and praying about
our problem, I got a call from some Young Life workers in
our city. They were trying to raise funds for scholarships
to their summer camps . . . and would I help out by speaking
to a women's group? *Would* I!

Public speaking isn't my thing—in fact, I don't particularly
enjoy it. But when I'm enthusiastic about something I'm willing to try. So try I did, and at that morning get-together we
raised enough money to provide several young people with
camp scholarships. And yes, our young friend got one of
them. What's more, while he was at camp he became convinced that God loved him . . . his response was so full and
natural that his life became a whole new ball game. . . . Now,
that's satisfaction!

A woman's life has seasons, and I'm about to enter a new one.
Our older sons are away at college, and the other two children
are following close behind. In a few years our house will be a
much quieter place. I'll have to be adaptable, for I'll be
needed in different ways. With four children in college at the

same time, I may be needed to help provide bread for our table, and I may find myself working outside our home for the first time in twenty years. . . .

And when the children are educated and on their own—what then? Ah, what then? Which of our dreams will we turn to? So many times over the years Louie has said, "When the children are grown, let's. . . ." So it's not a question of "What then?" but "Which one?" Which new thing? Which ministry of faith? Which adventurous service? For when your children are grown and no longer need you the same way they once did, there is always a world full of need outside your door.

Needs . . . needs . . . that's what this Beatitude is all about . . . our own needs and those of others . . . reaching out toward each other to share our love and faith. Yes, we need each other . . . our spirits hunger and thirst to make contact with each other . . . to touch each other's lives, just as Jesus did. This is living in the spirit. This is hungering and thirsting after goodness.

God has a place and a task for us, no matter what our season of life. You and I will always be needed . . . somewhere—by someone—and *that* is our fulfillment.

Happy is the woman whose heart yearns for the deep things of God. . . . This woman seeks for spiritual riches rather than the things of this world . . . she knows that there are others with needs greater than her own, and she is not satisfied simply to look after her own family's well-being. Her love and faith reach out to those around her, and through her God is able to touch the lives of many persons. The happiness she knows will be deeper and greater and more lasting than anything this world can offer her.

5

Happy are the merciful, for they will have mercy shown to them!

Matthew 5:7 PHILLIPS

Blessed are the merciful: for they shall obtain mercy.

Matthew 5:7 KJV

The Generous Women

The simple, direct words of our Lord have a way of digging into my complacent life and stirring things around. Like leaven in a loaf, they will make me stretch and grow. It's not an altogether comfortable experience—change rarely is. Shall I come back to the Beatitudes another time? Find something else to do? There are so many things. . . . No. Without change, there can be no growth. So it must be.

Right away I run into trouble. I'm not sure what *mercy* is. Or how it works. Or what it will do to my life. Mercy can mean kindness—compassion—forbearance. . . . But the word is hardly used anymore and my mind keeps tripping over it. It's too dramatic, too big, for everyday life and seems to belong to a crisis—". . . God, have mercy on a sinner like me"

(Luke 18:13). Yes, it belongs there. *Mercy* is a God-sized word.

Perhaps another word, another translation, will help. Yes, here it is: *generous.* That's a person-sized word. *Happy are those who are generous with others. . . . God will be generous with them.*

All right, then, what about generosity? As I turn the word over in my mind I immediately think of giving—giving things, money, time. "Happy birthday, dear!" "It's just what I wanted!" "Sure, I'll help out." "We gave at the office."

And yet, something tells me that Jesus was talking about a deeper, more demanding kind of generosity. What else can I give? My hands, my mind, my attention, my love, my understanding? Even more? *Happy are those who give lavishly of themselves. . . .* Yes, I think that's what Jesus meant.

Suddenly my thoughts race back through the years. . . . My husband and I were very young and everything was new. Life seemed to come rushing at us all at once and we met it eagerly, head-on. Lou was in his first church, and the congregation was new, too. The sanctuary wasn't built yet, so having nowhere else to go we held our meetings in our home—two of the weeklies were men's prayer breakfasts at 7:00 A.M.! People were constantly stopping by with ideas, concerns, problems. And then there was the phone, always the phone. It would be understating the situation to say that my plate was full, and so was my house! As a minister's wife there was much for me to do, and I was also the mother of four children, all of them under the age of five. I loved my life, but it was wearing me out. I was hungry for rest and quiet, and there was none in sight.

Worst of all, I was starved for my husband. Longingly I recalled our student days in Edinburgh when we used to walk for miles—talking, moving fast to brace ourselves against the chill wind blowing in from the North Sea. We had been so close then, but now I practically had to wave to him from across the room. I was proud of Lou and the work he was doing. I was glad to share him with our family, our congregation—with the whole world, if necessary. But I needed him too!

It's never wise to hold your feelings in. They have a way of bursting into the open when you least expect it. That's what happened to me. I should have told my husband then how I felt, but I didn't want to burden him with my problems when he already was carrying so many others that were bigger. And so I kept quiet—until one night when we were getting dressed for the evening services.

Lou had come home very excited about a new project. Ordinarily I loved listening to his plans, his hopes, and his dreams, but that night my own frustration began to well up inside me. As he went on enthusiastically I could hear our front door opening and closing as the early birds began to arrive. I knew I had to speak, to tell my husband how much I needed him. *Right now?* something inside me said, disapprovingly. *Yes, now!* I thought, but instead of words, my tears came. (I don't cry often, but at the right moment it seems to work wonders!) Again I tried to speak and although I don't remember much of what I said, my husband apparently got the message. I was hungry for him!

It was Lou's response that made me remember that night years later, for he was truly generous. He waited until my tears stopped and he listened to me, which wasn't easy to do with one hundred people sitting in our front room waiting for the service to begin. Then he was generous in his attitude as he shared my need, saying he needed me too. He was generous in his action as he promised, with God's help, to give me my time—no, to make sure we had *our* time together. And through the years, he has been generous in his determination to keep that promise. In spite of his hectic schedule, and often against enormous odds, he has kept our special times and our short trips away together as something sacred that must not be violated.

Many times I have heard my husband turn down invitations to meetings, speaking engagements, and almost anything that happens to fall on our night. "No, I'm sorry," he'll say, "but I have an important appointment for that night and I want to keep it." And with those words he tells me "I love you" better than all the flowers and heart-shaped boxes of candy in the world. He knows I don't want things—I want him. And he wants me.

You really don't have to go far to get away. There are hundreds of glamorous places in the world and hundreds of exciting ads telling you how to get there and how much fun you'll have. Travel is a treat and I love it, but it's expensive. Sometimes a man and wife simply need *to be*—and *to be* together. How often we forget about that because we put other, more material goals first in our lives It's normal, I suppose, for a wife to want to help her husband get ahead, to make his dreams come true, but what good is worldly success if a man and his wife are strangers by the time they achieve it? Maybe a wife can do more than support a husband's ambitions. Maybe she can remind him that their life needs its quiet moments away from the pressures of work and even those of family. Stillness, when it is shared with someone you love, can be a very rich experience.

I'm grateful for the many moments of stillness Louie and I have known together. Believe me, it wasn't always easy to arrange them during our busy life, and there were times when we thought it would be simpler to forget the whole idea. But we didn't, and I hope we never will.

Sometimes we were so broke that after we paid a baby-sitter to come in for the evening we didn't have a cent left to spend on ourselves. But we didn't mind. We went for long, long walks in the lovely hills where our first church was being built.

Now we walk the beaches of La Jolla, often between midnight and dawn if there seems to be no other time we can call ours. Sometimes we talk, eagerly pouring out all the feelings that have waited to be expressed. Sometimes we don't say a word — and that's all right, too.

Getting away on short trips together has taken real ingenuity, especially when the children were small. With a little luck we could "child swap." That meant we would take care of our neighbors' children while their parents went off together for a weekend — and then a few weeks later they would return the favor. Having sleeping bags and bodies all over the house was a treat for our children, and for me it was easier than squeezing money from our budget for a baby-sitter.

Recently some friends came up with a wonderful offer. They have a guest house and simply gave us the key to it. Now, when we put aside a day and a night — or even part of a day — for ourselves, we arrange for someone to look after the children, pack a bag, hop in the car, and drive four blocks to "the little house below." It's quiet, convenient — and free!

The time we take for ourselves may seem like a little thing, but I think it makes the difference between our being turned on or turned off to each other. It has helped to make our marriage a daily happening instead of a situation that exists. In giving us the time and the opportunity to be generous, it has blessed us with great happiness. (Thank you, Louie, for hearing me out that night. . . .)

I wonder, though — have I always responded to my husband's needs as generously as he has to mine? I'm thinking of the times when he comes home unexpectedly for a half hour between counseling appointments, after a funeral, before a wedding. Sometimes I can sense that he wants me to stop whatever I'm doing and sit down and listen to him, or perhaps just be with him. Whenever I do, I'm glad. But very often I don't. Very often I'm too busy *doing* something to take time out to *be* someone to my husband. Those are the times I am not generous with myself. Generous with my services, yes, but not with *me*, and at that moment my husband couldn't care less about my talents as a homemaker. He needs me as a friend, as a woman, as a lover—yet he has to play second fiddle to a vacuum cleaner.

Like most women I like a clean house, but sometimes I think there can be too much housework and not enough home. We've all heard wives of late-working husbands say, "I don't want his money—I want *him*." Yet, I wonder how many husbands would like to say, "Forget the house—I want a wife."

I admit I have a problem with neatness. I think it comes from being an only child and being brought up by my mother and grandfather. Affluent we were not, but we were very clean and neat, which is not so difficult with only three in the family. I grew up with a built-in sense of order, which is rather pleasant to live with when you're all by yourself. But when you're part of a large, busy family, when your daughter sews and enjoys crafts, when your three sons make surf boards in the garage and model airplanes in the attic, when your husband is a gifted do-it-yourselfer whose work doesn't allow him time to finish his projects on schedule—an overdeveloped sense of order can be a real drag.

My family is very generous with my passion for neatness, yet I know it bugs them. I'm trying to learn how to be more casual, but sometimes Lou has to take me by the hand and lead me away from a cluttered kitchen or an unfolded pile of laundry. "That can wait," he'll say. "This is our chance to do something as a family." He's right, and he's a good teacher.

Frankly, it bothers me to leave the dishes in the sink, and I don't like to see my husband run out of clean socks. But when my family says "Let's go," I have learned to ask myself,

"What's the worst thing that can possibly happen if I don't clean the kitchen?" Leaving my work undone has never lost me a friend or caused the sky to fall in or the world to come apart. It has enabled me to give myself to the people I love.

In exchange for a little dust on the tabletops, I now have a much bigger world to live in. I am part sailor, hiker, camper, researcher, painter, swimmer, flashlight holder, photographer, driver, skirt measurer, and critic-at-large. I can lend a hand, a foot, a shoulder, or an ear to many things that did not exist for me a few years ago. What's more important, I feel I am woman, wife, mother, friend, companion, confidante, and occasional umpire. That's about all I can handle.

Now I'm beginning to understand why Jesus urged us to be lavish in our giving. It's because generosity is a magical quality that seems to increase as it is used. I'm pretty convinced that nervous breakdowns don't come from overwork (or overgiving), but from worrying about all the work or keeping track of all the giving.

I find that the more I am able to give myself to my family, the more I have to give. I do not wear out. I am not used up.

Neither am I diminished as a person. I don't feel I am an appendage of my husband or my children. In giving of myself I am finding out who I am—and there is more to me than I thought! I am part of my husband, and for a season I am part of my children. I am an influence in their lives. They need me. They need what I am and what I have to give. And in responding to those needs I am discovering myself.

Again, it's a matter of words and what they mean to us. If I think of a need as a demand, I'm going to resent it and pull away. But if I think of a need as an open-armed invitation to share the love and life of someone dear to me, I can only be grateful it came my way.

When a woman is married she has a special and very beautiful opportunity to make generosity meaningful in a physical sense. I'm not talking about the sharing of tasks in a home, important as these are. No, right now I'm thinking about a man and woman who are very much in love, whose lives are joined in the sight of God, and who freely give their bodies in a joyous ministry to each other.

These days we hear so much about sex *before* marriage and *outside* marriage, that you'd think sex is exciting only when it's illicit. The momentary tingle, the tang of guilt, the sudden splurge of passion—these are all we hear about sex. But there is so much more and it is so much better.

Sex doesn't make the marriage, but it can certainly break it. Some marriages, too many marriages, suffer from an incomplete sex life. But that isn't the way married sex *has* to be. It's not at all what it *can* be. There are other kinds of marriages, marriages that constantly grow in honesty, friendship, goal sharing, love, and the physical expression of that love. These marriages have soul!

Sex not only gives life; it celebrates the life God gave each of us. It is a powerful force that can become terribly destructive if it is cut off from its natural environment, love. Then it can become unprincipled, fickle, selfish, hateful, even violent, almost as if it wants to destroy the life it was meant to serve. This is the kind of sex we read so much about.

Only in a marriage—a marriage where love is—can sex develop into the delightfully positive force God meant it to be. Here is where the excitement of sex really is. When a man and a woman make a lifelong commitment to love and cherish each other, they are giving themselves the time they will need to dismantle the barriers of restraint, shyness, defensiveness, and selfishness that exist between all human beings. It cannot be done in a night or with a rush of passion. It takes time to know and be known.

In a marriage a man and a woman can discover the thrill of trusting each other so fully that their freedom of expression reaches undreamed-of heights. Their intimacy becomes a sanctuary, a place where the soul of their relationship can grow through their physical oneness. No matter how many others they may share life with in the circle of family and responsibilities, they have a small private world where they can offer each other their trust, their vulnerability, and the unrestrained affirmation of their love.

Generosity in the physical relationship of marriage brings each partner great dividends. In giving of themselves they also receive in kind, and this reciprocity of love is beautiful beyond words. A marriage with a good healthy sex life can also weather all kinds of pressures from the outside.

It sounds very stern to urge Christian wives to submit themselves to their husbands (Ephesians 5:22). Here again it's a matter of words and what they mean. How much better it is to think of *submitting* as *giving*. And how much better it is to think of sex as an opportunity to give our love to our husbands in every possible way—emotionally, physically, mentally. Perhaps this is the way to achieve a truly spiritual expression of love.

Yes, generosity enlarges my life and brings me closer to my family. But there is a world outside my front door, and I live there too. It needs a part of me, just as my family does—and I need it!

My mind turns to the national and international scene. I wonder what would happen between nations, between races, between just plain human beings if the generosity of Jesus were applied to all our relationships. It wouldn't be easy, because when Jesus gives, He gives totally, with no strings attached. Could we Americans, for example, give aid to an emerging nation and resist the desire to tell its people how to live their lives? Could we really put their interests ahead of our own if we had to make that decision? If we could, and if people all over the world became convinced that we wanted everyone to reach his full potential as a human being, how different the human and the international scenes might be.

Right here in our own country there are so many ways we could be more generous with each other. We mean well, but sometimes we don't give well—or enough. If only we could go beyond the giving of our resources and time. If, for instance, we could help our black brothers achieve the goals they set for themselves instead of offering them our goals, we would be on our way to becoming one nation under God.

I'm thinking of a lesson I learned a couple of years ago while doing some volunteer work on one of our city's ghetto programs. Yes, like most other cities, we have a ghetto, and like most other cities we're trying to do something about it. The program I was working with was a truly happy experience for everyone involved in it. It was successful, I feel, because it was a program *for* black people, *headed* by black people and *run* by black people. I and others like me helped in small, practical ways—such as sitting on a board—but only when needed and asked. It cost us very little in terms of time and money, but we did have to give something of ourselves. We had to give way.

When I really open my eyes to what is going on around me I see that the spirit of generosity is growing . . . in the young people of our church who gave up their Easter vacation to go to Mexico where they and the local young people rebuilt a school; in some of my busy neighbors with large families of their own who somehow squeeze out a few hours each week to tutor children in depressed areas. I almost gasp when I visualize the potential for generosity among our retired citizens.

It's strange, isn't it, how life becomes stale and meaningless when we think we have nothing left to give? So it was with some of the older people in our community. But then the rest of us realized that we were wrong and so were they— their lives were far from finished. Our city needs them more than ever and they need the challenge service offers. "Give us of yourselves," we said. "Give us of your experience, your wisdom, your love for mankind. This is your great opportunity to serve."

Some of these people thought they were beyond the age of involvements. The brightness had gone from their eyes and they were sitting back, resigning themselves to a dreary, monotonous future. But now they're alive again because they're being used creatively in a whole new revolution.

I see retired schoolteachers tutoring minority children on a one-to-one basis in the tutorial program held in our church. I see retired businessmen sharing their years of experience with men who want to start businesses of their own. I see retired builders, land investment developers, and lawyers working on low-income housing projects in all areas of our city—one of them sponsored by our church. Yes, the potential amount of generosity coming into the world is staggering, and I am caught up in the wonder of such thoughts . . . until some minor crisis with one of my children brings me back, back to the world where I live.

All right, I'm in my own backyard once more and I see I still have *much* to learn about giving. I have friends, neighbors; new people will be coming into my life. What can I give them? What do they need from me?

Perhaps the most generous thing I can do is to let them be whatever they are. In other words, I must not judge them. When my neighbor's political views turn out to be just the opposite of mine, I must not resent her. Not that we can't differ openly and honestly, but I must not try to change her into something I want her to be. If I am to be generous about our differences, I must respect my neighbor's ideas, much as I might dislike them. Somehow I don't think Jesus wanted us to manipulate each other.

Neither must I judge people by outward appearance. How a person speaks or looks, what he wears or doesn't wear, has nothing to do with what he is. This seems to be especially true of our young people today. As one song goes, "Look past the hair and into the eyes. . . ."

Some years ago my husband and I learned how important it is to take that second look. We went to a dinner party where all the other guests were either students or young people employed by the university near us. In fact, we were the only over-thirty people there, and we felt like real squares.

The moment we entered the room I felt my old habit take over. In one quick glance I had sized up everyone, or so I thought. And believe me, there was a lot to glance at—beards, long hair, bare feet, strange clothes. We have two boys in college now and they have really helped their mom reach the point where I don't even see these things anymore—but at that time I felt uncomfortable because I didn't seem to fit in.

Well, as the evening went on and the conversation became open and honest, we all discovered that our differences were quite superficial. One by one the barriers of age, dress, and life-style broke down and we took a second look at each other. We were very much alike. Beneath some rather alarming exteriors our fellow guests were warm, sensitive, concerned human beings who were very generous about accepting the two squares in their midst. My split-second glance on coming into the room had been all wrong. I realized, for instance, that the biggest hang-up didn't belong to the boy with the longest hair or the girl with the shortest mini. It belonged to me.

Friendships began that night as we shared our similar joys and concerns. We found we had our differences, too, but we were able to talk about them honestly. We were learning to give each other the right to be ourselves.

I can see now that generosity means opening yourself up to others. But what about those *others,* the receivers? They really have to be there, or our generosity would have nowhere to go. Giving is only half the action, and if someone refuses what we offer, it hurts. Perhaps, then, some of us need to work at being generous receivers.

I have learned a lot about receiving from the women in the congregations we have served, for they have been such beautiful givers in my times of need. I have learned still more from a good friend, a woman my mother's age. For some wonderful, unknown reason, God must have put me "in her basket," because she has done so many generous, kind, and truly helpful things for me that I've lost count. And that's the way she wants it.

At first it was hard for me to accept so much generosity. My independent streak got in the way and I began to feel uncomfortably indebted to my friend. I wanted to return her love in tangible ways, and of course I couldn't. Being a sensitive person, she realized how I felt and one day she had a talk with me.

"Colleen, I get a lot of pleasure out of doing things for you," she said. "If only I didn't have to worry about your feeling of indebtedness. . . . Think of the fun I could have!" I couldn't believe it. She made me feel that I'd be doing her a favor by accepting her deeds of love.

I did a little thinking and a little praying, and gradually my attitude began to change. I put myself in my friend's place and realized how I would have felt if someone accepted my generosity with a frown on her face. And if a friend returned my favor tit for tat—like some kind of duty—it would make my generosity look like a pompous gesture done just for show. No—since my friend gave freely and lavishly of herself, responding to my needs as she saw them, the best way for me to be generous was to become a good receiver. For there is another part to the Beatitude, isn't there? *Happy are those who are generous. . . . God will be generous to them.*

There is so much God wants to give us. He wants to show

us how to make contact with people, how to express our love for our family, our friends, our fellow man, and for the whole world. And as we open up to each other, we will be more open to Him. Then His Spirit can move among us, soothing our cares, ministering to our hurts, uniting us in love, increasing our awareness of each other. In short, God wants to teach us how to be happy. That's too good an offer to turn down.

Happy is the woman who is generous with her love and understanding. She knows that it isn't so much what she does, but what she is, *that is really important to her loved ones. And when the voice of need is uttered, however feeble it may be, she hears it. She listens, she comforts, she supports, she gives her love generously. Because she becomes a part of the lives of those she loves, and because her happiness comes from her generosity, she receives even more than she gives.*

6

Happy are the utterly sincere, for they will see God!

Matthew 5:8 PHILLIPS

Blessed are the pure in heart: for they shall see God.

Matthew 5:8 KJV

The Sincere Women

Pure in heart ... pure in heart. . . . What do these lovely, familiar words mean to me, a busy wife, a mother, a woman concerned about the world? Do they mean I am to be spotless, perfect? If so, I'll stop now — no need to go on.

But wait. Surely our Lord was describing something more — something more attainable for me. The concept of purity tumbles around in my mind. Then I look into the New Testament where I find that *purity* is mentioned twenty-seven times. Gradually I reject the idea that purity means perfection. Instead, it seems to mean genuineness, sincerity, honesty, a singleness of mind and purpose. Or, in the more concise words of Sören Kierkegaard, "Purity of heart is to will one thing."

Transparent is an even better word. Yes, I like that. To be pure in heart is to be a transparent person, a person with no shadows or double meanings, one who says what he means and means what he says. I like people who do that—people who don't hedge, who take a stand even if it turns out to be unpopular. I can think of many heroes who were transparent people.

But what about ordinary human beings meeting life's ordinary situations? What about someone like me?

I wasn't exactly transparent the other day, at least not at first. Going through the house, picking up the usual clutter, I came to one of our boys' rooms and stopped, surprised. The room was in perfect order! The bed was made, everything was put away, and each piece of furniture was where it belonged. I was so pleased.

When Tim came home from school I literally showered him with praise—"Good boy! You're a great guy to clean your room like that." He accepted my words casually. Well, I thought, we've always praised our children whenever we felt we could do it honestly, so why should he make a fuss over it?

I went back to my work, but something didn't feel right deep down inside me. *Pure in heart . . . pure in heart . . .* kept running through my mind. When you're pure in heart, you're honest about your feelings. You don't mean one thing and say another.

Well, I *was* honest, I told myself. I really do think Tim's a good guy. Yes, but "good" only because he cleaned his room? Did my son's goodness depend upon his neatness? No, of course not. That wasn't what I meant. Yet that's what I said.

It seemed like such a little thing, so I promised myself to remember it the next time I began to praise my son. Still, the not-right feeling persisted.

At that moment my son walked into the room.

"What I really meant was that you helped me a lot today by cleaning your room," I said. "My work was easier, and I felt you cared."

"Thanks." This time his response was warm and sincere, perhaps because I had become more real to him. My words of praise were related to a simple act, not to his entire being.

My son taught me something that day: I have to be transparent even in life's smallest moments. I have to express my true feelings, not the ones that rush in to cover up for what's really going on inside me.

That isn't easy to do today, when we live in a world that urges us to play it cool. "Don't wear your heart on your sleeve" —"Don't leave yourself wide open"—"Don't get involved." Sounds familiar, doesn't it? That's the kind of advice we all get from people who mean well. We may even catch ourselves saying the same words.

Jesus wasn't cool, and I don't think He wants us to be. When He calls us to become pure in heart, He's telling us that we have to take some risks. If we're going to express ourselves truly, honestly, that means we'll have to expose ourselves, be vulnerable. Someone may take advantage of us. We may be misunderstood. We may get hurt. That's part of being transparent. Nobody said it was easy.

I'm remembering one afternoon when I went shopping and got into a serious conversation with one of the store clerks. He was quite upset about the racial tensions in our nation, and particularly about the prospect of open housing. "They better not start coming in here," he said. "You wouldn't want one living next to you, would you?"

I liked that man and had known him for a long time. I didn't want to offend him, so it would have been easier for me to change the subject, pretending I didn't hear. But I did hear, and what he said troubled me. If I hadn't cared I could have passed off his comments. But I did care.

Gently, I tried to explain how I really felt—that "they" had every right to "come in here" or wherever they wanted to go—next door to me, or to him . . . that I hoped we all could begin to live as brothers and sisters, because we all are children of God.

The clerk was polite, but unmoved; our relationship became strained and it still is. Now I understand that reading sacred words is one thing, living them on a daily basis is something quite different. Expressing my real feelings may involve cost to me.

Perhaps, as I become more and more transparent, I will find ways to be open without offending. But perhaps not. Honesty is telling it like it is, and people don't always welcome it. At times I may have to hurt . . . or be hurt.

Jesus, I know You understand, because You lived through it. You weren't one of those "Now I have to be frank with you" persons who used truth like a dangerous weapon. But You *were* honest, no matter what it cost You. Remember when You told Peter that he would deny You? And he had just promised that he would never turn away from You. But You had to tell him the truth about himself, and later he understood why. You were telling Peter that he wasn't perfect, that he was even a coward at times—*and that You still loved him.*

Because You were honest, sometimes You had to hurt people . . . the scribes, the Pharisees, some of Your followers and Your dearest friends, even Your family. But Your honesty was always combined with love, and I think that's what made the difference. . . . You hurt only to heal, and everyone could see that love was Your motivation. It must also be mine.

Now I can see what You are telling me in this Beatitude. It's not enough for me to get rid of the shadows in myself. And it's not enough for people to be able to see clear through me.

They have to be able to see through me to something else. I must let God's love be visible through my transparency.

Wanting to express ourselves honestly doesn't make it happen. It's not that we're deceitful, at least not deliberately; but we're in the habit of speaking abstractly rather than personally. We've been taught that it's good manners to leave our feelings out of the things we say. And so we try to ignore our feelings entirely.

What a mistake that is! You can't ignore your emotions. Turn your back on them and they'll poke you in the ribs. Run away from them and they'll trip you. Slam a door in their faces and they'll break your windows.

Besides, what's so wrong about feelings, anyway? God gave us the capacity to feel and He must have had His reasons. Here in the Beatitudes He tells us how to appreciate feelings, understand them, and use them. He is reminding us that feelings can become vital lines of communication between one person and another. When we become transparent, there will be no obstacles between us.

Because it is so difficult for us to give up the defenses we put between ourselves and others, we need help in tearing them down. We just can't do it alone. That's why the pilgrimage toward transparency isn't a walk for loners. I know, because I've been on that journey for the past few years and I would have turned back many times had it not been for those who walked with me.

It's harder to lean than to be leaned on. It's harder to take the extended hand than to reach out with your own. It's easier to comfort than to allow ourselves to be comforted. We would rather dry someone else's tears than expose our own sorrows. And yet, we can't really reach someone else until we ourselves have been reached.

My family has helped me discover what my real feelings are. Now that the children are older, we have our own group encounters right around our dinner table—or anytime, for that matter. I remember one evening when I was in the kitchen packing the next day's lunches while my youngest son was keeping me company. I had the feeling that something was on his mind. He was talking casually about school, his friends, nothing in particular, until finally he got to the point. He was having a problem with one of his teachers. He couldn't put his finger on what it was, but he knew they were at cross-purposes and it bothered him.

I listened, wanting to help him sort out what he felt, but not knowing how. My impulse was to soothe him, to minimize the problem. . . . "Don't worry about it, son. It'll all work out" —"Maybe you're exaggerating the situation"—"Try not to think about it so much." No, that wasn't what I really felt, and I caught myself before I allowed the moment to slip by.

When Jamie began to talk about his problem, I remembered something that had happened to me a long time ago. For a split second I had an urge to share it with him, but I hesitated because it wasn't exactly my finest hour I was going to describe. Perhaps it's only human for us to want to present only the best parts of ourselves to our children, and so I almost hid my real self behind a lot of meaningless clichés. But then I realized that my son had had the courage to be honest with me. He had been totally transparent, and I simply had to respond to him in the same way.

So I told Jamie about a conflict I had had with one of my high-school teachers. It happened so long ago, yet as I described it I could still feel the pain of it.

I had a teacher who didn't like me. I'll never know why, because as far as I knew I had done nothing to earn her hostility. Perhaps I reminded her of someone else. Whatever the reason, she made my life miserable with her belittling remarks. I actually dreaded going to her class every day, knowing that she'd humiliate me in front of my friends.

It would have been wonderful to tell Jamie that I finally got through to my teacher and that we had a nice, long talk that cleared up all our misunderstandings. But that wasn't what happened. No, I just had to suffer through that year in school and go on to the next.

But I did learn something from that unhappy situation. Almost everyone I knew in school seemed to like me as much as I liked them—but there were a few exceptions, and there always will be. Life is like that. Now and then you'll run into someone who just doesn't like you, perhaps for reasons neither of you can understand, and there isn't anything you can do about it. Yes, it hurts, but that's all right. Life goes on . . . and we can learn and grow through our hurts.

I could see that my son was interested and also a little surprised. He had heard (too often, I'm afraid) of my past successes. But at that moment it was important for him to hear about one of my failures because it made him realize that I knew how he felt. There I was, standing at the sink while he was sitting across the room, yet we were holding each other's hand as surely as we ever had.

It's this self-censorship, this holding back of parts of ourselves that seems to be the greatest barrier between human beings. I think it even prevents us from getting to know ourselves. Too often we build up false images of what we are until we become convinced that they are real. Then it's especially hard to face the truth, to see ourselves clearly, transparently. We're afraid we won't like what we see, and we think others will feel the same way. So we go along, handing out our counterfeit selves—and then we wonder why we can't touch each other anymore.

A few years ago several of our church members felt that they wanted to reach out toward each other, but couldn't. They decided that they needed help. And so they began— very cautiously—to work with each other in small groups.

Now I know what the word *group* brings to mind. We think

of people behaving peculiarly, even sensationally, perhaps letting too many restraints down along with their hair. We thought of those things, too. But we went a little further and found out that there are many kinds of groups, some more constructive than others. It depends on what people want to get out of them, who leads them, and what the members put into them.

Our church groups have a distinct advantage. We don't get together to tell each other sad stories; we aren't interested in weird experiments; we aren't looking for company in our misery. We are Christians trying to experience Jesus Christ and His fellowship with one another. . . . We want to experience it more deeply and directly. We are seeking Him in ourselves and in each other. In short, we are trying to help each other become our genuine selves.

We're also lucky in that we have Gordon Hess, a young and dedicated pastor with a real gift for group leadership. Gordy has had a lot of experience in group encounter work, but he's not what you'd call a "professional facilitator." Neither are the rest of us professionals, and that's good, because we know we are all in this life together . . . and there's no such thing as a "professional person." As Gordy puts it, "Christ calls us to be real, not religious. Our purpose is to hold hands with each other as we walk through this difficult and sometimes lonely life. Because we belong to God, we belong to each other—we need each other."

In the beginning I had conflicting feelings about being in a group. On the one hand I longed for the close-up fellowship a small group offers, because in a large church there is such a need for more than the Sunday-morning hello. But on the other hand I was timid about this new experience. The truth is, I was scared! But Gordy, sensitive friend that he is, forced my hand by asking me to join the first training class for leaders of small groups. Actually, that was our first group . . .

and once I got my feet wet, I was there to stay. Since then I've been involved in women's daytime groups. Women from nineteen to seventy have been transformed from faces in the Sunday-morning crowd to my sisters in Christ, with whom I share life. The love that flows among us is a very special gift from God.

The groups I have been in over the past few years have been honest and supportive. There have been painful moments when I was forced to look at the flaws in my being which the others helped me to see . . . but even then I knew that I was loved and accepted as a person created by God. And there have been moments of utter joy over the discovery of something worthwhile that I could share with others.

It has taken time and patience, but in our group work we have learned to express our fears, our hang-ups, our delights. Gradually we are able to express the most important part of ourselves—our love for God and for one another. At last we are coming to the place where we can share each other's burdens (Galatians 6), which is what Christians are meant to do. Prayer has also been a very real part of our experience, and believe me, after the searching moments we share with each other, our prayers are not just a lot of pretty words. They are real, and they come from deep within us.

Some amazing things have happened to us as we became more honest with each other. I have seen personalities emerge and spiritual wounds heal as we allowed Christ and His kind of honesty to work through us.

Anne's experience is a good example of what can happen in a Christian group. The first time I spoke to her we were total strangers. She and her husband had serious problems and, having heard about our church groups, she called me to ask about them. She sounded desperate, and when she began to cry I nearly lost my own composure. We couldn't accomplish much on the telephone, so we arranged to meet a few days later.

Anne and her husband Carl had been married about twenty years. They had four fine children and a home that appeared — from the outside, at least — to be happy and secure. Anne and Carl were very close and their love for each other was deep — no problem there. When it came to sharing their faith, that was something else.

It was startling for them to realize that they had such a problem at all, considering their backgrounds. Both came from Christian homes. When they met, Anne was the daughter of a minister and Carl was a young seminarian interning in her father's church. They fell in love and were married when Carl graduated from seminary. Anne, at eighteen, went from minister's daughter to minister's wife, a simple enough transition — or so she thought.

She kept telling herself that her life was trouble-free. And why shouldn't it be? She knew all the answers — she had memorized enough Bible verses to fit anything life might bring her way, she could study the Scriptures in depth and find their prescriptions for her problems, and she knew every hymn in the book. Going through the motions of her role was a snap.

But inside Anne there was another person — a woman who could not squeeze life into a narrow mold. This inner person needed more than memorized Bible passages to sustain her faith. She needed to know the living Christ Himself and to feel His influence in her life. And, not understanding how to reach out to Him, she waited for His touch. When it didn't come, she began to doubt that He existed.

The doubts increased secretly for many years until finally Anne couldn't stand being a skin-deep Christian any longer. One day she told her husband how she felt. Understandably, Carl was hurt and confused. Never having known such doubts himself he was unable to deal with Anne's. He seemed to think he could compensate for her loss of faith by spending more and more hours alone in his study praying, reading the

Bible, and meditating. Rejected and filled with guilt, Anne rebelled against religion altogether—no worship, no prayer, no mention of God.

Everything else in her life began to come apart after that. She and Carl disagreed on how to bring up their children. Carl, a gentle, loving parent, seemed to get closer to the children, whereas Anne, a strict disciplinarian, felt she was turning them off.

The reason Anne decided to get in touch with one of our church groups was that she had a particularly serious argument with her husband. As usual it led to a discussion of Anne's doubts about God. As she was trying to explain them, Carl interrupted her angrily. "For God's sake and the children's, find out what you *do* believe!" he said. He asked her if she realized what a bad example she was setting for their children. Filled with hatred for herself and convinced that she was a failure as a mother, Anne ran to her bedroom. Sobbing, not even realizing what she was doing, she began to cry out to God, asking Him to show her where to turn. That's when she remembered reading about the work our groups were doing.

Anne was such an unhappy woman when I met her. Just talking about her problems was a big step for her to take, and I admired her courage. It meant that she had to come out from behind the facade that had sheltered and imprisoned her all her life. She was presenting herself—doubts and all—as honestly as she possibly could. It was not an easy thing to do, especially by herself. What made it even more difficult was that Anne saw herself as an ugly, unlovable person—when, in fact, she was truly lovely.

I reached out and touched her. "You're coming into your own as an individual, Anne. That's wonderful!"

She was quite surprised. I could see that she expected some sort of reprimand.

"It's all right," I said. "God meant you to be an individual — it's about time you got to know yourself the way He does."

Still she couldn't believe her ears. I understood how she felt. I had seen this happen many times in our group — it had happened to me.

"God loves you very much, Anne," I told her. "And He loves you the way you are. So do I."

She began to cry again, but this time they were tears of relief. I suggested that she join one of our women's groups where she would have the help and support she needed as she searched for her authentic self. I could see that the prospect was both promising and frightening. It was like a door held open to her, a door that led to — who knows? For a moment she struggled with her fears and then she won out over them.

That night Anne told her husband about joining the group. When she saw the tears come to his eyes she realized how much she had been hurting him over the years — and how much he really loved her! Holding each other tightly, they felt the warmth and deep sense of caring that had been missing for a long time. Changes were already happening in Anne's life.

Our women's group helped Anne in many ways. "They accepted me even when I told them about my doubts of God," she said. But she still found it hard to share her problems with Carl. His self-confidence and his complete spiritual tranquillity made her ashamed of her own uneasiness. Gradually Anne began to realize that the best way to communicate with her husband was for both of them to join a couples' group where they could face their problems together.

It worked. As the communication lines between husband and wife began to open, they revealed that Anne wasn't the only one with problems. Carl had a few of his own, and as he became more aware of them he began to sympathize with what Anne had been experiencing. She was no longer alone.

During the past year Anne and Carl have faced situations and crises that would have wrecked them if they had remained so far apart. But now they are able to help each other through life's rougher moments. They not only feel their love for each other—they *live* it.

Their children have gained most of all. Anne and Carl can see now that the most important thing they can do is to let their children know how much they love them. If they have different ways of showing their love, it doesn't seem to matter—the children know how they feel.

And God? Somehow, through receiving God's love as it came to her through others, Anne has found God. She has had the encounter she desperately needed and it has given her the courage to be herself. She is not afraid to let others see the person God created. In other words, she is becoming a transparent human being.

"Sharing my faith and my life with friends who really care has been the most wonderful experience of my life," she told me recently. "I feel as if I'm floating on a cloud of friendship —a deep, warm friendship with Jesus."

Now you can understand why I'm convinced that Christ-centered groups can be a real help along our pilgrimage to transparency. Anne is one example, and there have been many others. Of course, group work is only one way, and it's not for everyone. A good friend of ours, who has come alive as a person and a believer during the past few years, says, "I don't need a group—my whole life has become a group experience." And he's right—just being with him is an exciting encounter with honesty. This should be the end result of every group experience as well.

It really doesn't matter how you become a transparent person. The important thing is that it happens. And when it does it will turn your life into a daily adventure as all the routine, familiar things take on new and deeper meaning.

The other day I saw what a difference it made when I applied Jesus' concept of honesty to a very small incident. It was panic hour at our house, which means that I was preparing dinner, the children and their friends were home from school, and the telephone was ringing endlessly. One call was from a new young woman in our church who asked me to attend a women's meeting with her later that week.

It sounded like fun, except that I already had a full week. So I hedged, but I felt pressure in return. I knew that if I said *yes* my family would get the short end of the bargain. This was not my season to major in ladies' meetings, yet I felt the old temptation to give in to social pressures in order to please my caller. And then I reminded myself—*to be pure in heart is to be perfectly honest about your feelings.* I decided to say *no* and explain why.

At first there was nothing but silence at the other end of the line. Then the young woman said, "Well, it's a good thing you're a minister's wife today and not fifty years ago when ministers' wives were not only asked but *expected* to do everything!"

My own honesty was such a relief that I was able to appreciate hers. "It sure is," I said, and laughed.

She laughed too. We talked on—she understood. She might not have but she did. And I had a new friend.

At dinner that night I felt unusually gay and free. Conversation was animated and the children were hilarious. We all felt especially close to each other. Our happy time lingered on into the after-dinner hours of cleanup, homework, lunch packing—often the hours that take the last bit of starch out of a wilted day.

Later, when the house was quiet, the children asleep, and my husband still busy at the church, I saw that my Bible was open to Matthew 5 where I had been reading earlier in the day—*Happy are the pure in heart . . . the transparent people.* Truly, God had spoken to me through His Word.

As I looked ahead to the next day I found myself wondering what new adventures were in store for me. And so it can be—for all of us, each day of our lives.

Happy is the woman who is honest with herself, with others, and, above all, with God. This woman has given over every conscious area of her life to God, and has asked Him to reveal to her the inner areas of fear and bitterness that need to be healed. Between her and her fellow human beings, there is no barrier. In her there is no tension, for she seeks to hide nothing from God or man. Because she is a transparent person, her Lord is able to shine through her life and be visible to those around her.

7

Happy are those who make peace, for they will
be known as sons of God!

Matthew 5:9 PHILLIPS

Blessed are the peacemakers: for they shall be
called the children of God.

Matthew 5:9 KJV

The Peacemaking Women

PEACE . . . ah, yes, we see the word often these days—in
symbols, on bumper stickers, on Christmas cards, and on
buildings. One friend of ours uses it on his personal statio-
nery, another has it written boldly across his front door. It's
all around us—yet, what is it, this *peace?* And who are today's
peacemakers? Whoever they are, Jesus says they are happy
people, and they belong to Him. *Happy are the peacemakers . . .
they are the children of God.*

Is peace something quiet, unruffled—perhaps unreachable? Are the peacemakers those calm, unshakable people
I often wish I could be like? And is there really a place for
peace in this turbulent, pulsating world?

The word *peace* makes me think of summer vacations, of

93

long hours when at last I don't have anything special to do; when the weather is warm and beautiful and I have the time to hear the breeze moving in the trees. Yes, that's peaceful— but throw in a little rainstorm . . . let school begin again and fill my days with busy moments, and exit peace! At least, *that* kind of peace.

But that's okay—because that's not the kind of peace Jesus is talking about in this Beatitude. The peace we find in this world is totally dependent upon time, place, and circumstance. It comes and it goes. Jesus was talking about *real* peace, the peace that comes from God. He spelled it out for us: "I leave behind with you—peace; I give you my own peace and my gift is nothing like the peace of this world" (John 14:27). Once we have God's peace, it doesn't leave us, no matter what happens in our lives or in the world around us. It's always there, deep inside us. God's peace is . . . a sense of occupancy in the heart . . . a feeling that Someone is there all the time— a spiritual reaching out for God's hand and finding it there. That is peace.

Surely, then, if we are to become peacemakers, we must first of all be at peace with ourselves. For if we're at war on the inside, we'll carry the battle out into the world. As Jesus said, "If a household is divided against itself, it cannot last" (Mark 3:25). And neither can we—our inner conflicts can bring the walls of our being down around our ears.

That's what happened to some people I knew years ago. They were very unhappy in their church because they objected to the minister's "politics in the pulpit." For instance, one Sunday he asked them if they could buy love and justice— and they thought the love theme sounded a bit like some kind of Communist propaganda. They thought a preacher should preach the gospel—but apparently without applying it to life.

Well, they left the church and went to another one that was known for its strict emphasis on worship and its lack of social involvement. But still they weren't happy. They had just as many complaints, although for different reasons. It was obvious that these people would never find peace anywhere until they found it within themselves. Wherever they went, they took their inner frustrations with them . . . and they became disturbers of peace.

When Jesus lives within us, His love brings the warring elements of our selves together into the whole persons we were meant to be. He frees us to be the "you" of you and the "me" of me. We can shake hands with our selves . . . we have peace.

There's also something about inner peace that makes us want to spread it around. We want to bring it into our relationships with other people and eliminate the barriers between us. But that isn't always easy, and sometimes the process isn't what we usually think of as "peaceful." It may mean uncomfortable, even painful exchanges between us.

A few years ago Louie and I were visiting friends from another parish we had served. It was what we call a "warm-fuzzy" night—comfortable old friends combined with interesting new people to meet.

At Louie's table there were several new acquaintances . . . one of them was a gifted artist whose work we both admired (but couldn't afford). Her name was Gail and she was a lovely woman, full of grace as a person. From her husband, with whom I was sitting, I learned that she also had a busy home life—when I asked about the size of their family, his answer was simply, "Boys—and numerous!"

Gail seemed to be a gal with everything. But of course we didn't know what was going on inside her . . . and at that moment she was in the midst of a terrible struggle between her home and her career. At first she had thought she could handle them both—and do a creditable job in each area. Then came the days when she couldn't cope, and the short straw always seemed to go to the boys and her husband.

Actually we all have days like that, even when we don't have a budding career to squeeze into our lives. But Gail was convinced that she was having more than a healthy share of difficulty and she was afraid it was hurting her family. And so, the night we met her she was carrying a heavy burden of guilt in her heart.

I didn't know how Gail felt until about a year later. Louie was one of the speakers at a regional ecumenical retreat, and Gail and her husband were there representing their church. It was wonderful to see them again, and I was especially delighted to learn that Gail and I were in the same small group which was to meet every morning for discussion and sharing.

At our group's first morning meeting we went from one to another, trying to put words around who we felt we were and what we thought was our main priority as a Christ person. Everyone shared—except Gail. Throughout the meeting she blinked back tears. No one questioned her, but her silence let us know she was hurting. After the meeting she stayed behind, and I could see that she wanted to talk. When we were alone she told me what was bothering her. . . . And would you believe it? *It was my husband!*

Apparently, at that "warm-fuzzy" dinner party almost a year ago, Louie had said something that had cut Gail deeply . . . had seemed almost cruel. He had spoken of the need to balance career and family . . . and of the danger that a profession might take up all of a person's life energy, leaving human relationships, and the family in particular, with the crumbs from the table. His remarks seemed innocuous enough, but to Gail—at that sensitive moment in her life— they were crushing. Her mind began to play tricks with her. . . . "Louie knew something"—he didn't. "My husband must have talked to him"—he hadn't. "Louie thinks women shouldn't have careers"—wrong again! Silently, all those months, Gail had kept her hurt inside herself until now it had festered and grown out of proportion.

I understood what Gail had done, for I could remember doing the same thing . . . being hurt, usually through a misunderstanding, and instead of talking it out immediately, I embraced the hurt feelings—suffering inside for days, weeks, even months. Why do we do such things, when it's so much nicer to embrace a friend instead of a hurt?

Clearly, Gail had misunderstood Louie. I knew his feelings on the subject, and I realized that he hadn't been talking to Gail specifically, nor to women in general. He was speaking about all people . . . about businessmen who make money their god, about ministers who make success their thing—about himself and me, for we were having our own struggle to keep the balance between work and family.

During those months Gail had felt guilty and censured—and so unnecessarily. I tried to tell her that, but she wasn't about to be convinced, at least not by me.

It was a long day, waiting to see Louie alone. First there was lunch, and then the "discipline of silence" until dinner. (That really *was* a discipline for me that day!) Next came dinner, then evening vespers—and finally, cabin time! At last I could tell Louie about Gail.

When I told him, he was concerned . . . concerned that Gail had been hurting for so long . . . concerned that she was hurting still. Late as it was, he grabbed his flashlight and went looking for the cabin where Gail and her husband were staying. He was gone a long time and I fell sound asleep.

The next morning at breakfast Gail's husband—a gentle giant of a man—rushed up to us and hugged Louie. "Louie, Louie," he said, "there is peace between my house and yours!"

Peace had been made the night before when Gail and Louie talked out their misunderstanding on the porch of Gail's cabin. At first it had been awkward and difficult for both of them. Now they were very tired and would need an extra cup of coffee. But the important thing was that they had been willing to suffer the discomfort that led to mutual understanding . . . to *shalom*, the peace that comes after the honest struggle. And then, as they talked, they really heard each other . . . they had become peacemakers.

Only when we have peace within ourselves can we mend these breaks in our relationships with others. Only when Jesus makes us whole can we begin to see that the world itself needs to be made whole.

A peacemaker is an absorbent person. When malicious words and gossip hit him, they go no further. . . . Instead of reverberating in excitement, he is like a great silencing chamber . . . gossip hits him and is absorbed. Yes, he may feel the sting of it, but he doesn't pass it on. He smothers it with forgiveness.

I'll never forget seeing such a magnanimous spirit in action. Some years ago, while Louie and I were studying in Scotland, Billy Graham came to London to hold a crusade at the Harringay Arena. Since we had known Billy and the team back home, we were asked to come from Edinburgh to work with Dawson Trotman in follow-up—which we did for eight wonderful weeks.

One night several of us squeezed into a small British car to accompany Billy to the arena. Billy was preaching that night and I remember wishing he could have had a quieter ride, but we were excited and talkative. Then one of our group began to tell Billy about some unkind, terribly unfair comments an ecclesiastical leader had made about him in the newspapers. Apparently our fellow passenger felt it his duty to repeat them to Billy, but believe me, if I'd had a muzzle I'd have used it! I felt hurt for Billy and I wondered how he could possibly get up and preach after hearing such things.

For a long time Billy sat quietly. Then, thoughtfully and simply, as though he were speaking partly to us and partly to Someone Else, he said, "God bless that man. If I were in his place, I'd probably feel the same way about me."

As far as Louie and I can recall, that was all he said — but we have never forgotten it. Many times, finding ourselves in similar situations, it has helped us to remember his words and his attitude. (Thank you, Billy!)

Jesus, now I understand what You meant when You said, "Love your enemies, bless them that curse you . . ." (Matthew 5:44 KJV). I always wondered how I could throw my arms around someone who deliberately hurt me. But now I know that it *is* possible — if I am a peacemaker. There is a difference between the action and the person . . . I don't have to love them both. You are telling me to love *the person.*

Peace in our mind . . . peace in our close relationships . . . that's a good beginning. But if peace ends there — on the inside — something is *very* wrong. Peace is a precious commodity, a part of our inheritance in Christ, but if we seek it simply for our own comfort, it will lose its purpose.

We must remember that we aren't called to *keep* peace, but to *make* peace. The inner peace Jesus gives us equips us to go out into the world and bring its warring forces together.

Keeping peace is passive . . . "Don't rock the boat" — "Don't get involved in controversy" — "Sweep unpleasantness under the rug." Peace keepers often hide from problems, crying "Peace, peace!" when there is no peace, and no one to make it. By ignoring conflicts, they actually make them worse.

"Making peace" is active, involved, aggressive. Peacemakers can see past personalities to the issues that must be resolved. They are strong people who can take moral stands. They bring sanity out of chaos and confusion.

Sometimes it takes more than one person to make things

whole. In our town the University on occasion will hold open meetings where people with conflicting views can discuss a controversial issue. Our congregation also holds open forums that serve a similar purpose . . . they give people an opportunity to speak out on some highly emotional subjects.

But sometimes our discussions get pretty heated, and at times it seems that we're only making a situation worse by talking about it. Then—always from somewhere among us—comes a peacemaker, a person whose vision extends far beyond our personal interests to where the real problem lies. His clarity of mind, his integrity, and his courage seem to lift the rest of us up to his level where we, too, can see more clearly.

Yes, our world needs peacemakers. Not only do they bring us together—they also seem to bring out the good in us all. And perhaps that's the element that will hold the pieces of this world together someday. . . .

As I go through the house straightening up, I like to let my mind run free. One morning recently I was thinking about peacemakers. . . . Who are they? I mean, specifically—what do they do in life? What do they look like? Where would we find one if we needed one? And how would we recognize one in a crowd?

Certainly a sincere evangelist is a peacemaker. His entire life is given over to reconciling man to God through Christ. But we all can't be evangelists in that sense, can we? Some of us—many of us—have no talent for speaking to masses of people . . . some of us must simply let God's peace work in our lives and pray that it will fall like good seed in the lives of those we touch each day. If we use every opportunity we have to bring man closer to God and man closer to man, then *we* are the peacemakers—each one of us.

My thoughts were interrupted when the phone rang. It

was Sue, a friend I don't see very often . . . actually, I don't have to, because our friendship is always there when either of us needs it. That day Sue needed it . . . she was crying. I waited, not knowing what to say, but I used those moments to pray for my friend and for Ed, her husband. Their marriage had been in trouble for years. They had serious financial problems and both of them were working to keep their two older children in college. . . . There was a crisis in the life of a younger child . . . and during the past few years there had been a siege of illness and surgery in the family. Life had been rough for Sue and Ed, and instead of bringing husband and wife closer together—as rough times can do—it had driven them far apart.

When Sue got control of her tears and was able to talk, she told me that their situation had come to a head the previous day. She and Ed had a terrible argument. In desperation they went to a mutual friend of theirs and ours—a minister who is now a clinical psychologist. This man is truly gifted by God in the art of counseling, and generously filled with the love of the Holy Spirit. He was just what Sue and Ed needed.

First, he asked Sue and Ed to be specific about all the things they resented in each other. Painful and humiliating as it must have been, they did it . . . and there it was—all the years of ugliness and hurt out in the open.

Then the counselor asked them to be equally specific in describing all the good things they saw in each other . . . the things that had drawn them together in the beginning, the things that had made their marriage last for twenty years, and the things that were still there. And as they probed among the ruins of their life, they began to see that there was still a lot to love in each other. As Sue put it, "We really have so much to go on."

I realized then that Sue's tears came from joy, from the relief of knowing that she and Ed could become whole again, in time. Our friend the psychologist had been the peacemaker in their fragmented relationship.

Now Sue and I prayed for God's final touch of healing, for she and Ed had done many things to hurt each other, in the way that only a husband and wife can hurt, and there was a deep need for forgiveness on each side. But they would have help. Jesus is the expert Forgiver and Forgetter, and because He had come to live *in* them, He would do this *for* them.

I hung up the phone with a feeling of gratitude for all peacemakers everywhere. And I prayed that when I had the opportunity to serve, I would be ready.

Ready? Am I ready now? There really isn't any perfect time to be ready to bring people together. Jesus is always ready . . . we simply have to let Him use us.

But some conflicts are so big . . . where do we begin to reconcile them? I'm thinking about war . . . after all, you can't really think about peace without thinking about war. What can I do about it? What can we ordinary people do to end war?

I hate war . . . so does everyone I know. The fact that I have three sons may have something to do with the intensity of my feelings. Yet I felt the same way before I had sons. But I also hate tyranny and manipulation of persons . . . there lies the moral conflict each of us must work out for himself.

Still, there are things we can do as peacemakers. We can pray for the leaders of our nation and for those of all other nations. We can pray for the men and women who have the enormous responsibility of making decisions that affect the lives of so many others. May they be sensitive to the forces that lead to peace . . . may they be strong enough to suffer the discomfort of reconciling differences . . . may they *respect*

honest differences and not make conformity their only aim
. . . may they, too, pray for guidance.

War does more than kill. It commits atrocities on the hearts
and minds of the people who stay behind while their sons go
off to fight. A Japanese-American friend of ours went
through a cruel ordeal during World War II. One day he was
a respected friend and neighbor—and the next day he was
whisked off to an internment camp as a so-called national
security risk. Many German-Americans suffered similar experiences. After the war, the Russians became the bad guys
. . . and then the Chinese. That's what happens when we
allow ourselves to become part of war's hate syndrome.

We can support our country without hating those who dis-
agree with its policies . . . because, for peacemakers, there is
no enemy. We can aim to be like Jesus, hating the forces that
cause war, but never hating our fellow human beings who are
caught up in it.

But wars don't have to start . . . we don't have to hate or
destroy. There is another Way. . . .

In the closing scene of the film version of the novel *Ben Hur,*
the young Palestinian Judah Ben Hur is reached by Jesus the
Christ. And Judah, a man whose life had been filled with hate,
bitterness, and revenge, says simply, "He has taken the sword
out of my hand." That's exactly what Jesus does when He
comes into our lives. He takes the swords out of our hands.
We no longer want to hurt . . . we want to heal. With His
love in our hearts, we shall be able to make peace . . . and as
God's children, we shall be unable to make war. That's the
other Way. . . . At least, in my own personal struggle of conscience, so it is for me.

*Happy is the woman who truly longs for peace—within herself,
within her family, and throughout the world. For she knows that
strife begins within the human soul where parts of ourselves are at*

war against each other. Beginning with herself, she asks God to help her end the conflicts that lead to destruction. From there, she seeks to reconcile the differences that exist among all human beings, even in the midst of love . . . perhaps even in her own family. Deeply happy is this woman when she sees that God is the Way to peace, and that through her words and witness she can be used by Him as a peacemaker.

8

Happy are those who have suffered persecution
for the cause of goodness, for the kingdom of
heaven is theirs!
And what happiness will be yours when people
blame you and ill-treat you and say all kinds of
slanderous things against you for my sake! Be
glad then, yes, be tremendously glad—for your
reward in heaven is magnificent. They persecuted the prophets before your time in exactly
the same way.

Matthew 5:10–12 PHILLIPS

Blessed are they which are persecuted for righteousness' sake: for theirs is the kingdom of
heaven.
Blessed are ye, when men shall revile you, and
persecute you, and shall say all manner of evil
against you falsely, for my sake.
Rejoice, and be exceeding glad: for great is
your reward in heaven: for so persecuted they
the prophets which were before you.

Matthew 5:10–12 KJV

The Suffering Women

Persecution . . . what a grim word. I don't even want to think
about it. I flinch from it . . . it reminds me of the early Christians and the suffering they endured.

But persecution still exists, and many of us later Christians
suffer for our faith. The acts of torment are more subtle
than those the Romans used, but they can be very painful

. . . the social stigma we're given when we refuse to join or-
ganizations that exclude certain people . . . the looks of
guests at a dinner party when we don't laugh at their dehumanizing jokes . . . the ridicule a young person gets when he
refuses to go along with the group in unhealthy experiments.
Love itself disturbs some people.

Chip, chip, chip—that's the way it goes these days . . . hundreds of little persecutions that chip away at our spiritual
complacency, reminding us that we are not our own. We belong to Jesus, and there is a price we must pay. . . .

If we're humble—the proud and arrogant will call us foolish.

If we're tamed by God—those who are self-made will call
us weak.

If we're transparently honest—we will irritate those who
feel uncomfortable with the truth.

If we're generous, and those around us seek revenge—we'll
be known as a soft touch.

If we believe that God's ways are the best ways for mankind—we'll be called prudes.

If we're peacemakers when others want war—we'll be
called weaklings, even traitors.

Just as Jesus was persecuted, His followers will meet with
opposition along the Way. Unavoidably the Christian life
will be a rebuke to some—and people don't take kindly to
being rebuked.

Christians were made to give and receive love—not to hate
or lie in wait for an enemy. That's why, of all things in life,
persecution is the hardest for us to bear.

But why does anyone have to suffer? Is it God's way of
reprimanding us when we do something wrong? And if we
do all the right things, will we automatically be exempt from
this pain?

Intellectually we all know that the answer to those questions is *no*. Yet we often behave as if it were *yes*. Let suffering come into our lives and we begin saying, "What have I done wrong?" Or worse than that—"Why is God punishing me?"

Suffering is a stubborn fact of human life. It comes to everyone, without discrimination. But not all suffering has value—what we suffer *for* can make a difference. Jesus didn't say, *Happy are you when you suffer*—period. He said, *Happy are you when you suffer for right causes.*

If I were to tally the score, I'm sure I'd find that most of my suffering has come from doing something wrong to my brothers and sisters in life and not from doing something right for God. I have goofed more often than I like to admit ... I've been thoughtless ... I've hurt people ... I've been selfish ... and when I realize what I've done, I suffer. There is no joy in this kind of pain.

But even when I make careless mistakes I can feel God at work in me ... showing me my weaknesses ... pushing me to admit I was wrong ... stretching me ... and then finally giving me the grace to forgive myself. So there is some good in this kind of suffering, after all—yet it's not the kind Jesus is describing in this final Beatitude. When He says we will find joy through our pain, He is speaking about the kind of suffering we will know only when we stand with Him and walk His Way. It is the outcome of *living* the Beatitudes.

How easy it is for me to nod my head and say, "Yes, that's right!" Making it part of my life is something else. I find it very hard. When Jesus tells me not only to anticipate trouble but to "jump for joy" when it comes—that's hard. It will mean far more than nodding my head.

I think of Joachim, a man we met in a work camp in Europe some years ago. . . . He and his family suffered the loss of many material things because he was determined to fulfill his call to preach the gospel.

I think of our friends who, because they are Christians, are speaking out against white supremacy in countries where it is a government policy. They are suffering as a result. In a recent letter one of them assured us, "Please believe that we are all in good heart. Our Christian faith, thank God, enables us to face persecution with equanimity and cheerfulness."

I think of the martyred Stephen in the Book of Acts. . . . I think of the African evangelist who spoke to our congregation recently and told us about the persecution Christians have suffered in many parts of his continent . . . and how they were filled with forgiving love for their persecutors even in the midst of their agony.

Yes, even today some Christians are giving their lives for Jesus Christ . . . and good things *do* come out of suffering when He is present.

I think of Corrie ten Boom and her sister, Betsie, imprisoned in the terrible concentration camp, Ravensbruck, during World War II . . . two young Dutch girls enduring inhuman brutality and coming through it spiritually triumphant. In *The Hiding Place* Corrie ten Boom describes her prison ordeal and the amazing change that came into her life:

> But as the rest of the world grew stranger, one thing became increasingly clear. And that was the reason the two of us were here. Why others should suffer we were not shown. As for us, from morning until lights-out, whenever we were not in ranks for roll call, our Bible was the center of an ever-widening circle of help and hope. Like waifs clustered around a blazing fire, we gathered about it, holding out our hearts to its warmth and light. The blacker the night around us grew, the brighter and truer and more beautiful burned the word of God. "Who shall separate us from the love of Christ? Shall tribulation, or distress, or persecution, or famine, or nakedness, or peril, or sword? . . . Nay, in all these things we are more than conquerors through Him that loved us."
>
> I would look about us as Betsie read, watching the light leap

from face to face. More than conquerors. . . . It was not a wish. It was a fact. We knew it, we experienced it minute by minute—poor, hated, hungry. We are more than conquerors. Not "we shall be." We are! Life in Ravensbruck took place on two separate levels, mutually impossible. One, the observable, external life, grew every day more horrible. The other, the life we lived with God, grew daily better, truth upon truth, glory upon glory.

God invaded Corrie ten Boom's time of persecution, and He will do the same for us—*whenever our cause is right.* Few of us will ever go to prison for our faith, but at some point in our lives persecution will present us with a choice—do we enter in or back away? do we say *yes* or *no*? do we live or die? And by that, I don't mean only physical death, for there are other ways to die.

If we believe that the cause is right, if we are willing to suffer for the moment because God has given us eyes to see beyond now to what will follow, what then? What help will there be? What guarantee do we have that we will find strength, peace, and joy at the end of the road?

A very good friend who has known more than a little suffering in life says, "We all will suffer persecution if we follow Jesus—but we must choose our hill wisely." In other words, we must be sure in our hearts that the cause we are willing to suffer for is His. For without His presence, there can be no joy in suffering.

But if we believe that the cause is God's—what then? How can we be sure He'll stand with us?

At this point I feel a little inadequate to write about this Beatitude. So many others could speak with depth of their experiences, while mine seem shallow. But Jesus doesn't tell us to *seek* suffering and persecution—only to expect it, accept it, and find joy in it when it comes. The portion that has come to me is small, and couldn't really be called persecution, but in my times of suffering God *has* brought me a strange kind of joy, and this is what I want to share. . . .

One day, without warning, it happens—you're not looking for trouble . . . you don't want to make waves . . . but all of a sudden you have to put your faith where your mouth is. . . . You do something that seems simple, uncompromising— and the world turns upside down. . . .

A few years ago we moved to a new church in a very beautiful, very affluent town. The town was changing . . . research centers were popping up all over the area, and the University of California had built a campus there. New industry brought new people, new ideas, new life-styles. Clearly, the town was on the growing edge of a changing American society. Its newness was part of what drew us there . . . it was also what repelled many of the established residents. That's the *where* of the situation. Add to this the *when*—the year of a bitter debate concerning open housing in California which wasn't the most welcome subject in a town where there were reports of a so-called gentlemen's agreement to keep "certain elements" out. And the *who?* The new minister and his wife, who didn't have the sense to do as they were told and stay away from controversy.

Within a short time after our installation Louie preached a group of sermons that applied the gospel to life—to *our* life in *our* town! In one sermon he read from Colossians 3:11: *In Christ there is no Jew or Greek, male or female—we are all one.* And then he ended with a question. . . . If we believed in this oneness, could we actually deny *anything*—housing, jobs, education—to *anyone?*

A few weeks earlier I had been asked to join an Open Housing committee, and of course I did. I worked with some of our most dedicated citizens—dowagers, domestics, faculty wives, realtors, and just plain *hausfraus* like me. I had no idea

I was headed for trouble until one day there was a picture of our committee in the newspaper. Immediately a member of our congregation took me aside and said, "No minister's wife should ever get involved in such a controversial thing!"

Well, Louie did, and I did, and now the repercussions began. First there were phone calls from friends who felt sorry for us . . . then there were angry callers who wanted to put us in our place. On the Sunday Louie preached on Colossians 3:11 I just got back to the house when the phone rang—it was my first obscene call! I guess I'm pretty "cream cheese" because I was so shocked, all I could say was, "Why, sir! God bless you!" and hang up. Then there was the message telling us, "Go back to Harlem where you belong" . . . and the endless stream of hate literature, parts of it underlined especially for us.

It went on for months. Normally I'm a mail hound, but by that time I dreaded going to the mailbox. And there were other things, too—things that were hard to take, because they hit my vulnerability center—my family.

In the beginning, when Louie became aware of the hostility, he was angry. I remember walking the beach with him for hours . . . we were asking ourselves—and God—if this was one of those times when we were to shake the dust from our feet and move on. There were places to move on to, and certainly we were tempted, but always the sense of call and the urgency to do a job right where we were won out. Our decision was simply to do as the gospel says—and take the consequences.

Then I saw something happen in Louie's life. . . . Something was coming in from the outside. His times of quiet and prayer were rewarded with peace and love . . . peace regarding what had happened, love for the opposition. It didn't seem natural—that's what I mean by "Something from outside." It was Christ's own Spirit.

I knew then that the cause was right. There would be no turning back.

That was eight years ago, and I wish I could tell you that once we turned the corner, everything was beautiful. Everything wasn't, but many things began to be.

It was still hard to lose people because they didn't like a church that was "involved"—but it was good to gain new people who wanted a church precisely because it was. It was still hard to accept bigotry in some people—yet it was so good to find that in some people it wasn't bigotry at all, but rather an honest difference of opinion as to the role the church is to play in the world. It was still hard to be criticized by the fringes of the community, one side calling us "radical com-symps" and the other "gradualists"—but it was good to sense an inner freedom that caused us to care less about what either side said. It was more important that people had the time and the opportunity to change.

And through all these glad-sad years, many exciting things were happening—the Greater Parish Ministry, born of our Minister of Missions' dream of churches working together to meet the human needs of *our* people in *our* city . . . lay people trained and sent out as evangelists in our own congregation and community . . . new classes to make the mind stretch . . . a new contemporary worship service added to the two traditional Sunday-morning services . . . on Friday nights a chapel service of prayer and praise led by laymen . . . a youth program that makes your spirit zing, as young people from the church and from the streets of our town come together in the Sun House, getting to know each other and their Lord . . . the choirs growing in all ways, young people encouraged and trained to use their talents for God—their flutes, recorders, violins, bells, trumpets, and guitars—surprising us with joy in our services . . . and best of all—*love* . . . love being felt and expressed, love touching and healing lives . . . a true baptism of love through the Holy Spirit.

Yes, during all these years God has been at work, and probably more in us than anywhere else. We have been pulled and pushed and made to grow, and He has been more than faithful. He has never left us without help.

During our most difficult days, help came in many forms, most of them unexpected. God was telling us that we weren't alone.

One Sunday a visiting minister came to speak at our church. He was a man everyone loved and respected. Although I had never met him, it took all of two minutes after our introduction to make me feel he and I had been friends for a long time. He was old enough to be my father, widely traveled, and very charming.

Our guest was easy to talk to and as we lingered over Sunday dinner Louie and I told him about the crisis in our lives. If we were looking for sympathy—and I suppose we were—we didn't get any from him. Instead, this urbane, sophisticated man lifted our wounded spirits with words spoken quietly, almost to himself. He said, "In all my years of ministry, whenever the going gets rough because of preaching and living the gospel, I just turn my mind to my Lord. And when I think of *Him*, and all He went through—the ridicule, the misunderstanding, the betrayal, and then the cross—for *me*, for old me, I can't get too worked up about what I may be going through at the moment. I just think of my Lord—and it helps."

Our friend left town that evening and we didn't see him again, but his words stayed with us. They were like good seed in our hearts. Help had come gently, but unmistakably. Thinking of our Lord during our time of suffering made the wounds easier to bear. Looking at Him got our eyes off ourselves and gave us perspective.

We had lived through a difficult time—no, more than lived through it. We felt not only alive but strong . . . and very much at peace.

While that particular phase seemed over, and a beautiful new work of the Spirit was begun, the experience had left scars deep inside me. I wasn't aware of them until much later.

It happened on a rare quiet afternoon at our house. Everyone else was off somewhere, and I was about to splurge on an afternoon to myself. I was savoring the time to read . . . about five books I had already begun stared at me from my bed stand. I reached for the smallest one, a slim volume on praise, hoping I would have the satisfaction of finishing it. I read for most of the afternoon and I was almost at the end of the book when a feeling of excitement came over me. I was expectant, eager, as if something important was about to happen. As I read I came to a quote from 1 Thessalonians 5:16–18: "Rejoice evermore. Pray without ceasing. In every thing give thanks: for this is the will of God in Christ Jesus concerning you" (KJV).

The words seemed to speak directly to me, and in response I began thanking God for all the beautiful and happy things in my life:

For my husband. . . . What do you say when, after twenty-two years of sharing life, you feel more love than when you first began—not *less*, but *more!* And not just love, but its handmaidens: Honesty and freedom of expression . . . the things that stretch a relationship and allow the soul within to grow. I thanked my God for Lou.

For our children, each one so unique, so full of his and her own special brand of joy and potential. I almost ached with love as I thought of Dan, Tim, Andie, and Jim. . . .

For my mother's healing . . . because now this wonderful woman who had worked so hard—and alone—to raise a daughter would have a chance to enjoy her retirement years with her good husband. . . .

For Louie's parents—so incredibly active and used by God in their "retirement" ministry. . . .

For our special friends, the ones we call our "warm fuzzies," the ones with whom we share our life and ministry. . . .

For our congregation . . . if our first years among these people were hard, the recent years more than made up for them. We were among a loving, ministering core of believers, sharing their faith and trying to live the gospel we all believed in. . . .

There were so many things to thank God for . . . they kept coming to my mind, one after another. I had never known such a full heart. But when I thought I was through, the Spirit let me know that He was not through with me . . . I heard no words, but the feeling was very clear—*There is more!*

In my mind I answered, "But, Lord, I've thanked You for *everything*—for *all* the good and lovely things in my life—honestly!"

Again there was that feeling—*There is more!*

I went back to 1 Thessalonians 5:16–18—". . . In every thing give thanks: for this is the will of God in Christ Jesus concerning you." And again the words seemed to speak directly to me. They weren't telling me to thank God for all the beautiful and lovely things in my life. They said, ". . . In *every* thing give thanks. . . ." *All things*. . . . Did that mean even the hard, the painful things? Was I to thank God for the times of suffering, too? Yes—that was the "something more." The Spirit seemed to confirm it in my heart.

Now, if you were like me, you'd be thinking, "Wait a minute—that would be insincere. It doesn't make sense." To thank God for the good that comes out of suffering is realistic—but to thank Him for the suffering itself—well, I just didn't understand. Yet I knew that there were times when I had to respond to God in a simple, childlike way, or my faith wouldn't work. This was one of those times.

And so I began—thanking God for all the hard and bitter experiences of the past years. One by one, I relived them,

and as I named them aloud they seemed so petty . . . the
letters, the phone calls, the looks. As God brought them into
my mind I was able to let go and give them to Him—with
thanks. Then it was finished, and I was spent. But I felt whole.
Deep inside me something tender had been touched by a gentle, loving, healing Hand. While I still didn't understand what
had happened, I knew that thanking God in all things had
done something for me that I wasn't able to do for myself.
Yes, I felt a kind of joy. . . . I knew then that this final Beatitude was as real, as practical, as right for today as all the
others.

As the burden was lifted from my heart, I felt love re-
placing it . . . love for those who had helped, forgiveness and
love for those who had hurt . . . understanding for their motives, compassion for their prejudices. I was free . . . and the
kingdom of heaven was mine.

*Happy is the woman who knows that God stands with her in
times of suffering and persecution. This woman can be unjustly
criticized and won't jump to her own defense . . . she can take
slander without lashing back . . . she can even accept the misunderstanding of friends. She can do all these things because of Christ.
When there is bitterness in the deepest parts of her heart, she asks
Him to take it from her. At that moment, when she can say, "Bless
them, Lord, for they know not what they do," the kingdom of heaven
is hers.*

9

> You are the earth's salt. . . . You are the world's light. . . .
>
> Matthew 5:13, 14 PHILLIPS

> Ye are the salt of the earth: but if the salt have lost his savour, wherewith shall it be salted? it is thenceforth good for nothing, but to be cast out, and to be trodden under foot of men.
> Ye are the light of the world. A city that is set on an hill cannot be hid.
>
> Matthew 5:13, 14 KJV

The Salty Christians

I've just come in from another walk along the beach. This time my body doesn't tingle from the chill winter wind . . . now I'm warmed by the sun, for it is the eve of summer.

When I started out this morning I was thinking about the words that follow the Beatitudes. . . . "You are the earth's salt," Jesus said to His followers. And I wondered if He was saying, "If you live these Beatitudes, then you *will* be like salt to the earth."

As I wondered—and walked—I found myself on a lonely stretch of beach . . . no surfers, no sun worshipers, absolutely

117

no one but me. Suddenly I had a delicious urge . . . with the sun warm on my back I wanted to run into the sea. I wanted to let the waves wash over my tired body and clear the haze from my mind. Ordinarily my children have to pull me into the ocean unless the water is lukewarm, but today my need for refreshment was greater than my desire for creature comfort. I wasn't dressed for the occasion, but my shirt and shorts were expendable. In I went.

It was wonderful! Laughing, squealing, feeling the swells lift me and then being tumbled about by a breaking wave . . . for a few lovely minutes I was fourteen again! But the best part was coming out of the water, my clothes dripping wet, and plopping onto a warm bed of sand. Pure joy . . . one of the best feelings in the world, and today it was mine!

Lying there, I could taste the salt around my mouth. Here and there on my arms and legs were little telltale spots of white. Salt . . . salt. . . . What was Jesus telling us?

We take so many things for granted in our world that sometimes we lose sight of their real value. Surely salt is one of these. It's essential, yet very ordinary. We see it on every table, every cook uses it without even thinking about it. Still, there must be something special, something meaningful about it.

Again, it helps me to imagine myself back in the days when Jesus spoke these words. Yes, already there is more substance to *salt*—for in those days you couldn't just pick up a box of salt (iodized or plain) off your supermarket shelf. Salt came from great distances, carried on the backs of camels in long caravans along dangerous routes. Since there wasn't a lot of it, it was used carefully. It was expensive and people paid the price, because no one could do without it. Salt was essential to purify, preserve, and flavor food. There were no refrigerators in those days, no tin cans or sealed packages—in fact, there wasn't very much food. And without salt, there might be starvation.

Purity, preserving, flavor . . . perhaps these are also the qualities of a "salty" Christian. . . .

Purity . . . in a world that has abandoned many of its moral standards, the salty Christian will hold onto God's loving guidelines — not because he *has* to, but because he *wants* to. He knows that God's Way is the only way to a better life.

During the past few years several young people have lived in our home — sometimes for a few days or a week, and sometimes for a year . . . some for happy reasons and some for sad ones. No matter who, or why, or for how long, each one left the special gift of his or her personality in our hearts. One of them, after struggling to make sense out of the changing moral values she found in her world, came to this conclusion: "Not from a sense of 'oughtness' or 'shouldness,' but from a purely practical approach, God's ways are best." She was becoming a salty Christian. . . .

Preserving . . . we preserve things to keep them from rotting, from souring, from going bad. That's why Jesus wants us to be like salt rubbed into society to keep it from going bad.

How's that for a challenge! In a world like ours, where do we begin? I guess the best place is right where we are . . . in our homes, in our community. We have to begin by making contact with people. We have to get involved in the events that concern us. We can't hide in the church and mingle only with our Christian friends.

We won't always be comfortable out in the world. . . . The rubbing in of salt may rub us, and others, the wrong way. And we must be willing to be used up. . . .

Two friends of mine, both of them devoted mothers, had a close brush with the drug problem in our town. It happens to many parents, and many turn and run scared. Not these women . . . they wanted help for their own children, yes, but they also wanted it for all children. So they did something about it . . . they went to the head of the Probation Department, the head of the Welfare Department, and the Chief of Police, and with their help and support they set up a Youth Services Bureau for kids with a drug problem—or any other kind of problem. And now, thanks to these two salty Christians—and to God, to whom they give all the credit—a lot of our young people are being "preserved."

We don't have to look far to find the spots that need salt. And as we are used up, we'll be replenished . . . there is no end to the supply, for our Source is inexhaustible.

Flavoring . . . now, this use of salt is the easiest for me to understand. I love to cook, to spice things up, and of course I couldn't get along without salt. In fact, any complaints I get in the cooking department are usually, "Hey, Mom, a little heavy on the salt, don'cha think?" Salt brings out the flavor of food and sometimes I overdo it . . . but when I use just the right amount—ah, how it enhances the meal!

Jesus said that we Christians are to be to life what salt is to food. We are to add flavor and spice . . . to be real people, full of fun and joy.

Robert Louis Stevenson once wrote in his journal, "Went to church today, and was not greatly depressed." Ouch! Bland, flavorless people *can* be depressing, and Christians are the last people in the world who should be that way. We should be the happiest people because we worship a living Lord . . . and when the worship service is over we should carry our joy with us into our daily service out in the world.

I don't like to see blandness in the church. It makes people think that God squeezed all the fun out of the life we gave to Him. He certainly didn't . . . in fact, He introduces us to a deeper level of joy.

In our congregation we have a real swinger . . . an outgoing, warm, delightful woman named Tony. During the past year she opened up her life to Christ, and I'm happy to say that she is still a swinger . . . she just swings in a new direction. Tony radiates so much energy and gaiety that it's fun just to be around her. She's salty . . . in the way that every Christian should be.

The sun's healing rays drenched me with warmth . . . its light was so bright in my eyes that I had to roll my head from side to side. It reminded me that Jesus also said, "You are the world's light. . . ."

Jesus, *You* are the Light of the world . . . yet here You are, telling us to glow. If You mean we should generate our own light from within . . . well, I just can't do it. I don't have what it takes. If I am to shine, I'll have to borrow light from You. . . . My life will be Your lamp.

Somewhere I read that the houses in ancient Palestine were very dark because they each had only one small window. A lamp was simply a bowl filled with oil and a floating wick, and it was kept on a lamp stand in a prominent place in the house. Remember . . . there weren't any matches in those days and relighting the lamp was pretty difficult, so lamps were left burning most of the time. When people left the house they placed an earthenware bushel measure over the lamp which allowed it to burn safely while they were away. But when they returned, the lamp was immediately uncovered so that it could bring light to everyone in the family.

That's what Jesus is telling us to do . . . to keep our light in the open where it can be seen—and where it can help others to see. In other words, if we are going to live the Beatitudes, we must do it openly . . . this is where privacy ends. Our light must burn brightly in our attitude toward our fellow human beings.

Light is a powerful force that pushes back the darkness. But there are places where light will not go . . . it stops at a closed door. And so must we. We can go just so far. Some people will resist our faith . . . some will run from Jesus . . . some have been in darkness so long they're afraid of the Light. It's right for us to push back the darkness, to bring God's light out into the world, but we have to respect the closed door. The individual will is the key to the door—and only the person whose will it is can open it . . . and when he does we can be ready to flood the area with His brightness.

Light has a nourishing quality . . . when I think of plants seeking the sun, I realize that light helps living things to grow. So it is with the light-filled Christian who shares his faith with those around him. He gives them food for the growing spirit. . . .

Today there are a lot of windows in our houses. We push a button and our homes are flooded with light . . . dimmer, brighter, whichever we choose. We have soft lights and highlights. Many things have changed, but we human beings are still the same. We still need the Light of the world. And we especially need Him in our homes.

How important it is for a mother and father to be light-filled Christians . . . to give their children an environment of warmth and nourishment where they can grow into the persons God wants them to be. How important for a husband and wife to give light to each other, for they too must continue to grow as loving human beings. Sometimes, when I'm weary from stretching, from growing, I see the light of my husband's faith and it gives me energy. Hopefully my light reaches him as well.

And there are others who need our light . . . our friends, the people we work among, our neighbors in the world. If we meet them in an attitude of love, they will grow . . . and so will we. I've seen it happen. . . .

Fred Williams is a member of our church executive staff. Thirteen years ago he came to our town after graduating from a black university in the South where he was trained as a teacher. Then he learned that teaching wasn't really what he wanted to do. He had a large family to support, so he took whatever job he could get, and he became our custodian. He was a good one—and he had other talents as well.

In the years that followed, some of our key lay people and staff realized that Fred Williams was capable of taking on executive responsibilities. So, when our business administrator died, Fred was made Building and Property Administrator. He is responsible for budget control, building use, protection, insurance, and supervision of all church property. His judgment and recommendations are highly respected by our church officers. He has also shown a remarkable ability to work with all age groups, sometimes firmly, but always with love.

Fred continues to grow . . . as an executive, as a trusted counselor, as a Christian, as a man. Recently he said, "I've never felt so full . . . not only as a Christian in my faith, but with *all* people. The trust I feel from the staff and people here—well, it's given me confidence in myself. I feel free to *be*."

Fred grew in the radiance that came through a few light-filled Christians . . . and this is what Jesus wants all of us to do, all the time. He wants us to reflect God's love until it shines throughout the world.

"Let your light shine like that in the sight of men. Let them see the good things you do and praise your Father in Heaven" (Matthew 5:16). There is no better way for us to do this than to be the lamps for His Light. And we become His lamps—fitted and ready to transmit His Light—by letting our lives be shaped by the Beatitudes. These are the attitudes that ought to be.

As I enjoyed the last few moments of sun and sand I felt rich and full and glad. God had spoken to me about my life, my goals. I want to be a loving, sensitive wife, a freeing mother, and a caring woman in my community. But there is more—much more to my future. I was created to do something magnificent—and so were you. We were designed before the beginning of anything—and everything—*to bring praise to our Father in heaven.* What a great and beautiful goal!

I stood up and brushed the sand from my arms and legs. As I walked along the beach toward home, I felt washed by waves of hope, expectation, love, and joy. In my heart the Spirit whispered of the goodness of life and confirmed that the best was still ahead. For over twenty years I had walked—sometimes stumbling—along the Way with Jesus. Yet so much more was to come.

My tender skin told me that I had had enough of the sun for one day. But my heart—newly tender from the touch of the Spirit—told me that I had only just begun with the Son of God.

Happy is the woman who is used by the Lord to warm and enliven the human spirit . . . and whose life becomes her daily witness to His immeasurable goodness.

THE
CHRISTIAN
FAMILY

Larry Christenson

GUIDEPOSTS ASSOCIATES, INC.

Carmel, New York

DEDICATION

To my wife, Nordis,
and to our children,
Timothy, Laurie, Stephen, and Arne,
for the joy they have given me
as a husband and father

Foreword

Here is the book that I have been waiting for, for a long time. There is a great need for a book on family life that covers a wide range of problems from a Biblical point of view.

In this book, Larry Christenson puts into words many of the thoughts and convictions I have had as regards the Christian family.

I *know* there is a great lack in most families in this day. I know, because many of the thousands of teenagers that I contact in my ministry have gotten into problems because of a deficiency in their family life—Christian or non-Christian.

I want this book to be read widely, by pastors, by teachers, by students, and above all, by parents! I believe that if the message of this book were applied on a large scale, it would turn the tide of delinquency in our country and help rescue this generation.

I believe in this book because I believe in the man who wrote it. He is a man who practices what he preaches. Also—this book appeals to the practical streak in me. Intelligent teenagers must read this book. It is the best I have ever read on the subject.

David Wilkerson

CONTENTS

PART ONE: God's Order for the Family

CHAPTER ONE: God's Order for Mates   3
CHAPTER TWO: God's Order for Wives   15
CHAPTER THREE: God's Order for Children   37
CHAPTER FOUR: God's Order for Parents   44
CHAPTER FIVE: God's Order for Husbands   100

PART TWO: Practicing the Presence of Jesus

CHAPTER SIX: Jesus, the Family's Savior
   and Lord   121
CHAPTER SEVEN: The Priesthood of Parents   129
CHAPTER EIGHT: Our Family, a Witness
   for Jesus   165

A Special Acknowledgment

During a trip to England, while browsing through a collection of out-of-print books, I came across a little volume by Dr. H. W. J. Thiersch, entitled *Christian Family Life*. It was originally published in German in 1854. The English edition was translated by S. R. Gardiner, and was published by the Thomas Bosworth firm in 1856; a second English edition was brought out in 1880. The Thomas Bosworth firm is no longer in existence, and the work has now passed into "public domain" in any case.

Nevertheless, I do want to acknowledge my indebtedness to this splendid little work on Christian family life.

As I read it, I found many of Dr. Thiersch's thoughts running parallel to the experience of our own family and congregation. I thought that many of us could be helped by having this voice from a past generation speak to us.

Since I quote or paraphrase him at a number of places in this book, I have taken note of it by a special means of punctuation. Rather than footnote each reference, *I have put an asterisk at the end of each paragraph which is taken or adapted from his book.* I have allowed his sometimes antiquated expression to stand as it is in most cases, to maintain the flavor of the period. My hope is that this form of 'dialog' with a man from an earlier generation will enrich the reader's appreciation and understanding of Christian family life.

Please remember, then, that a paragraph ending with an asterisk indicates a contribution by Dr. Heinrich Thiersch, a German pastor and professor of theology who lived in the middle of the Nineteenth Century.

Other Acknowledgments

Acknowledgment is gratefully made to the many people who have spoken and corresponded with the writer over the past several years on the subject of Christian family life—especially the members of my own congregation, Trinity Lutheran Church, San Pedro, California. Their suggestions and insights have been most helpful in developing the material for this book.

We also gratefully acknowledge our indebtedness to the following publishers and/or authors for quotations from their works:

Dr. Lester Breslow, director of the California Department of Public Health, for his statistical information, and interpretation, on the relationship between divorce and various physical and mental ills.

Christianity Today, an interview with Elton Trueblood, January 6, 1967; and the article, "Love, Honor, and Obey" by Andre Bustanoby, June 6, 1969, quoted by permission.

The Collegiate Challenge, the article, "What's the Next Move?" by Tom Skinner, copyright 1968 by Campus Crusade for Christ International. Used by permission.

Good News For Modern Man. Copyright by The American Bible Society. Used by permission.

Head Masters Association, London, England, for material from the joint report of the Head Masters Association and the Association of Head Mistresses, outlining the respective roles of teenagers and adults in contemporary society.

The Healing Light by Agnes Sanford, published by Macalester Park Publishing Company, St. Paul, Minnesota. Used by permission.

The Houston Chronicle, the article, "12 Rules for Parents for Raising Juvenile Delinquents," copyright January 12, 1960. Used by permission.

How to Discipline Your Children by Dorothy Baruch, Public Affairs Pamphlet No. 154, quoted by permission of the Public Affairs Committee.

Hurlbut's Bible Storybook; *The Amplified Bible*. Quoted by permission of the publisher, Zondervan Publishing House, Grand Rapids, Michigan.

Ann Landers, for a quote from her newspaper column on child guidance.

Letters and Papers from Prison by Dietrich Bonhoeffer, the chapter entitled "A Wedding Sermon From a Cell." Copyright 1967 by SCM Press Ltd, British edition; The Macmillan Company, New York, American edition.

The Living New Testament, published by Tyndale House, Wheaton, Illinois. Used by permission.

A Man Called Peter by Catherine Marshall. Copyright 1951 by Catherine Marshall. Used with permission of McGraw-Hill Book Company.

The March of Faith by Lindley Baldwin, published by Bethany Fellowship, Inc., Minneapolis, Minnesota. Used by permission.

"The Meanest Mother in the World." Reprinted by permission of Radio Station WIBR, Baton Rouge, Louisiana.

The National Observer, for an article by a medical doctor emphasizing the need for external controls in the raising of children.

Please Don't Eat the Daisies by Jean Kerr, published by Doubleday & Co., Inc. Used by permission.

Dr. Max Rafferty, California State Superintendent of Public Instruction, for his article, "The Parent as Dropout." Used by permission of the author.

Signs of the Times, the article, "The Time to Love" by John Drescher, June 1969. Used by permission.

This Week Magazine, the article, "Don't Let Them Grow Up Too Fast" by Booton Herndon, January 26, 1958; and the article, "Fathers Shouldn't Be Mothers" by Dr. Bruno Bettelheim, April 20, 1958.

Unequally Yoked Wives by C. S. Lovett. Available from Personal Christianity, Box 157, Baldwin Park, California 91706.

Capt. Robert Vernon, Youth Service Unit, Los Angeles Police Department, for his observations on the need for stricter discipline in the home.

Voice in the Wilderness, the article, "The Blessing of Work" by Thelma Hatfield; and the article, "The Training of Children." Published by Voice Publications, Northridge, California. Used by permission.

"We Need a Woodshed Revival" by David Wilkerson. Used by permission of the author.

The Scripture quotations in this publication, except where otherwise noted, are from the Revised Standard Version of the Bible, copyrighted 1946 and 1952 by the Division of Christian Education of the National Council of Churches of Christ in the U.S.A. and used by permission.

Introduction

The choice of a title for this book is deliberately dull. It has no flash or zing. It is 'solid,' 'respectable,' perhaps a trifle boring. It is quietly unpretending. It merely designates those for whom the book is written (Christians) and the subject of inquiry (the family). Unless you are prepared to re-examine some of your most basic habits and beliefs about family life, don't bother yourself with this book. It cuts too deep. You will never finish it, much less put it into practice.

Dietrich Bonhoeffer, sitting in a Nazi prison cell, once wrote a wedding sermon for a niece who was about to be married. In it he said, "Marriage is more than your love for each other. It has a higher dignity and power, for it is God's holy ordinance, through which He wills to perpetuate the human race till the end of time. In your love you see only your two selves in the world, but in marriage you are a link in the chain of the generations, which God causes to come and to pass away to His glory, and calls into His kingdom. In your love you see only the heaven of your happiness, but in marriage you are placed at a post of responsibility towards the world and mankind. Your love is your own private possession, but marriage is more than something personal—it is a status, an office."

In Christianity marriage achieves a sanctity and significance which was not known in ancient times. The forgotten dignity of woman was brought to light, and its value acknowledged. Neither the Roman nor even the Mosaic law accorded the wife rights which were equally great and sacred with those of the man. In Christianity the wife, as well as the husband, has claim to be the perfect fidelity of the mate.

The wife ceases to be merely the helper of her husband in this present life, but is a fellow heir with him of eternal life (I Peter 3:7).*

And yet more than all this, the highest love of God to man was shown in the sacrifice of Christ. Through that sacrifice the Church came into existence. Between the Church and Christ there exists a bond of love more holy, tender, and firm than any which ever existed between God and man. In Christianity there is set before man and wife the task of representing upon earth the image of this union between Christ and His Church—an image of self-sacrifice, devotion, fidelity. In ancient times marriage at its best had been a moral relationship. In Christian marriage we see something higher still —a mystery (Esphesians 5:32).*

The Neoplatonic philosophers looked on marriage with gloomy severity—it was a contradiction to the spiritual nature of man. The most rigid sect of Jesus' day—the Essenes —saw marriage as a hindrance to preparation for the kingdom of heaven. But the Christian family is formed to be the very image of the future kingdom of God, in which the will of the Lord shall be done on earth as it is done in heaven. It is not only a school for heaven; in a certain sense it is the anticipated kingdom of God itself.*

In the Christian family, on a small scale, should be seen the wisdom and gentleness of command, the willingness of obedience, the unity and firmness of mutual confidence which will characterize the perfected kingdom of God. In an exact sense, this can be said only of the Christian Church; the Church is above the family. Yet there is no building up of the Church without the building up of family life. In Christian families men should joyfully acknowledge the blessing which God pours out through the Church. In Christian families, on the other hand, should the strength of the Church consist. The order and development which St. Paul follows in Ephesians is no accident. He begins with the loftiest counsel concerning God and the Church which we find anywhere

---

* See page vi in reference to *Christian Family Life,* by Dr. H.W.J. Thiersch.

in the New Testament. He then proceeds to the ordering of family life, for it is in the family life of Christians that the increase of the Church, and its approach to perfection, must be found. *

The Christian family, therefore, does not exist for its own benefit. It is created to bring glory and honor to God. The blessing of man is a derivative, a by-product. Those who stubbornly hold that their own happiness and convenience are the highest goals of family life will never understand God's plan for marriage and the family, for they do not grasp the underlying structure, the basic starting point.

Most books on family life start with man, then try to include God as a helpful additive. A kind of celestial STP, guaranteed to pep up sluggish family life.

This book comes at it the other way around. The family belongs to God. He created it. He determined its inner structure. He appointed for it its purpose and goal. By divine permission, a man and a woman may cooperate with God's purpose and become a part of it. But the home they establish remains His establishment. "Unless the Lord builds the house, those who build it labor in vain" (Psalm 127:1). The children receive their status as members of the family by His act. "God sets the solitary in families" (Psalm 68:6).

Thus it is not our marriage, but His marriage; not our home, but His home; not our children, but His children; not our family, but His family. This might sound like pious rhetoric, but it works itself out in thoroughly down-to-earth fashion. If Jesus is truly Lord in your family, it will influence everything from the way you decorate your house to the way you spend your summer vacation.

So we are going to consider the Christian family—without benefit of flashy title, with no promise that your life will be transformed inside of ten days. Rather, we will look with some care at what the Creator of family life has said about it. We proceed on the assumption that the One who created families knows something about them, and can offer the soundest advice. If one holds to the opinion that marriage is a social contract between two individuals—that and nothing more—he will not be interested in this book. But if you are willing to consider that marriage is more than this, that something mysterious and wonderful lies at the heart of it, that it is the creation of God, and achieves its highest potential and destiny within a structure which He has established, then you may find in these pages some things worth pondering.

The views presented in this book are based unashamedly on certain passages and principles written down in the Bible. We believe they are as true and valid today as when they were written—which is something our age finds hard to accept. Furthermore, the principles expressed here have met the test of centuries. They have met the test in our own experience.

A number of years ago a group of people from our church went on a "family retreat." The theme of our retreat was, "God's Order for Parents." Our only resource material was a seven-page tract on the subject, and this in turn was little more than a summary of Bible verses on the subject. It proved to be more than enough! As a result of that retreat, a number of our families began to look seriously at the structure of family life. We found ourselves calling into question many of the attitudes and practices in our present-day culture. Against the prevailing pattern of relativism and permissiveness, we began to see the biblical concept of order and authority. As the biblical principles were put into practice, we began to see a transformation take place in a number of families.

In our own family, *overnight,* we experienced a dramatic change in the atmosphere of our home—for reasons we will point out later on. This study and practice of the biblical principles for family living has continued, for it is a challenging and exciting venture, and there is always something further to be learned and experienced. We do not offer pat, closed-end answers to the many-faceted problems that face the family today. We merely share some of the basic principles which have quietly revolutionized our own families—and invite you to 'come along' in the adventure of discovering a new sense of direction, a new harmony and joy in your family life.

We have titled this book *The Christian Family*. A Christian has been defined as "someone who lives together with Jesus Christ." This is not a theological definition, but a personal one; it does not describe a Christian in terms of abstract metaphysical principles, but in terms of his everyday *experience*. This is precisely the direction we want to go in our investigation of family life. So we could extend that definition and say that *a Christian family is a family that lives together with Jesus Christ.*

The secret of good family life is disarmingly simple: *Cultivate the family's relationship with Jesus Christ.* There is no phase of family life left outside this relationship. There is no problem a family might face which does not find its solution within the scope of this objective.

How *does* a family cultivate its relationship with Jesus Christ? After all, it isn't like having a guest move in the house . . . or *is* it? But we can't see and talk with Jesus, can't communicate with Him . . . or *can* we, if we take the time to learn *how* one may communicate with Him? This is the purpose of our book: to suggest some of the ways that a family may cultivate its relationship with Jesus Christ. For the basic fact of the Christian religion is simply this, that its Lord is ALIVE.

The business of cultivating your family's relationship with Jesus has two parts to it, basically:

The first part consists of establishing "Divine Order" in the home. This has to do with the relationship of order and authority between the various members in a family.

The second part consists of "Practicing the Presence of Jesus." This is the adventure of sensitizing ourselves to the invisible presence of Jesus in the home—developing our capacity for spiritual perception—learning the practical ways in which we may intensify our awareness of His way and His will for our family.

Of these two parts, the second is the more important. It is

only as we 'practice the presence of Jesus' that our homes become truly Christian. Yet, establishing 'Divine Order' has a certain functional priority, for it helps create an atmosphere where we are *able* to practice the presence of Jesus. When we establish Divine Order in our home, it creates an atmosphere in which Jesus feels at home; the Holy Spirit is then able to do His work of teaching and leading us into the kind of family life for which God created us.

PART ONE:

God's Order for the Family

"Divine Order" is an order of *authority* and *responsibility* which is spelled out in the Bible:

"The head of every *man* is Christ, the head of a *woman* is her husband, and the head of *Christ* is God" (I Corinthians 11:3). "*Children,* obey your parents in everything, for this pleases the Lord" (Colossians 3:20).

God has ordered the family according to the principles of 'headship.' Each member of the family lives under the authority of the 'head' whom God has appointed.

The husband lives under the authority of Christ and is responsible to Christ for the leadership and care of the family. The wife lives under the authority of her husband, and

CHRIST, the 'Head' of the husband; Lord of the family.

HUSBAND, the 'Head' of the wife; chief authority over the children.

WIFE, the helpmate to the husband (Genesis 2:18); secondary authority over the children.

CHILDREN, obedient to parents.

is responsible to him for the way she orders the household and cares for the children. The children live under the authority of both parents. The authority over the children, however, remains essentially one. The dotted line indicates that the authority of the mother is a derived authority. She exercises authority over the children on behalf of and in the place of her husband. This has great practical significance for relationship between mother and children, which we will bring out in a following chapter.

Thus God has structured the family along clear-cut lines of authority and responsibility. It is important to recognize this structure at the outset, for it is so little understood in our day, still less practiced. Yet God has made the well-being and happiness of the family absolutely dependent upon the observance of His divinely appointed order.

Any change from that which His will has ordered only brings forth a misshapen form, for which there is no cure except a return to God's original order. *

-----

* See page vi.

CHAPTER ONE

God's Order for Mates

God's order for mates is nowhere more clearly and simply stated than in the Bible's very first commentary upon the man-woman relationship: "Therefore a man leaves his father and mother and cleaves to his wife, and they become one flesh" (Genesis 2:24). To "cleave to one's mate" takes in every aspect of the relationship between husband and wife. There is no problem which can arise between mates, the solution for which will not be found in a deeper grasp of what it means to cleave to one another, to become 'one flesh' with one's mate.

God made us male and female as a part of His basic creation. It is part of the innermost expression of God Himself. When He created mankind in His own image, He didn't just create man. There was something missing. So God said. "I will make a helper fit for him" (Genesis 2:18). He created woman. Now He had the whole thing. Man and woman came together in marriage, manifesting God's ideal of completeness.

It is God's intention, as a general rule, that man shall find a mate. This is even borne out by statistics. There's about the same number of men and women born in the world. After a war, when the male population is depleted, an amazing thing happens: in the next generation, there will be a bumper crop of male babies. This happened in Europe right after the war. Within one generation, the population was restored to balance again.

The Role of Sex

"For best results, follow instructions of maker." So advised a brochure accompanying a jar of common cold remedy. If such advice is good for the relief of a simple physical ailment, how much more it is needed for the relief of sick marriage relationships! Movies, television, novels, magazines, and billboards constantly bombard us with wrong ideas about sex. Sex is not an invention of 20th century Hollywood. It is a creation of the eternal, holy God, who also gave us definite instructions for its right expression in the relationship of marriage. Sexual union in marriage is a wonderful mystery of God. It occupies a relatively small space in the marriage. Even with young and newly married couples, the sheer amount of time spent in sexual activity is relatively small. Yet without that union the marriage is no marriage. It is like the spark plug of a car: small but essential; it sets the whole mechanism in motion.

We say that sexual union is a mystery, because no rational explanation can fully account for its powerful and pervasive influence in a marriage—indeed, in life itself. While is is primarily a physical act, it draws much more than mere physical sensation into orbit around it. While its primary purpose is procreation, this is not usually its immediate objective; indeed this result may actually be undesired, without diminishing the desire for union. It so merges and unites two human beings that the Bible speaks of them as 'one flesh,' yet no other human act so accentuates one's own identity and self-awareness, at such an elemental level. It is a deep and fundamental giving of oneself, a yielding of the procreative powers to another. Yet the more successful the relationship, the greater degree of self-pleasure obtained by both partners.

Christians tend to fall into two basic errors in their attitude toward sex. The one error is to regard it as a kind of necessary evil. This grows out of the old Greek idea that the body is essentially evil, and the way to be truly 'spiritual' is to subdue and suppress the body as much as possible.

This idea is not altogether absent from the New Testament.

In writing to the Corinthians, Paul makes a strong case for celibacy, then concedes, "If they cannot exercise self-control, they should marry. For it is better to marry than to be aflame with passion" (I Corinthians 7:9). As is true with many wrong ideas, there is undoubtedly an element of truth in the belief that evil has a special link with the body.

It is well to recognize the powerful potential for misuse which lies resident in our sexual appetites. In plain truth, our bodies are easily aroused to lust. This tendency must be guarded against all life long. But this should not cast a shadow upon the sexual relationship between husband and wife. God created man and woman with the capacity for sexual pleasure, and means them to enjoy this in marriage.

This first error—regarding sex as base, shameful, evil—finds no spokesman today. Not even the most conservative churchman would be caught holding a brief for Victorian prudery. Yet it needs to be mentioned, for it still holds a grip on the unconscious attitudes of some Christians. We can change a conscious attitude with relative ease. The unconscious tends to cling to old patterns with a stubborn will.

In reacting against this first error, Christians have tended to fall into a second, more subtle, error: This is the tendency to over-spiritualize sex.

Oh, we would never think of the hush-hush, naughty-naughty approach. No, no. We are far too enlightened for that. "Sex is beautiful." "Sex is wonderful." "Sex is a perfect blending of two personalities, an expression of love that takes in the whole range of man's being—at once a physical, intellectual, and spiritual encounter." "Sex is an act of total self-giving." "The sexual act is profoundly spiritual." "In the act of sex, a man and woman express the essential unity which overarches their separateness." All this may be more-or-less true, if one makes sex an object for intellectual dissection. But where is the husband who embraces his wife with high thoughts of "overcoming the separateness of their being in an act of overarching unity"? This is no man, but the invention of Christian apologists for sex, who imagine themselves commissioned to lift sex from the mundane level which it seems inevitably to occupy. Isn't there anybody around to say that sex is *fun*?

A woman once had the temerity to say this straight out while giving one of the inevitable "boy-girl relationship" talks without which no teenage Bible camp can pronounce a benediction. Some of the adult eyebrows went up, as though a dangerous secret had been betrayed. But afterward one of the girls came up and said, "I really appreciated your saying that it was fun. They always say how wonderful it is, but I sort of had the idea that you weren't supposed to enjoy it too much, because it was too holy."

The philosophers of sex seem unable to accept the fact that physical and emotional pleasure is the dominant feature of the sexual relationship. That does not seem dignified enough. So by words they attempt to lift sex to what they feel is a higher plane, describing it in almost transcendental terms. This spiritualizing of sex, however, does not make sex more spiritual. If anything, it is an anemic throwback to pagan fertility rites, which assigned mystic significance to sex.

The Bible indulges in no such philosophizing over sex. The *total* marriage relationship is pointed to as symbolic of the relationship between Christ and the Church (Ephesians 5:32). But when the sexual relationship *per se* is in focus, it is treated very practically for what it is—a physical act, with a strong emotional impetus.

It would be hard to find a more mundane handling of sex than the 7th chapter of I Corinthians: "The husband should give to his wife her conjugal rights, and likewise the wife to her husband. Do not refuse one another . . . lest Satan tempt you through lack of self-control." And this is the only chapter in the New Testament which offers specific advice on the sexual relationship in marriage!

Sex is one aspect of marriage. Like any other thing in the marriage, it should be done as well as possible, but it should not be allowed to color every other aspect of the marriage. By way of illustration: When the family sits down to dinner, the husband wants his wife to be a good cook. That's the service appropriate for that particular situation. When the children misbehave, the wife expects her husband to be an effective disciplinarian. If he is an ineffective disciplinarian, it does not make much sense for her to complain, "Yes, you like my apple pie well enough, but you won't take a hand with the children!" His appetite for her apple pie is perfectly good and genuine. That is not where the problem—or the solution—to his disciplining of the children lies. Yet the sex relationship is called upon to shoulder just such ridiculous responsibilities. "All you care about is sex. Why don't you turn off that TV once-in-a-while so we can just *talk*?" Again, the fact that one finds pleasure in the sexual relationship is perfectly in order. The problem of not taking time for talk is another problem, and should be dealt with in its own sphere.

Husbands and wives should expect their sex relationship to be a fun time together. Yet, paradoxically, a key to this is the total acceptance of their sexual relationship *as is*—even if it has some problems and disappointments. A good sex relationship may not come all of itself. It may take some time and some intelligent adjustment of attitudes.

One's response to the sexual relationship in marriage, like love itself, is far more subject to the will than we suppose. One does not have to wait for an ecstatic feeling. Even when one enters into the relationship out of duty, a happy relationship can grow and develop. Indeed, there are times in every marriage when one or the other partner enters into the sexual relationship more out of duty than passion. Such an approach to sex is not beneath the dignity either of the act itself or of the partners.

A woman who had a happy sex relationship in her marriage was listening to some friends complain that "all their husbands wanted was sex." "What you need," she said, "is a little more of the Bohemian here-I-am-go-ahead-and-use-me attitude." This may sound like a pretty prosaic attitude toward sex, but it offers greater potential for happiness than the unrealistic attitude which leaves everything up to the feelings. It is, furthermore, thoroughly consistent with the biblical counsel which says, "The wife does not rule over her own body, but the husband does; likewise the husband does not rule over his own body, but the wife does" (I Corinthians 7:4). In plain language this means that if one partner desires the sexual relationship, the other should respond to that desire. The husband and wife who adopt this kind of down-to-earth approach to sex will find it a wonderfully satisfying aspect of their marriage—for the simple reason that the relationship is rooted in reality, and not in some artificial or impossible ideal.

Separation and Divorce

According to society, marriage is a contract between two individuals, which can be dissolved if there is sufficient cause. With such a limited view of marriage, it's natural for society to find all kinds of excuses to dissolve the marriage relationship, and even to enter into marriage on a trial basis to see how it will work out.

When the Pharisees came to Jesus to test Him on the question of divorce, Jesus answered them, "Have you not read that He who made them from the beginning made them male and female, and said, 'For this reason a man shall leave his father and mother and be joined to his wife, and the two shall become one?' So they are no longer two but one. What therefore God has joined together, let no man put asunder" (Matthew 19:4-6).

The second chapter of Malachi tells us that God hates divorce. The Bible leaves no doubt that marriage is for life; separation and divorce are contrary to God's order.

We let that stand as a flat statement, even while we recognize the exception which Jesus cited, and also the one which St. Paul recognized.[1] The marriages which are dissolved strictly on the basis of the exceptions permitted by Scripture are minimal, and for a very good reason: Where even one of the partners is determined to live according to Scripture, the

---

[1] Matthew 5:32, I Corinthians 7:15. For a fine biblical study of this question, we recommend the book DIVORCE AND REMARRIAGE by Guy Duty, published by Bethany Fellowship, Minneapolis, Minnesota.

marriage will rarely come to such a pass. Quoting again from Bonhoeffer: "God makes your marriage indissoluble. He protects it against every danger which threatens it from without or within; God himself guarantees the indissolubility of the marriage. No temptation, no human weakness can dissolve what God joins; indeed, whoever knows it may confidently say: What God has joined together, man *cannot* put asunder."

A question occasionally arises which is so natural that no one can be surprised at it: 'If marriages are indissoluble, and if husband and wife are bound to one another for life, then an unhappy marriage is an evil of an inexpressible magnitude.' Yes, so it is: and so it ought to be. Let it not be said that such a punishment is too hard for the youthful levity which has determined the choice. That levity ought to undergo the hardest possible punishment, because it has made the most solemn and holy of all human relationships a matter of sport, of carelessness, and of sensual gratification. *

If a truly innocent person has to bear the burden of an unhappy marriage, there is hope for him even in his sufferings; and even these are, for a man surrendered to God, the most wholesome school of purification, and of discipline in virtue: the years lost for earthly happiness become gained for eternity.*

People who set up personal happiness as the chief goal and purpose of marriage will usually end up frustrated. For while God wants happiness and fulfillment for His children, He wants this to come about through His plan for us. Therefore, God does not shy away from asking His people to endure hardship, if this is the best way to achieve His purposes. It may well be that in order to preserve the stability of marriage as an institution of God, some people will have to endure an unhappy marriage. This is a lesser evil than the wholesale breakdown of marriage which we are witnessing in our own day. We may not be able to stem the tide of that in society at large. But Christian people can determine that they will live by God's laws, regardless of the prevailing standards in the world around them.

Nor should Christian pastors and counselors soften God's law out of a presumed compassion and concern for those caught in an unhappy marital situation. There come times when a Christian must be told to endure hardship for the sake of Christ, and this is such a time. The evils of divorce are great enough for the individual himself. In California, where the divorce rate is almost twice the national average for the United States, statistics show that general illness, alcoholism, mental illness, maternal and child health, and suicide are markedly higher among divorced persons.[2]

The laws in favor of divorce were in all probability made with a view to humanitarian interest. But it is the spirit of our age, and not the spirit of love, which is behind them. Because marriage is the precious foundation and cornerstone of all society, the destructive spirit of our age manifests itself most strongly in our divorce laws. No folly is so great or so fatal as this, to imagine that it is possible to throw morality to the winds, and to preserve religion; to loosen the marriage tie and to draw more tightly the bond of government; to give over to destruction the divinely appointed foundation of all human welfare, if only the self-invented props of the state be provided: iron oppression, and crafty espionage.*

But the greatest evil of all is that done to the authority and rule of Christ, for divorce flies in the teeth of His word: "What God has joined together, let no man put asunder" (Matthew 19:6). Christ spoke that word out of a deep knowledge of the central place which marriage holds in God's eternal plans for mankind. The person who tampers with so solemn a word of Christ does so at great spiritual peril. The Apostles did not hesitate in urging their people to sacrifice temporal happiness for eternal gain, nor should we. Better a lifetime of loneliness or misery than an eternity of regret.

Mutual Esteem

Mutual esteem, and a correct appreciation of the place which God has assigned to each, are the primary conditions of happiness in marriage.*

---

[2] Dr. Lester Breslow, director, California Dept. of Public Health.

To esteem one's mate is to see the mate as more than an individual, as one set in a sacred position by God. We esteem the person who occupies a high public office, out of respect for his office. How much more should we esteem that person set next to us in marriage; for to be designated 'husband' or 'wife' by God is to enter upon a position of highest dignity and trust in His Kingdom.

Esteem is an essential element of love. If it is absent, love ceases to be love; a mere passion remains. Mutual esteem protects a marriage from becoming a victim of the inevitable ups-and-downs which it will encounter. If a husband's tenderness and care for his wife depends upon the way she looks or the way he may happen to feel on any given day—if the wife's respect for her husband fluctuates with her moods, or her judgment as to how well he is satisfying her standards and expectations—that marriage is on shaky ground. Love has become the pawn of passing moods and feelings. God means for love in marriage to be built upon a more stable foundation.

God never commands a love involving intimate affection between two people on the mere basis of their natural attraction to one another. He does not bring a man and a woman into proximity with one another and then say, "Now, love each other; and when I see that your love is strong enough, then I will bless it with marriage." Falling in love is a wonderful experience, and where it is accompanied by modesty and restraint, God shares the joy of it. It may well be the thing that leads two people to marriage. But God does not build a marriage upon the foundation of that mere natural attraction. In the wedding sermon which he wrote to his niece, Dietrich Bonhoeffer said, "Just as it is the crown, and not merely the will to rule, that makes the king, so it is marriage, and not merely your love for each other, that joins you together in the sight of God and man. As high as God is above man, so high are the sanctity, the rights, and the promise of marriage above the sanctity, the rights, and the promise of love. *It is not your love that sustains marriage, but from now on, the marriage that sustains your love.*"

Romantic-love-as-the-only-viable-basis-for-marriage is one of the unexamined and therefore blindly followed axioms of our culture. We blithely assume that this is the only basis for marriage consistent with human freedom and dignity, and since "love" occurs in the formula it must also be more Christian.

In many cultures marriages are arranged by the families of the prospective bride and groom. Such a practice would be intolerable in our culture. It is inconceivable to us that a marriage contracted on such a basis could be a happy one. If it were, we would chalk it off to pure luck. Happy marriages, however, are not the invention of our culture. What *is* the invention of our own culture is the notion that romantic love is the only sound basis for a marriage. One might well ask whether our culture, following this notion, has produced fewer miserable marriages. The rate of divorce causes one at least to wonder.

In considering the structure of Christian marriage, the nature and place of romantic love needs to be re-examined. We tend to give it a status of autonomous authority over a marriage. Love is something that just "is": Either you have it or you don't, and there's not too much you can do about it. The disillusioned young couple discovers that "we just don't love each other anymore" and tearfully concludes that their marriage has lost its essential basis for existence.

Now love *is* an essential ingredient of marriage. But the marriage does not depend upon love for its continued existence. Rather, the love depends upon marriage for its continued existence. Marriage gives to love a situation of stability and permanence, wherein it can grow toward maturity. Marriage rescues love from the tyranny of strong but immature feelings. It forces a person to live out times of difficulty, and win through to new depths of love and understanding.

Love should never be allowed to tyrannize a marriage and threaten its dissolution. Couples who come to the despairing conclusion that "we just don't love each other anymore" should be told quite simply, "Well, start learning!" When

we have entered into marriage, God commands us to love
one another. Love, from God's point-of-view, is not the basis
for marriage, but the issue or outcome of a successful marriage. It is far more subject to the will than we suppose. We
help cultivate and develop love because we set our mind to
do so. In marriage, we are not the helpless pawns of love.
Rather, we train love to be the willing servant of our marriage.

This kind of love does not grow in the sandy soil of our
immediate feelings. It roots down into the rich subsoil of
mutual esteem. The woman holds her mate in the high regard which God has conferred on him with the name 'husband'; the man likewise cherishes the woman whom God
has honored with the name 'wife.' A reverence for the dignity and honor which God has bestowed upon one's mate
establishes married love upon an enduring foundation. Upon
this foundation can be built the kind of love which St. Paul
describes in I Corinthians 13—

> Love is patient and kind; love is not jealous, or conceited, or
> proud; love is not ill mannered, or selfish, or irritable; love does not
> keep a record of wrongs, love is not happy with evil, but is happy
> with the truth. Love never gives up: its faith, hope, and patience
> never fail. Love is eternal.

Marriage—A Mystery

The Bible looks upon marriage not as a social contract between two individuals that may be dissolved at will; rather,
it looks upon marriage as a mystery. St. Paul, writing to the
Ephesians, says, "For this reason a man shall leave his father
and mother and be joined to his wife and the two shall become one." Then he goes on and says, "This is a great
mystery, and I take it to mean Christ and the Church"
(Ephesians 5:31-32). In other words, your marriage—every
Christian marriage—is designed to be a reflection of the relationship between Christ and His Church.

Thus, contrary to natural thinking, much of the real joy in
marriage comes from *giving*, not *getting*. For marriage is
modeled on the relationship between Christ and His Church.

In every Christian marriage the world should be able to see that mutual giving and self-giving which characterize the relationship between Christ and the Church.

What opportunities present themselves daily to the man to give—to express toward his mate the love of One who gave up His very life for His Bride! What opportunities present themselves daily to the woman to give—to express the faithfulness of the Church as it is described in Ephesians 5:24 and 27, '. . . subject in everything to Christ . . . without spot or wrinkle, holy and without blemish!" This is not merely an ideal, but is the projected goal of the Holy Spirit with every Christian couple.

CHAPTER TWO

God's Order for Wives

"Ladies first" is a familiar quotation in regard to proper social order. The Bible applies the same principle when it speaks about God's order for the family, and it is probably no accident: In a family, the wife is the link between husband and children; when she lives according to Divine Order, it will tend to draw both husband and children into order. Therefore, in speaking about Divine Order in the family, Scripture addresses first the wife—

"Wives, be subject to your husbands, as to the Lord. For the husband is the head of the wife as Christ is the head of the Church, his body, and is himself its Savior. As the Church is subject to Christ, so let wives also be subject in everything to their husbands" (Ephesians 5:22-24). The very thought of 'being subject to' or 'submissive to' one's husband will stir up negative feelings within many capable and intelligent women who think of it in terms of being an inactive, insignificant doormat—

> Husband, husband, cease your strife,
> No longer idly rave, sir;
> Though I am your wedded wife,
> Yet I am not your slave, sir! (Burns)

To God, however, submission means something else. To be submissive means to yield humble and intelligent obedience to an ordained power or authority. The example He gives is that of the Church being submissive to the rule of Christ. Far from being degrading, this is the Church's glory! God did not give this law of wives being submissive to their husbands because He had a grudge against women; on the contrary, He established this order *for the protection of women and the harmony of the home.* He means for a woman to be sheltered from many of the rough encounters of life. Scripture knows nothing of a 50-50 'democratic marriage.' God's order is 100-100. The wife is 100% a wife, the husband 100% a husband.

God has given wives the opportunity to choose freely the submissive role, even as Jesus chose to be submissive to the Father. "Have this mind among yourselves, which you have in Christ Jesus, who, though He was in the form of God, did not count equality with God a thing to be grasped, but emptied himself, taking the form of a servant, being born in the likeness of man. And being found in human form He became obedient unto death, even death on a cross. Therefore God has highly exalted Him . . ." (Phil. 2:5-9). God honors not those who cling to their 'rights,' but those who choose freely to obey Him.

"A Good Wife . . . More Precious Than Jewels"

In *A Man Called Peter,* Catherine Marshall tells how her late husband tended to put women on a pedestal. She quotes the following from one of his sermons: "Modern girls argue that they have to earn an income, in order to establish a home, which would be impossible on their husband's income. That is sometimes the case, but it must always be viewed as a regrettable necessity, never as the normal or natural thing for a wife to have to do. The average woman, if she gives her full time to her home, her husband, her children . . . If she tries to understand her husband's work . . . to curb his egotism while, at the same time, building up his self-esteem, to kill his masculine conceit while encouraging all his hopes, to establish around the family a circle of true friends . . . If she provides in the home a proper atmosphere of culture, of love of music, of beautiful furniture and of a garden . . . If she can do all this, she will be engaged in a life work that will demand every ounce of her strength, every bit of her patience, every talent God has given her, the utmost sacrifice of her love. It will demand everything she has and more. And she will find that for which she was created. She will know that she is carrying out the plan of God. She will be a partner with the Sovereign Ruler of the universe."

Proverbs 31:10-31 presents the Bible's most complete and beautiful picture of what a good wife should be. She is capable, ambitious, a willing worker; she is kind, wise, trustworthy, cheerful, providing for her household and reaching beyond. She knows her worth. She uses to good purpose her intelligence, her physical strength, her God-fearing character. She makes life abundant for her husband, their children, and for the poor and needy beyond their family circle. A remarkable woman!

And what triggers all this creative effort? A husband who holds the whip hand over her and keeps her submissive? On the contrary, it is a husband who expresses his unqualified appreciation for her: "Her husband praises her: 'Many women have done excellently, but you surpass them all.'" Where a wife's submission becomes a harsh demand from the husband, God's Order has been thrown overboard, and a mere human authority remains. But where a husband fulfills also *his* role in God's order—which is to 'love his wife, and not be harsh with her' (Colossians 3:19)—then a wife's submission to him becomes a fountain of mutual love and devotion, a thing of surpassing moral and spiritual beauty.

> A good wife who can find?
> She is far more precious than jewels
> The heart of her husband trusts in her.

Submission—A Means of Protection

In the world a woman is subject to physical attack, and therefore needs her husband's protection. This is a basic, universal fact of existence and is written into the folkways of every age and culture.

A woman's vulnerability, however, does not stop at the physical level. It includes also vulnerability at the emotional, psychological, and spiritual level. Here, too, she needs a husband's authority and protection.

An irate neighbor bangs on the front door. When the wife answers it, the neighbor lets loose a stream of complaints because some of the fence slats between your two yards have been knocked loose, and this most certainly by your children and therefore the repairs are your responsibility.

"I'll speak to my husband about it," is the wife's reply. This is not an 'out,' but is the natural and proper response of a wife who is living under her husband's protection and authority. She is meant to be largely free of the emotional burden which comes from representing the family outward to the community.

Less recognized, but even more important, is a wife's need for protection from the emotional attacks of her own children. A mother should not have to ask, much less battle, for respect from the children. This robs her of the poise which enables her to maintain a spirit of calm and dignity for the whole household. It is the husband's responsibility to protect his wife from any abuse which the children might mount against her. Should the father overhear the slightest hint of disrespect toward the mother, or the least lapse of obedience to her word, he should put a stop to it at once and firmly. The children should always know that behind the mother stands the authority of the father.

Still vivid in my memory is a comic-serious incident from my own childhood. I had argued over something with my mother. As she left the room I shouted after her, "You're a big dummy!" My father had come into the room a few moments earlier. His arm shot out, caught me by the shirt front, and lifted me right off the floor. "Who's a dummy?" he demanded. Scared stiff I blubbered, "*I'm* a dummy, *I'm* a dummy, *I'm* a dummy!" My older brother burst out laughing, and my father could scarcely suppress a smile. My desperate retreat into self-incrimination salted the situation with enough humor to save me from a spanking. But I never forgot the lesson of that day: If I abused my mother, I would incur the wrath of my father.

A husband who protects his wife from the discourtesies and abuses of the children instills in them a sense of respect for womanhood. This, together with his own example of courtesy and considerateness toward his wife, is part of the legacy which every father should pass on to his sons.

Finally, and most important of all, a woman is also subject to spiritual attack. A husband stands as a shield and protector to his wife against assault from the unseen world of 'principalities and powers' (Ephesians 6:10).

Paul suggests this in I Corinthians 11:10, "Therefore she (the wife) should be subject to his (her husband's) authority and should have a covering on her head as a token, a symbol of her submission to authority, because of the angels." (Amplified Bible, RSV.) We know that Paul uses the word "angel" (*angelos*) to refer both to the loyal spirits of God (2 Thessalonians 1:7) and to the rebellious cohorts of Satan (I Corinthians 6:3, Romans 8:38). The context here may suggest that Paul has in mind the latter application of the word. It is not merely the propriety of the veil which concerns him. He recognizes that a woman who is unprotected by her husband's authority is open to (evil) angelic influence.

St. Paul understood that women are vulnerable to spiritual attack, especially along the lines of deception, and that their protection is found in coming under a man's authority. This is the reason for his otherwise puzzling advice in I Timothy 2:12-14, "I permit no women to teach or to have authority over men; she is to keep silent . . . For . . . Adam was not deceived, but the woman was deceived." Women can contribute much as teachers of children and of other women. They can prophesy and pray publicly (Joel 2:28, 29; I Corinthians 11:5), but they are not to formulate doctrine or to set themselves up as leaders over men in the church.

How much evil has come upon home and church because women have lost the protective shield of a husband's authority! We have let Satan beguile us into believing that it is degrading for a wife to be submissive and obedient to her husband's authority. The whole teaching is dismissed as a foolish vaunting of the "male ego," a Neanderthal vestige which our enlightened age has happily outgrown. The Bible, however, has no desire to exalt any ego, male or female. The Divine Order set forth for the family serves the elemental purpose of protection, spiritual protection. A husband's authority and a wife's submissiveness to that authority, is a shield of protection against Satan's devices. Satan knows this, and that is why he uses every wile to undermine and break down God's pattern of Divine Order for the family.

When a woman lives under her husband's authority, she can move with great freedom in spiritual things. Protected from many of the satanic devices which would come against her, she can move with power and effect in the life of prayer, and in the exercise of spiritual gifts.

God's intention is that a husband should stand between his wife and the world, absorbing many of the physical, emotional, and spiritual pressures which would come against her. It is the husband, not the wife, who is primarily responsible for what goes on in the home, the community, and the church. When he deserts this role, or when the wife usurps it, both the home and the community outside the home suffer for it.

The question naturally arises, "What about the single woman, or the widow? How does she receive protection?" The New Testament looked upon *the church* as the protector of "widows and ophans." (See Acts 6:1, James 1:27, I Timothy 5:3-16.) When a woman had the protection neither of a father (or male relative), nor of a husband, she was to look upon the leaders of the church as her spiritual 'head.' From them she would receive spiritual counsel and protection. Her material needs also become the concern of the local church.

It would be hard to conceive of a wiser arrangement for the woman who does not live under the direct authority of a father or a husband. The church has the requisite spiritual power and authority to be that shield and protector which a woman needs. And by committing this responsibility to a *group* (most likely the deacons, see Acts 6:3), the situation could be handled with due propriety.

This same principle could be put into practice if a husband were required by business, military service, or some other cause to be absent from his family for a period of time. The spiritual care and protection of his family could be committed to the leaders of the church. A man going on a business trip, for instance, can simply mention this to one or more of the deacons, and ask that special prayer be offered for his family during his absence. The family may also call upon the deacons, if they need any special help which would normally fall to the head of the house. Thus individuals and families may call upon the larger family of the church, so that no one without spiritual care and protection.

Submission—A Means of Social Balance

St. Paul wrote, "As many of you as were baptized into Christ have put on Christ. There is neither Jew nor Greek, there is neither slave nor free, there is NEITHER MALE NOR FEMALE, for you are all one in Christ Jesus" (Galatians 3:27-28).

Some people have taken this isolated text as a basis for teaching an indiscriminate social "equality" between men and women. But this is far from the Apostle's meaning.

In their relation to God as His children, in spiritual communion with Christ, in the possession of the Holy Ghost—in all these relations to God, and to the higher world—men and women stand on equal footing. *

Yet not one of the relationships which God has ordered for this world between man and man is thereby shaken from its place. Paul was certainly far from preaching a political equality of all men, or a division of earthly possessions in the sense of communism. As little did he think of speaking a word in favor of the modern plans for introducing an equality between man and woman. *

There is a firm, unalterable decree of God in the position of men and women. It was established by their creation, and is found in the nature of both. It was not overturned by Christianity; it is confirmed in the New Testament. Upon it rests the harmony of a Christian marriage. To acknowledge it seems easy enough. Yet it is a problem which few couples solve satisfactorily, and the failure to solve it is the cause of much unhappiness in the marriage relationship. *

According to the ideas of Eastern nations, the wife is depressed to the condition of her husband's slave. According to those of the romantic period, she was elevated to be his mistress. Both conceptions are erroneous, though the romantic notion is the nobler error. These two extremes still contend and cross one another in common life. Yet the purely Christian ideal is distinct from both. *

The Bible teaches a *subordination* of the wife to her husband. In this, both Old and New Testaments agree. This subordination is grounded upon the creation. "Adam was formed first, then Eve." It is further grounded upon the fall of our first parents: "Adam was not deceived (as long as he stood alone), but the woman was deceived and became a transgressor" (I Timothy 2:13, 14). After the Fall, upon each was laid a particular burden. The subordination of the wife was confirmed, indeed it was increased. God said to the woman, "In pain you shall bring forth children, yet your desire shall be for your husband, and he shall rule over you." To the man God said, "Cursed is the ground because of you; in toil you shall eat of it all the days of your life; in the sweat of your face you shall eat bread till you return to the ground, for out of it you were taken" (Genesis 3:16-19). *

We may strive against these words as much as we please. They are, and ever will be, the primitive law which has never ceased to be valid. Fallen man must submit to it, unless he would depart yet farther from God. No resistance avails here. These words are continually operating. These barriers stand firm. These burdens are laid upon us, and cannot be shaken off. *

Upon man is laid the authority to rule. But with it comes heavy care and hard labor upon a cursed earth. In every earthly calling he must taste something of the bitterness of that curse. Gladly would the man allow the rule to pass out of his hands—if at the same time he were released from the care and responsibility. The number of men who have abdicated their position as heads of their households bears testimony to this in our own day. *

The woman is not afraid of the toil, but desires the rule.

The continual self-denial of her own will is her heaviest trial.*

Thus the burden of both man and woman is chosen for them, so as to fall most heavily upon the natural inclinations of each. In the natural state, man and woman find the burden to be truly a curse. If it is unbearable, it is not to be wondered at, *for it should be so. The yoke should be so heavy to them that they cannot bear it without God's help. The burden of this life should compel them to seek God.**

If they do this, then a hidden blessing opens up in the curse. The burden becomes only half as heavy. It serves as a purification. It shows itself as the ordering of Divine wisdom and love. It is a preparation and education for the kingdom of God.*

Many otherwise sensible people try to force marriage to function contrary to its nature. A person who would drive a car off a cliff, expecting it to fly, would present a ridiculous, if not a tragic, spectacle; flying is altogether contrary to a car's nature. God has assigned a certain role in marriage to each partner. These respective roles are a part of the basic nature of marriage. To ignore them, or devise our own substitutes, is to invite a marital crack-up.

"But what if the husband's decision will head the family into disaster? Doesn't the wife have to take a hand when such a situation threatens? Are there no limits whatsoever to this business of submissiveness?" (One can hardly suppress the question!)

The Bible says, "Wives, be subject to your husbands, as is fitting in the Lord" (Colossians 3:18). Clearly, the Apostle means that it *is* fitting or proper for the wife to be subject to her husband. Yet there is the implication that her obedience must be 'in the Lord,' i.e., must not lead her into anything which could directly be called sin. This does not mean that a wife may go against her husband's authority when there is mere disagreement over some matter relating to the spiritual life of herself or the children.

Andre Bustanoby, Baptist pastor in Fullerton, California, points out that both Peter and Paul state the command for a wife to be submissive without qualification (Ephesians 5:24, I Peter 3:1). "Peter's use of Sarah as an illustration of obedience is notable," he says, "since Abraham twice, in order to protect his own life, denied that Sarah was his wife and allowed her to be taken into a ruler's harem (Genesis 12:10-20, 20:1-8). The implication is not that a wife should allow her husband to sell her into prostitution if he wishes. But by stating the case absolutely, both Peter and Paul forestall capriciousness in the matter of submission."

A church in Brazil, which has experienced a great awakening, has had to face the problem of women who come into the faith, while the husbands remain outside—some indifferent, but some openly hostile to the faith. Some husbands have forbidden their wives to attend church or take part in church activities. The leadership of the congregation has told the wife to accept this, and trust God to change the husband's heart. And a number of men have thus been won to the faith.

This is a difficult case, for one might argue with some justification that worship touches the very heart of our faith, and here 'we must obey God rather than men' (Acts 5:29). Yet it illustrates how far God will go in honoring His own Divine Order for the family.

In all of this, however, it is important to distinguish between *submissiveness* and *servility*. A wife who sees that her husband's judgment is wrong or unwise should tell him so—with all respect, but freely and honestly. The judgment, wisdom, and opinion of a loving wife is one of a man's greatest assets. It saves him from many a foolish mistake, and it is his privilege and responsibility as a husband to receive the wise counsel of his wife. The wife who says quietly, "Do whatever you think is best"—never offering an opinion even when she sees that her husband is heading the family for trouble—is not being submissive, but foolishly servile. She must tell him her thoughts fully and make her case as strongly as she can, never laying aside her respect, but never concealing her honest doubts about a particular decision. When she has done this, *then* she may let the decision rest with her husband, trusting God to give him good judgment.

Submissiveness is not a matter of mere outward form but of inner attitude. A wife can be a person of strong, even outspoken opinions, and still be submissive to her husband's authority, if deep down she respects him and is quite prepared and content for him to make and carry out the final decision. On the other hand, a wife who scarcely opens her mouth with an idea of her own, never questions her husband's decisions, and goes along with all his schemes no matter how foolish, may underneath it all nurse a deep and sullen rebellion. Sooner or later God will put her in a situation where this will break out into the open and have to be dealt with, for God is interested in the condition of the heart, not merely in our outward behavior.

In spiritual things, especially, a wise husband will welcome the counsel and opinion of his wife. Women often have a more direct, intuitive grasp of spiritual realities than men. Klaus Hess, a Lutheran pastor in Germany, has put it thus: "In physical life, the man begets a new life while the wife bears it and brings it forth. In spiritual life this is often reversed: the woman begets a new vision, sees a new dimension of spiritual reality, and the man must then patiently bring it forth in its practical out-workings."

If a wife sees, for instance, that the family is sliding away from God—neglecting family and private prayers, skipping church, becoming too involved in other outside activities—she must share this insight freely with her husband. To *see* this is a revelation of the Holy Spirit. It may be that the husband is not truly aware of its implications, for the sins of omission are peculiarly deceptive. It is no breach of submission to say these things to her husband, even urging him to take a hand in setting things right again. Indeed, if would be wrong if she were to remain silent. For if she feels that the Holy Spirit has given her understanding in a particular matter, she is obligated to share this with her husband so that he may weigh it in his considerations. The spiritual health and direction of the family is fully as dependent upon the insight and concern of the wife, as upon the authority and protection of the husband.

Submission does not mean that one remains piously silent, 'leaving everything in the husband's hands.' Submission to authority means that you put youself wholly at the disposal of the person who is set over you. This is the meaning that the Apostle Paul sets before the Christian in his submission to God: "Yield yourselves to God . . . and your members to God as instruments of righteousness" (Romans 6:13). And this is the submission on which the husband-wife relationship is modeled. If a wife withholds her understanding and feelings on a matter, she is being less than submissive, for she is not putting these things at her husband's disposal.

When she has made her thoughts fully known, *then* she may rest the decision with her husband and with God. Nor should she try to force her own understanding and opinion through at any cost. But fully and freely express her thoughts she can and must, else the family will be denied the very blessings which God intends to channel through her.

Thus the subordinate role of the wife does not stifle her personality. On the contrary, it provides the best environment for her creativity and individuality to express itself in a wholesome way. It is God's way of drawing upon her gifts of intelligence, insight, and judgment, without at the same time burdening her with the authority and responsibility of decision. The subordinate role of the wife is necessary not only for her own well-being, but also because it contributes to maintaining a balance both within the family itself, and in society at large.

Dr. Bruno Bettelheim, noted psychologist and author, director of the Orthogenic Center for disturbed children, warns that too many husbands are becoming 'assistant mothers' in their own homes. "Take child care," he says. "In countless families, the father is merely 'mother's little helper.' She exhorts him, 'Why don't *you* change the baby?' 'How about feeding him while I go shopping?' 'Get him dressed, I'm busy.' It's condoned by many family experts. They urge today's father to be a part-time nursemaid so that he will be 'emotionally enriched' as mother is.

"But this is foolish advice. Male physiology and psychology

aren't geared to it. Not that there's anything wrong with a father occasionally giving baby a bottle, if the situation requires it or he enjoys it. What's wrong is thinking that it adds to his parenthood. When a man tries to be a 'better' father by acting like a mother, he is not only less fulfilled as a father, but as a man, too. A father's relationship with his children can't be built mainly around child-caring experiences. If it is, he's a substitute mother—not a father!

"Similarly, under this 'petticoat rule,' if a tired father is bludgeoned into serving as a kitchen aide and handyman, it doesn't enrich his fatherhood either. Actually, a wife who shifts her unpleasant household chores to her husband is downgrading her own activities in her children's eyes.

"Many well-intentioned fathers turn over their pay checks to their wives who then give them an allowance—pretty much as a child gets one. This 'mother knows best' practice shows that a husband thinks highly of his wife. But it also implies to a child that Pop is just another silly boy child in the family.

"This blurring of mother-father roles can have harmful effects on children. Because many fathers now wash dishes, bathe the baby and perform other traditional female tasks, their sons often don't know what it means to be a man. If mother and father do the same chores, a child doesn't have a clear father or mother image. No wonder so many boys and girls are mixed up about their roles in later life."

It is the responsibility of both partners in a marriage to see that the husband and wife roles do not become confused. Men have been as guilty of abdicating their role as head of the home, as women have been of usurping it. It is not easy to remain submissive to one who palms off his responsibilities upon you, and refuses to take the lead in family affairs.

The emancipation of women has brought many needed reforms, but has had the unfortunate side result of robbing women of securities and protection which are their right. Women today are put upon to shoulder financial problems and worries in the family, to spearhead civic programs, to take the lead in raising the children, to represent the family to the community, to make major family decisions, to be the spiritual leader in the family. All of this is contrary to Divine Order. A woman is not normally equipped by nature to sustain this kind of psychological and emotional pressure and still fulfill her God-appointed role as wife and mother. The fact that women can do some of these things with technical competence only camouflages the irreparable damage —to woman, to family, to society—of this departure from Divine Order.

The Church has not been the least to suffer from this trend toward the feminization of our culture. As men have abdicated their role as the spiritual heads of their families, more and more of the responsibility in the church has fallen upon the women. They teach the Sunday School classes, run the Parent-Teachers Association, do most of the visitation, carry by far the lion's share of the work-burden in the care and upkeep of the church buildings, take the lead in prayer and Bible Study.

The men, having deserted their post, now feel out of place in the church. They turn over to their wives things like family devotions, church activity, spiritual guidance for the children. It becomes a vicious circle: Things having to do with spiritual life have taken on a feminine image. Girls dominate church youth groups, as their mothers dominate the church. Boys grow up to follow in their fathers' footsteps, and soon learn that 'when I become a man, I can put away childish things.'

What a far cry this is from the rugged Christianity of the New Testament—where men dropped whatever they were doing to follow Jesus; suffered misunderstanding, hardship, persecution, and even death because they had found in Him a Master who commanded the uttermost of their loyalty and love. Can you imagine Peter sending his wife to the Temple to make a defense for the Christian Way before the Sanhedrin? Of Paul letting his sister handle the gift-offerings which had been gathered for the poor in Jerusalem? Make no mistake: Women played a vital role in the early Church; the spread of the Movement was not a little dependent on their faithful work and witness. But the 'government' of the

Church was in the hands of the men. They did not palm off this responsibility upon their women.

The Church will regain power and spiritual authority in direct ratio as men reassume their place of leadership. A church which finds men gathering in the early morning hours for prayer; has men teaching the upper classes in Sunday school; sets apart Christ-dedicated men to go and visit its own members, as well as the unchurched; gathers a council of spiritually mature men around the pastor of the church, not merely to vote on how much of a raise to give the church custodian next year, but to help set the spiritual tone and direction of the congregation—this is the church which will restore God's intended balance to the Body of Christ. And none will more delight in this than the women, for the lack of male authority in the church is in some ways even more painful than its absence in the home. A woman sitting with her children in church, while her husband sits at home, is one of the loneliest creatures in the world. Perhaps nowhere else does she feel quite so keenly her need for a 'spiritual head' as in the presence of God, who established this Divine Order.

God has given to women great talents and abilities. Their intelligence is equal to men, their stamina and emotional endurance often greater. He does not want women to bury their capabilities. But He wants to channel them.

A wife's primary responsibility is to give of herself, her time, and her energy to her husband, children, and home. This does not mean that women cannot have responsible positions of leadership and still be in God's plan. Indeed, God seems to have peculiar honors for women: they were the last to linger at the cross, the first to come to the tomb. It was to a woman, Mary Magdalene, that Jesus first appeared after His resurrection. The Old Testament tells of Miriam, who was instrumental in saving Moses' life while he was a baby; Deborah, who gave leadership to the Israelites as prophetess and judge; Esther, the courageous queen who saved her people from death. The New Testament, too, speaks of prophetesses, such as Anna (a widow) and the (unmarried) daughters of Phillip. Lydia, one of the early converts under Paul's ministry, was a businesswoman. But she who is "blessed among women," the most honored woman of all time . . . the mother of our Lord . . . was just a humble woman who found fulfillment as a wife and mother in the home where God had set her.

Submission—A Means of Spiritual Power

A wife is more than a mother, housekeeper, cook, counselor, and chauffeur. She will not find the deep places of her heart satisfied with bowling, bridge, PTA meetings, or even church work. On the other hand, if her sole source of happiness lies in her husband or her children, she is also doomed to disappointment. God did not intend us to find satisfaction apart from Himself. A wife who puts Jesus first will be a joy both to her 'lord' and to her Lord! (See I Peter 3:6.)

A radiant wife, who once sought escape in intellectual pursuits, recently disclosed her secret for finding fulfillment in life: "It's doing what Jesus wants me to do!" She went on to say that Jesus can change our attitudes; He can even change the routine tasks that were once a drudgery into a joy. "Be rooted in Christ, not in your husband; then you are free to be a worthwhile person, a good wife." Jesus gives you the invitation to take your anxieties to the cross, and to leave the reforming of your husband in God's hands. The wife who is trusting God is not nagging her husband.

Submission is much more than an outer form; it is an inner attitude. It is more than a veiled head; it is a heart veiled with honor and reverence for the husband. Beware of making pious public prayers for an "unsaved" husband!

It is not uncommon that a wife's spiritual awareness and concern runs ahead of her husband's. But right here is where a wife comes into danger. She uses this as a pious excuse for becoming unsubmissive to her husband's authority. She feels that only by taking an active "spiritual lead" in the family can she assure the proper upbringing of the children and the eventual enlightenment of her husband. A great deal of unsanctified rebellion can masquerade behind this kind of pious spirituality. ("The heart is deceitful above all things,"

Jeremiah 17:9.) Even more important, it does not accomplish the desired end, but actually frustrates it. The husband is driven further away from an interest in spiritual things. Whereas in a continued attitude of submissiveness the wife has at her command a spiritual power with God—guaranteed results. "You wives, be submissive to your husbands, so that some, though they do not obey the word, may be won *without a word* by the behavior of their wives, when they see your reverent (to the husband!) and chaste behavior" (I Peter 3:1-2).

A woman once came to her pastor with the complaint that her husband was so unspiritual that she didn't know whether she should go on living with him. She had tried and tried to get him to come to church, to hold family devotions, to quit using profane language, etc.—all to no avail. He made sarcastic remarks about her spiritual activities, and it was beginning to rub off on the children. She even wondered if it was right to go on having marital relations with him because of his blasphemous ways.

The pastor reassured her that the marital relationship did not hinge upon her husband being a Christian. (See I Corinthians 7:13.) But he went further. He said, "Now I see something here. Twice this week your husband has offered to take you out to dinner—gave you a chance to get away from the kitchen and the kids—and you turned him down."

"Why, yes, that's right," the woman admitted. "I—I was so busy—had things to do . . ."

"The problem isn't with your husband, but with you. You're a rebellious wife. You resent your husband's authority over you. What you need to do is go home and apologize to your husband, ask his forgiveness for being an unsubmissive wife. Quit lecturing him on religion—leave that to God. Cook him his favorite meal. Settle down to the business of being a wife who is 'subject to her husband in all things' (Ephesians 5:24)."

The advice jolted her, but she accepted it and acted upon it. About a week later the woman's husband dropped in on the pastor.

"Say, you talked to my wife about a week ago," he began.

"Yes ..."

The man's face broke into a broad grin, "I like that!" he said.

The man began coming to worship services, ended up becoming a deacon in the church. What the wife had failed to achieve by her own direct efforts, God brought about as she became submissive to her husband's authority.

C. S. Lovett calls this "woman power," in his practical little book telling women how they can witness effectively to an unbelieving husband. "Her nice behavior is tread upon," he says, "preaching is forbidden, brute strength impossible, argument futile, nagging dangerous—what can she do?"

Lovett offers what he calls the 'nutcracker technique.' "Can you picture the two jaws of a nutcracker bearing down on a shell?" he asks. "See how the hinge joins the arms providing the leverage? Simple? Now consider God's nutcracker. It has two jaws also. One is called LIGHT, the other WORKS. The Holy Spirit hinges the arms together, making the pressure possible. Get your husband in a place where you can use LIGHT and WORKS together and you have him in the spiritual nutcracker.

"For example, let's suppose your husband prefers fresh-brewed coffee. But you have been giving him instant coffee. It's more convenient. Now you plan to submit to his preference. Doing so is an ACT of submission, a WORK. Yet that is only one jaw of the nutcracker. Two are needed for a squeeze. So you bring the coffeepot to the table, holding it so you can fan the aroma toward his face. He reacts, happily. 'Say, it looks like we're going to have some real coffee for a change!' Now for your LIGHT, the other jaw, 'I've been asking the Lord to help me be a better wife to you, dear. And He put it on my heart to do something just to please you. So ... courtesy of Christ ... you'll get fresh-brewed coffee every morning.'

"There! Now your light shines! You have put WORDS with your WORKS. You can see what that coffeepot is going to suggest to him every morning after that. This is but one illustration. There are hundreds of things a wife can DO and SAY for a LIGHT/WORKS squeeze with God's nutcracker. What is so precious is—it works! It is Christ-honoring and the Spirit does the actual squeezing. Before long your husband is meeting the Lord at every turn. He soon finds that all of the delight and joy of his home is due to Jesus. How much of that can an unsaved man take before his resistance shell cracks? Every shell has a breaking point."

Human wisdom would urge a woman to rise up and take matters into her own hands when she sees the family floundering, with no spiritual leadership coming from the husband. The Word of God counsels a better way: Remain submissive to her 'head,' and trust that her husband's own 'Head' (Christ) will take charge of the matter, and act.

To be active, clever, and religious are noble qualities in a woman; but the energetic woman who holds down her husband in inactivity; the clever one who silences him and by the brilliancy of her conversation makes a show of his dull insignificance; and lastly, the religious one, who allows others to remark that her husband is less enlightened or awakened than herself, are three disgusting characters. Yet is the last, especially when in combination with the second, the most disgusting of all.*

As a woman may be superior to her husband in natural understanding, so also may be the case with her Christian enlightenment. And indeed it is more common to find piety in women than in men. Their minds are more accessible to Christian truth, as was seen to be the case everywhere at the first spread of Christianity. And with them the continuance of faith has often been found, in which even the first disciples of Christ were surpassed by the holy women in the Gospel. So too, it is more usual in a time of estrangement from the faith, that the women return to it before the men. And it far more often happens that a Christian-minded woman has to suffer from her husband, than the opposite.*

Let us then imagine the case in which this incongruity is found in the most conspicuous and striking manner; genuine and deep piety on the part of the wife: worldly-mindedness, unbelief, and tyrannical harshness on the part of the husband. Yet the position of the wife, according to God's ordinance, is not in the least altered thereby. Her duty toward her husband remains exactly the same: she is none the less bound to pay him reverence than if his character had been the gentlest and most enlightened. By her Christian knowledge, this duty is not lightened, but impressed upon her the more. As certain as the marriage bond is indissoluble, so certainly the command of obedience in marriage stands irrevocably firm. The authority which He hath appointed, let no woman assail, especially under the pretext of an especial love to God.*

Rather, let her continue to show modesty and reverence towards her husband; gentleness, silence, and submission in all things which are not sin in the proper sense of the word. In these virtues lies the true acknowledgement of Christ; in their violation, the denial of Him.*

She must see Christ in her husband. She must by a continual act of faith hold fast to this, that in honoring him she honors Christ, who has set him to be her head. Upon all who bear the dignity of ruler, judge and father, there is laid something of the dignity of Him who is the Ruler, Judge and Father. Thus does it rest also upon the husband as the head of the house.*

Does she believe in God, and in a Divine guidance? Let her acknowledge this guidance even in the sufferings which her husband may cause her. Let her yield herself to them with the certainty that this is the school wherein she has to learn patience, the hardest of Christian virtues. In this school of obedience she will learn that Christianity—the only one which God will acknowledge—which stands not in word but in power.*

Let her place her hope in God and know that her husband is placed to be a blessing to her, and there is no blessing for her to be found except as she humbly attaches herself to him. If this contradicts her low opinion of her husband, and her high opinion of herself, and appears utterly illogical to her, then let her take heed lest in despising him she despise God, and cut herself off from God's appointed source of blessing for her. Let her not suppose that those things which flatter her wishes and feelings will forward her progress in the kingdom of God. Rather, let her look for help in those very hardships which the Divine education decrees for her. Until she has done all this, let her not wonder that no change takes place in her husband. But when she has, she shall see the miracles of God.*

Let her renounce the inclination to make known in words all her (spiritual) feelings and experiences. If she has attained to a beginning of Christian knowledge, let her not be in a hurry to win her husband to it by eloquent testimony. Let her beg of him to go with her to hear the preaching of the Gospel, but let her not attempt to teach him herself. SUCH AN ATTEMPT WILL AND SHOULD FAIL. From one evil springs a second which is greater; her persuasions change into complaints and lecturings. Displeasure, coldness, and estrangement follow, and the foundation of a lasting mischief is laid.*

Yet there is a way to his heart. It is toilsome but sure. It works upon the conscience. It is slow and quietly unpretending, but it has a victorious power: It is the pure behavior of a patient, silent, hoping, loving wife. Even this testimony a man may for a time misunderstand. He can misinterpret the noblest conduct, and thereby seek to erase the impression from his conscience. But there comes a 'day of visitation' sent by God, and not by man. The veil is taken from before his eyes, and he, like one initiated into the mysteries, looks with wonder upon the mystery of a deeply Christian personality till then hidden from him. At the right time, for his own blessing, will he acknowledge it, and will thank God for the patience with which his suffering wife has endured.*

A group of men were once studying the Bible together—a passage dealing with the marriage relationship. Each one wrote down the thoughts which came to him during a time of silent meditation. Then they shared with one another what they had written.

As one of the men studied the passage, he was moved to think about his own marriage. He put down his thoughts in the form of a prayer, and this is what he wrote:

"Lord, I do thank you for my wife, Kristin. I praise your Divine plan and providence which led me to her. I thank you, Lord, for her patience and perseverance and prayers through twelve Christless years of marriage. I praise you, Lord, for your salvation which finally came even to me—through her patience, and perseverance, and prayers.

"Lord, set your guardian angels over her and protect her.

"Thank you, Lord Jesus."

This is a beautiful tribute to a patient wife. But it is more than that: It is also a testimony to the power of God acting through His own appointed channels of Divine Order. The wife lived out her role of quiet submission to her husband, trusting God to work in his life. God honored her faith. He saved her husband. But more than that: The husband then moved in to assume the role which the wife had 'kept open' for him, in faith. He became in fact her 'head,' her shield and protector: With true spiritual authority he calls down upon her the blessing of heaven, the protection of angels. This is Divine Order at work for the blessing of family, church, and nation.

Wives, rejoice in your husband's authority over you! Be subject to him in all things. It is your special privilege to move under the protection of his authority. It is within this pattern of Divine Order that the Lord will meet you and bless you—and make you a blessing to your husband, your children, your church, and your community.

CHAPTER THREE

God's Order for Children

Obedience, the Key

God's order for children is compassed in a single command: "Children, obey your parents in everything, for this pleases the Lord" (Colossians 3:20). A child's relationship to Jesus thrives in direct relation to the obedience which he gives to his parents. Jesus lives and works in the life of an obedient child. An obedient child is therefore a *happy* child. The child who knows exactly how far he can go is relieved of a heavy burden.

His old nature will sometimes chafe under the parents' authority. Like our six-year-old Arne, who one day stomped his foot and declared, "We're the only family that has to have goodness!" But where this authority is exercised in an atmosphere of love, a child soon comes to accept it as "right." He will even look with horror or disdain upon the other children who act disrespectfully toward authority. Our oldest son attended a school which had strict discipline. One of his friends transferred to another school where the discipline was lax. One day this friend came back to visit some of his pals, and reported with utter disdain: "The kids run the school!"

A child may test his parents' authority, to see how far he can go. He may feel quite unhappy in a particular situation where his own will is at odds with his parents. But deep down he wants to know that the parents' authority will stand firm, that he can depend upon it.

A teenage boy once told me that his father had laid down the rule that he couldn't get a driver's license unless he brought his school grades up. The boy had resented this, threatened to run away, and generally made life miserable for the whole family. But as he talked about it, a sheepish grin crept over his face, and he said: "I guess I really wouldn't respect Dad if he didn't follow through on it."

A child may strain at parental authority, even rebel against it, but he will rebel even more—though often in disguised ways—against a lack of parental authority. For though the old nature is still active in a child (see Romans 7:15), his relationship with Christ is also active. When he persistently disobeys his parents, he experiences a deep discontent in his spirit, for his relationship with Jesus has been clouded.

Every parent has had the experience of watching a child grow more and more disobedient until the exasperated parent finally bursts out, "You're just *asking* for a spanking!" If only the parent realized how literally true that is, he would not have to tune up to the point of exasperation. The child's understanding is not mature. He cannot articulate the reason for his discontent, for he does not have an intellectual grasp of it. But his spirit nevertheless has a clear intuitive grasp of the basic issue: His discontent is related to disobedience; he is too young and weak to command this obedience himself, but must look to his parents to do it for him.

Not many children will grasp this intellectually, like the seven-year-old who said to his father after a sound trouncing: "Thank you, Daddy. That did me good!" But every child will know a deep contentment of spirit when he is helped to walk in the ways of obedience.

So-called modern methods of child-raising make much of a child's intuitive sense of right and wrong, of fairness and unfairness. Great burden is laid upon the parent to deal fairly with the child, to always give the "right" command; the implication being that a child can and will and *may* rebel against a "wrong" command.

The Bible, however, does not say, 'Children obey your parents when they are right.' It says: 'Obey your parents in the Lord, for this *is* right'—even if they are wrong! (See Ephesians 6:1.) The child who obeys a 'wrong' command will still bask in the light of God's approval. In the long run, he will be a happier and better adjusted child than one who is given the freedom to challenge and question the parents' authority. For the obedient child is living according to Divine Order, and therefore participates in a deep sense of harmony and fitness.

Surely a parent must seek in every way to deal fairly, rightly, and in tenderest love with his children. But parents are human and fallible. Furthermore, most people become parents while they are still quite young. They have not attained a great deal of wisdom, and certainly not in regard to raising their children. Something as important as a child's obedience cannot be made to hinge upon the perfection of a parent's judgment in every situation. The child is not responsible for weighing and evaluating the parents' decisions—obeying those which he deems right, and rejecting those he does not agree with. The responsibility of decision rests with the parents. The child's responsibility is simply to obey.

The time in life comes all too soon when the child grows up, and *will* be responsible for judgments and decisions. But God has so structured the family that a child is relieved of the responsibility for judgment and decision, other than the one simple command to obey his parents. Only in this way can he be protected from wandering or rushing down innumerable bypaths of foolishness, ignorance, and waywardness.

Some friends of ours have eight children, and they all love ice cream. On a hot summer day, one of the younger ones declared that she wished they could eat nothing but ice cream! The others chimed agreement, and to their surprise the father said, "All right. Tomorrow you can have all the ice cream you want—nothing but ice cream!" The children squealed with delight, and could scarcely contain themselves until the next day. They came trooping down to breakfast shouting their orders for chocolate, strawberry, or vanilla ice cream—soup bowls full! Mid-morning snack—ice cream again. Lunch—ice cream, this time slightly smaller portions. When they came in for mid-afternoon snack, their mother was just taking some fresh muffins out of the oven, and the aroma wafted through the whole house.

"Oh goody!" said little Teddy. "Fresh muffins—my favorite!" He made a move for the jam cupboard, but his mother stopped him.

"Don't you remember? It's ice cream day—nothing but ice cream."

"Oh, yeah . . ."

"Want to sit up for a bowl?"

"No thanks. Just give me a one-dip cone."

By suppertime the enthusiasm for an all-ice-cream diet had waned considerably. As they sat staring at fresh bowls of ice cream, Mary—whose suggestion had started this whole adventure—looked up at her daddy and said, "Jeepers, couldn't we just trade in this ice cream for a crust of bread?"

This was a harmless adventure, which helped the children to see where their own judgment could land them, if their parents didn't do some directing. It simply illustrates the fact that a child makes his judgments from an extremely small base of knowledge and experience. The parents' world is a puzzle of contradictions to a child: Mama doesn't have to take a nap—and she does. Daddy could buy all the suckers he wants to—and he doesn't. When Mama and Daddy have friends over, they just sit and talk. They almost never play games or climb trees. Given the logical premises of his own little world, a child's unguided decisions will inevitably lead him into difficulty, even serious difficulty. And that is the reason that God protects him by putting him under his parents' authority.

In the command of obedience given to children, there is no mention made of any exception. It must be set forth and impressed upon them without any exception. "But what if my parents command something wrong?"

We know well that there are fathers and mothers who have led their children into sin. There are commandments which the child too must know, and to overstep such commandments would no longer be 'obedience in the Lord.' Children who are led astray by their parents to take part in crime are, according to the principles of the criminal law, liable to lighter punishment, though they do not escape altogether. A child who has reason to fear such things must arm himself with trust in God, not with thoughts of rebellion. God has given the commandment to honor father and mother. If this comes in contradiction with another commandment, God will provide a way of escape. The child must call upon God to preserve him from the sad necessity of refusing his obedience. God cannot leave such prayers unheard. His guidance will make all things result in good. *Faith in a living God is forever the complete termination of quibbling, hair-splitting, or mental reservation over the issue of obedience.**

Parents will inevitably make some wrong decisions, give some poor commands. Whenever this occurs, and is recognized by the parent, it should be confessed and corrected. We should never hesitate to confess a genuine mistake, and ask forgiveness of our children, fearing that this will undercut our authority. Our authority does not derive from ourselves, or from our flawless performance as parents—nor does it derive from our children's acceptance of that authority. It derives—as does all true authority—from the one who stands behind us, backing up our authority. The authority of a sergeant depends upon the captain who backs him up; the authority of the captain depends upon the major of the regiment, and so on. The authority of parents depends upon God, who has set them as authorities over their children. Therefore, when a parent makes a mistake, the question is not, "How will the child react if I admit this?" The question is rather, "What will God think if I try to hide this and bluff it out?" God honors honest and open repentance—in child or parent. The fear that you will lose status and authority with your child by confessing a sin is the devil's lie. On the contrary, your authority is actually confirmed and strengthened when you have the courage to be as honest and demanding of yourself as you want the child to be with himself. For then you are the kind of authority whom God *can* back up!

I once punished my oldest child for something of which he was not guilty. This came to light later on, and I saw that I was without excuse in the matter. I had acted hastily, and had not gotten the facts straight. I wondered what I should do. He was going through a difficult age, and I was wary of anything that might upset the balance of authority in the family! (How jealously we protect our pride, thinking thereby to preserve our authority. God can well establish our authority without any assistance from our ego!) Finally I took the boy aside and said to him, "Tim, I'm sorry I spanked you for that, because I see that it wasn't your fault, and I should have found out first. I can't unspank you . . . but will you forgive me?"

He put his arms around me and gave me a big hug and said, with that blending of the appropriate and the inane which in children somehow has a logic all its own: "That's okay, Dad. Say, can I have a peanut butter sandwich?" The next morning he was more cooperative and obedient than he had been for some time. The authority which I had been so worried about had not been weakened; it had actually been strengthened, for now it was rooted in honesty.

The authority of parents is not their own authority, but one given them by God. When parents realize this, they will not be hesitant to admit their mistakes—indeed, they will feel the necessity of it, for only thus can God continue fully to honor and back up their authority. On the other hand, the realization that God has invested them with authority will encourage a parent not to weaken that authority out of a false sense of unworthiness.

All authority is from God, but it is given for the good of those under it. Since Christ came not to be served, but to serve, the character of authority has changed—for all who enter into His mind. Now authority becomes a service, and subjection is submission to being served.*

No one may clothe himself with authority. But whoever has received authority from God must hold it firmly. He must have faith in it and must maintain it, out of faithfulness to God, not for selfish reasons. God has established that authority for the sake of the children, to attain certain ends. Nor should the parent set it aside through weakness and a morbid delicacy in sparing those set under him.*

Parents must maintain their ground upon the knowledge that they are in the right. They must demand obedience for what they know to be right.*

It seems at first sight to be simple obedience to the will of man. Yet it is already obedience to God. For in submission to the parents' will, children learn to submit to a will higher than their own. Submission to parents is a school for the independent and direct obedience to God which they will have to render when they no longer live under a parent's authority. It is for this that we educate our children—that in their own time they may follow the will of God, and the guidance of His Spirit, not from external force, but from conscientiousness, and an impulse from within.*

To learn obedience is to learn a basic law of spiritual life. For God's authority often comes into our life through human authority. When we know our position under authority, we can relax; relaxation and trust help one to be receptive to the Holy Spirit. We may teach and reason with our children however much we please, and still hold them back from a genuine encounter with God, unless with our teaching we have also instilled in them a sense of obedience.

Children: Obey your parents! This is God's plan for you. In obeying them, you obey Him. Thus you will know the presence and blessing of Jesus in your life.

CHAPTER FOUR

God's Order for Parents

The most succinct, yet comprehensive, summary of a parent's calling is found in a single sentence which the Apostle Paul wrote to the church in Ephesus: "Do not provoke your children to anger, but bring them up in the discipline and instruction of the Lord" (Ephesians 6:4). The Apostle thus summarizes God's Order for Parents under the aspect of three basic commands: *Love, Discipline, Teach.*

This simple outline of parental responsibility is patterned after God Himself. Some schools of philosophy would reduce religion to a 'projection of the father-image'; man feels over-awed by the universe in which he finds himself, so he projects his desire for security and protection upon a 'heavenly father.' The Bible, however, puts it in exactly reverse order. It is God who projects an image—His own image—upon man. He created man in His own image (Genesis 1:26), and part of the image of God in man is found in this, that we share His fatherhood.[3] God is *the* Father. All earthly parenthood derives from Him. And He deals with us, His earthly children, according to this same threefold pattern.

"If we sin deliberately after receiving the *knowledge* of the truth, there no longer remains a sacrifice for sins, but a fearful prospect of *judgment,* and a fury of fire which will consume the adversaries . . . the Lord will judge His people . . . it is a fearful thing to fall into the hands of the living God" (Hebrews 10:26, 27, 31).

---

[3] "Father," in this generic sense, includes also the mother, just as the term "Man" includes Woman, cf. Genesis 1:27.

He begins with *teaching:* He gives us a "knowledge of the truth." Where the teaching is rejected or ignored, He disciplines and the discipline is not light: It is a 'fearful judgment.' Yet this discipline is not at variance with His love, but in support of it:

"My son, do not regard lightly the discipline of the Lord, nor lose courage when you are punished by Him. For the Lord disciplines him whom he *loves,* and chastises every son whom He receives. . . . God is treating you as sons; for what son is there whom his father does not discipline? If you are left without discipline, in which all have participated, then you are illegitimate children and not sons" (Hebrews 12:5-9).

In these verses we see the order reversed, yet the basic threefold pattern remains clearly evident: *Teach, Discipline, Love.* This is the way in which the eternal God expresses His fatherhood. He is the perfect Father. He is a model for all those who are privileged to express the image of His parenthood here on earth.

TEACH

"Train up a child in the way he should go, and when he is old he will not depart from it" (Proverbs 22:6).

Glenn Clark, one of the great teachers on the life of prayer in the past generation, said that every child comes into the world with "sealed orders." Every human being has a unique destiny to fulfill. When one is 'born again' into the Christian community, this same truth prevails. The Apostle Paul describes the Church as the "Body of Christ," in which each individual member has a unique place and function—as the eye, the ear, the foot have a unique place and function in the body. Every person comes into the world, and comes into the Body of Christ, with "sealed orders"—a unique destiny to fulfill. Part of the calling of a parent is to help the child unseal his orders—discover what it is that God means him to be and do. We are to train up the child not simply in the way that any and every child should go, but also in *the* (specific and unique) way in which *he* should go.

This means that parents must deal with each one of their children under the creative leading of the Holy Spirit. All parents have to adjust to the sometimes difficult realization that each one of their children is different—and tend to become more so as they grow older. This does not mean that a family becomes the arena for a rampant individualism, but it does mean that the differences in the character and make-up of the children betoken differences in the destiny which God has appointed for each one of them.

Parents must be on guard lest they visit upon a child something of their own desire and ambition. It is not uncommon that a parent will try to live out some aspect of his own life through the life of his child. A mother who was gay and popular as a teenager may try to relive some of this by coaching her daughter into this same role. If the daughter is like her mother in this regard, no harm is done. But if her daughter has a different set of sealed orders—is quiet and retiring—it can cause untold suffering and frustration.

The public school can accommodate individual differences only to a limited degree. The parents, however, must repeatedly ask not only, "Am I doing right?"—but, "Am I doing right *for this child?*" "Is my teaching helping to train up *this* child in the way *he* should go?"

Instruct

The teaching of our children begins with thorough instruction. It may be instruction in table manners, in tieing shoes, in moral values, in driving the car. Patiently and lovingly we should teach our children what we expect of them. It is the parents' responsibility to see that a child understands exactly what is expected of him. Not only must he understand mentally, but he must also be helped and shown how to carry out a command correctly, how to do a good job of it!

This is especially true in building good work habits. Most parents are guilty of issuing orders without a corresponding effort to show and teach exactly *how* it should be done. Time and effort spent at the initial stage will save hours of time lost through a habit of slipshod performance. A parent has no right to expect diligence and good workmanship in the child if the parent will not invest time and effort to instruct the child thoroughly.

Even little children can begin to have their jobs and chores around the house. A four-year-old can systematically empty all the wastebaskets in the house. Six- and seven-year-olds can set the table and help with the dishes. As each new job is assigned, the necessary instruction should accompany it. If the four-year-old spills some papers, emptying the wastebasket into the trash barrel, the mother must take the time to lead him back and have him pick up every paper. The first time or two it would be quicker and easier to do it herself. But those spilled papers should not be looked upon simply as some trash to be picked up. *They are a training experience for the child.* Besides, a little time invested at this point will be repaid many times over as the child builds the habit of neatness and thoroughness in doing his work.

Nothing is so helpful in the training of a child as the opportunity for significant work. One of the real problems connected with the urbanization of our culture is that our children have fewer work opportunities. Nevertheless, parents must see to it that their children develop good work habits. Work around the home must be given over to the children as soon as they are able to handle it. The time which they have for play and leisure must be carefully proportioned against meaningful, necessary work. Younger children spend proportionately more time at play. As a child grows older, an increasing proportion of time should be given to work, moving toward the biblical standard given for the adult: roughly one-seventh of one's time for leisure, six-sevenths for work (Exodus 20:9-10). "Work" in this sense includes also the responsibilities which a child has outside the home, e.g., school, school activities, sports, paper routes, baby-sitting, music lessons and practice time.

One of the simplest preventatives for juvenile delinquency is the building of good work habits. The great majority of delinquents have too much free time. They have not been required to shoulder genuine responsibility. A municipal judge put it succinctly thus: "We have found that football players don't get into trouble during football season. They are too tired at night to do anything but fall into bed. After the season, they start to roam around and some of them turn up at juvenile hall."

Thelma Hatfield, a retired Lieutenant Commander in the Navy Nursing Corps, writes wisely of the need for building good work habits in children:

"It is obvious by the way most parents react when this subject is mentioned—usually a sort of blank, unimpressed look—that they do not realize the necessary part of discipline that is supplied by nothing other than plain ordinary *work*. Had not God opened the eyes of my understanding a very few years ago, I would not either. When I reached my fiftieth birthday, I still had never learned to *like* to work. What a pity! Then God moved in my life, and before long I found myself going from 4:30 a.m. till 11:00 at night with hardly a moment in between for rest or leisure. I can't tell you what this did for me—I could write reams about it! And, by the way, one of the blessings was health. There is no tonic equal to motion for the physical body.

"Parents, you must *teach* and *train* your children so they will *like* to work, or at least when faced with a piece of hard work be able to get in and do it without suffering oppression. You can rear them in Christian doctrine and culture, and by God's grace they will be 'born again'; but if you do not train them to work they will never amount to anything for God or themselves or for you. A lazy Christian never did anything for God.

"We acquire knowledge through book learning, but we learn wisdom through hard work. There is no substitute for the valuable 'transfer wisdom' learned from work. In years gone by children washed breakable dishes and if they broke one they were very apt to get a trip to the woodshed. This taught them to handle things carefully. Unfortunately, our plastic dishes are not such good teachers, for they can slam bang them at will.

"As Johnny learns to work quietly and efficiently in order

to accomplish a task, he is taught organization of himself as nothing else will. And never underestimate the value to character building afforded by a sense of actual *accomplishment*. Then, too, in growing children, work—and, of course, directed educational and recreational activities as well—automatically take care of a lot of discipline problems by using up exuberant energy which otherwise becomes like a motor-in-action, which neither you nor the child can control.

"When you set your child to a long and tedious piece of work, do not permit him to dispute and enlarge upon redundant details in order to build obstacles, or to be just generally irritable because he must work, thinking he will wear you out and soon be able to leave the job undone. If you are not firm here, this spirit will *possess* him and when he is an adult and expected to make something of himself, he will fail, because he was trained to avoid and oppose that which is unpleasant. He will be doing exactly what he was *trained* to do in his younger years; but the trouble is, it will now be on such giant-like proportions that parents usually fail to recognize it as their own training.

"Why do you suppose so many young people turn to various forms of lawlessness and depravity in order to make a living? The poor souls were permitted to play, play, play, from early morning to late at night for eighteen years. They have learned nothing but foolishness—colossal and stupendous foolishness. Can they suddenly face the discipline of weariness and the mundane involved in making a living? *It is too late.*

"Work tires our bodies and leaves us glad for moments of repose. Young people, who at an early age are thus disciplined, will not be devising evil upon their beds. It is a common sight today to see a mother running absolutely wild, straining every fiber of her body trying to keep abreast of all the family work details, while the ten- or twelve-, or even sixteen-year-old daughter sits around primping her hair and posing in the mirror. Don't say she's too young. In earlier days a child had to stand on a box when he or she learned to wash dishes. That is the age children should learn to accept responsibility.

"From early years, girls should be learning to wash their own clothes and sweaters, helping mother and sacrificing themselves for their family by keeping the house, cooking, etc. How will a boy or girl give of themselves later on when God or duty calls? If there has been no early training and sacrifice, they will be unable to yield. *If we do not learn obedience in small things, we will lose our ability to be obedient in the large things.*

"I have in mind a family where the child was not obligated to do anything but what pleased his fancy. He was made the center of attraction and when small was allowed to indulge in all sorts of wee-sized vandalism throughout the house and grounds. When an interested person saw what was taking place in that child, he tried to speak to the parents. However, they could not be approached. The friend had scarcely broached the subject when he was silenced by their angry and superior attitude.

"Years later when this child was the literal embodiment of the devil, and totally incorrigible, the parents in tears were ready to talk hours on end to the same friend regarding their trouble. The kindly man did not have the heart to shake his finger under their nose and say, 'Remember when I tried to tell you!'

"Many times a person standing off to the side can see vital needs of which even well-meaning parents are totally blind. Humility and wisdom will listen to advice and warning before the awful indisputable *facts* force upon us the same conclusions. When a child goes wrong and is given over to the devil, the parents will *search* for someone to talk with regarding the burden of their broken and bleeding hearts. They will lift up their voices and weep, but they will find no place of repentance, though they seek it with tears. 'Whatsoever a man soweth, that shall he also reap' (Galatians 6:7). It will be far too late then. Oh, may God help us to take heed in the early years when something can be done.

"Any day of the week you can drive through our cities and see the youth—boys with their tight pants, blonded long hair, rebellious spirits; and girls with their dyed stringing hair, their ragged-legged pants and painted faces. They walk leisurely, looking about trying to decide what they will do for some self-gratifying excitement today—and that which follows testifies that it was spawned in hell.

"In the hearts of these young people there is no thought of industry, or work, or getting ahead. They are consumed by an endless desire to amuse themselves. I tell you the spirit one sees in their eyes and faces is fearful indeed. Why? Why is this? A large part of the answer is simply no work in their early tender years. They had no training to work, often never so much as the responsibility of daily emptying a waste basket.

"I know of a young lady who openly and flagrantly boasts that she is lazy and does not want to work. The terrible scrapes the poor soul has already been in would break a mother's heart and she is still tobogganing on the hell-bent downward plunge, taking her little girls with her. Oh, the pain in the heart of that girl's mother. Much could have been done to correct this in those early tender years by a good strong and continuous diet of solid work. This would have conditioned her so she could now hold under the pressures and grind of making an honest living, rather than being almost forced by her own inner weakness to choose the easy and questionable way.

"In contrast, I have in mind this moment a young lady who has gone away to school and must work for part of her way. I have no fear but that she will meet the challenge and move right along, because she learned to work in her home. Terry will have no problem with adjustment, for that adjustment was effected when she had to wash dishes, scrub the floors, clean house, iron clothes, help tend the babies, since childhood.

"I know a young man who, being the eldest of four children, had to wash dishes at home regularly. As soon as he could find work, at ten or twelve years of age, he was out learning how to hold down a job. His father was a faith missionary and money was scarce. Jim had to work for his clothes, his books, his needs. I have a suspicion these parents would have pursued the same course even though the need had not been so urgent. In his teen years he washed dishes at Bible Camp to pay his way; then worked every inch of his way through five years of college—and this was no inexpensive state college either.

"Jim never had trouble finding work, for he knew how to work and people soon discovered it. To pay his way while in school, he washed dishes each summer on a train—mountains of dishes. When confronted with having to work so hard, he did not draw back and turn tail to take cover in some waywardness. He had washed enough dishes in his young years— this was a breeze to Jim. In fact, he gave praise and glory to God for the job!

"I tell you, Jim's parents are proud of him. Oh, parents! Don't you see it! Don't you see it! Young people today are to be pitied. They cannot help going wrong when they are faced with the difficult things of overcoming in life, for they have been *trained* to go the easy and careless way.

"If you have started wrong, stop now and make the change. Naturally, the older your children, the more difficult it will be, but take hope for the job isn't as hard as it may seem—if you realize the mountain-size need and if you have a will to do it. Actually, it is difficult at the beginning, regardless of the children's ages. You will have to lay many other things aside for the first few short years; but is it not worth any price to see the children God has given you to raise for Him grow up to glorify Him and live happy, useful lives?

"With determination, a sweet and gentle spirit, as well as authority—and praying night and morning for God's help— begin at once. In a short time the whole household will be geared to their chores and responsibilities. You will find a beautiful pattern taking shape, with all rising early in the morning to have time for devotions because each one will be giving a hand with the needed labors of the hours to follow.

"Children will be learning obedience from their labors, their little spirits being subdued as they learn to rule their spirit. Also Mother and Dad will not be so tired and exhausted, because Johnnie is now taking care of the lawn, etc., and so on it goes. Love will flow from parents to children and from children to parents, because all things will be in order."

In the Second Part of our study, we will consider specifically how we may cultivate the spiritual life of the child in the family. But here should be said something about instruction in virtue and moral values.

Truthfulness, faith, and modesty are the three cardinal virtues of youth. With guidance they are not difficult of attainment, and they are the foundation of all genuine Christianity. This must begin with the parents themselves. A deep disgust of untruthfulness, unbelief, and immodesty must first be deeply rooted in the parents. Then it can be imparted to the children. When these three virtues have taken root in the child, a parent has the greatest consolation as he watches his children grow up and leave the home.*

Lying and concealment of the truth are to be reckoned in the child as sin. They are different than the common faults of childhood. They do not spring from haste, lack of reasoning, or impulsive desires. They are practiced with premeditation, cunning, and cold calculation. Lying, therefore, deserves a far heavier punishment than greediness; it is already a sin of the second power.*

Every lie is a sin, but it is the greater sin in proportion to the authority of the person to whom the lie is told. A lie to strangers . . . to brothers and sisters . . . to parents—children themselves recognize in these a gradation of fault. A lie to the parents weighs the heaviest, because the parents' dignity is more sacred; their right to demand the truth is greatest of all.*

Why such a severe attitude toward lying? Because of its tremendous implication for the spiritual life. In all those who perish, lying is the true ground of their condemnation. "And this is judgment, that the light has come into the world, and men loved darkness rather than light, because their deeds were evil. For every one who does evil hates the light, and does not come to the light, lest his deeds should be exposed. But he who does what is true comes to the light, that it may be clearly seen that his deeds have been wrought in God" (John 3:19-21). The eternal fate of man is decided in those depths of the heart where lying and truth are in conflict with one another.*

But how shall a child be upright towards God, if he has not practiced uprightness with his parents? What more sacred task have we than to protect our children against temptations to lying—to offer battle for life or death against the lie when it shows itself in them—and to allow anything else to find a place in them rather than this rising love of darkness?*

Therefore, above all, let no lie be found in our own mouths! Our truthfulness towards our children is as high a duty as theirs towards us. Never leave unfulfilled our promises and our threats. Answer them seriously, so they may depend on our answers. This is what builds in them a love of the truth.*

The capacity for faith in the soul of a child is a sacred inheritance. God commands man to believe. Faith and trust are as certainly virtues as is thankfulness.

Skepticism is no virtue. The art of doubting is as much a desolation of the heart as unthankfulness. Unfortunately, we live in a generation which holds skepticism to be a sign of knowledge and even moral superiority. In many universities, skepticism is skillfully applied to all holy things. Make yourself a master of skepticism! It is the devil's shaping tool. It carves out a character of mistrust, suspicion, slander, and continual negativism.*

Modesty is the third principal virtue. Parents must watch over it in their children. They must employ reasonable means to insure the cultivation of modesty, establishing and maintaining standards of dress, conduct, and speech. Exhortation and prayer are not enough. Yet, after all watchfulness, we must look to God for a continual miracle of Divine protection in the midst of the moral breakdown of the last times.*

Immodesty, when it finds a place in the fancy, *scares away the Holy Spirit*. It is the hidden ground of modern discontent, and of modern unbelief. For when the Spirit of God is gone, then truth and faith are gone, and peace also.*

It seems that our generation has become almost "shock proof." The most insulting immodesties in manner of dress, in speech and innuendo, troop boldly into our homes, our schools, yes, even our churches with scarcely an eyebrow being raised. Here parents must instruct their children with great care and patience, impressing them with the standard of modesty which is proper for a Christian boy or girl.

It does no good to bewail the low moral standards which the world has come to in our day. The world is not interested in modesty. A Christian must establish his own standards regardless of the standards which prevail in the world around him. When a culture begins to disintegrate morally, the people of God must expect that the difference between their way of life and the world's will become more and more pronounced. If we are not prepared to accept the disapprobation which this may bring, then we had better ask ourselves seriously whether we are prepared to be followers of Jesus at all.

Parents must carefully monitor the television, movie, and reading fare of their children. They must establish and maintain modest standards of dress. If a Christian mother cannot buy dresses for her daughter which are attractive, yet modest, she may have to resort to sewing or altering them herself—or, better yet, teach her daughter to do so. But let the mother first be certain that her own dress and conduct are modest. To surrender to the world of fashion, at the expense of modesty, betrays a spineless faith which knows nothing of the call to holiness.

Do Christian mothers, who themselves dress in a provacative fashion which in former days was ventured only by prostitutes, and watch their teenage daughters go off to school slaves to the same prevailing fashion—do they realize the moral potential in this rising tide of immodesty? Have they so far lost touch with their men, that they no longer believe them to be men? Or care that they remain men?

Immodesty does not encourage merely lust. That is bad enough. But continued and increasingly brazen immodesty leads to unnatural lust. A mother was dropping her teenage son off at high school one day. A group of boys were lounging on the steps of the auditorium. An attractive girl, with a short, short dress, started up the steps. The mother thought to herself, "Now there will be some ogling." To her amazement, the boys scarcely glanced at the girl. She later mentioned this to her own son. He said, "Oh, that's old hat. Every time a girl sits down you can see practically everything. You get used to it."

At first blush this might seem to be an encouraging reassurance: "We do, after all, adapt ourselves to these changing styles. Our grandfathers probably had the same reactions when the floor-length gown gave way to the knee-length dress." There may even be an element of truth in this. But there is also the more disquieting fact that blatant and continued immodesty dulls one's natural responses to the opposite sex. It is no accident that the trend toward immodesty parallels the rise in perversion and homosexuality. Men become sated on natural sex through overstimulation, and so take up with unnatural and perverse behavior. The surest guard both of morality, and of the healthy desire which leads ultimately to marriage, is modesty.

Set Rules

Teaching of any kind involves establishing certain rules. Here we must recognize two opposite and equal dangers: No firmly set rules on the one hand, and an oversupply of petty regulations on the other.

A troublesome anarchy, and an overburdening of children with rules and prohibitions are apparently two contradictory evils. Yet they are akin to one another. And they are equally unsatisfactory.*

Where there are no rules, firmly set and kept, a child's life is tossed about on the shifting tides of feelings and impulse —either his own or his parents'. Children thrive on set order and routine. They may strive against rules for the simple reason that they are yet undisciplined; they are subject to passing whim or impulse. Yet they depend, knowingly or unknowingly, upon their parents to establish order in their lives. The child who grows up never encountering a firmly set rule to which his will and behavior must bend, is a 'deprived child' in the most elemental sense: He has a lazy and undisciplined parent. Let's face it: It takes effort, will, and determination to set and maintain rules. *For the moment* it is usually easier to give in to a child's pressure to set the rules aside. But the result is increasing anarchy in the home, and an upset of Divine Order.

The time is past due when parents reassume control and do so by establishing and maintaining firmly set rules. Away with the nonsense that says, "I can't do anything with the child!" Of course you can. What you mean is, "I can't do anything with the child without taking time to see it through —without some effort—without giving up some of my own pleasure and privilege—without losing my popularity—without a modicum of trouble." Well, take the time, accept the trouble, accept even the withering blast of unpopularity with your own child. You'll get it back with interest in a few years, when your child thanks God for a parent who had the gumption to set down some sensible rules and stick to them.

Dr. Max Rafferty, State Superintendent of Public Instruction in California, blames 'dropout parents' for much of today's juvenile delinquency: "We've been soft when we should have been tough. Permissive when we should have cracked down. Generous when we should have been stingy. Noninvolved when we should have been up to our ears." Dr. Rafferty's questions and comments probe uncomfortably some of the areas of parental neglect—

"1. Do you give your teen-agers more money than they need for lunch, school supplies and the Saturday night dance? You know you do. That's why so many of them today own expensive college pads, drive expensive little foreign cars, smoke expensive pot and go to expensive hell.

"2. Do you know where your high schoolers are and what they're doing every minute they're out of school and away from home? If not, why not? In this connection, please spare me all the popularly corny rationalizations about Junior needing to learn independence and self-reliance. Hah! Independence and self-reliance are the last things in the world our offspring need to learn. They're positively bristling with these sterling qualities, like so many adolescent porcupines.

"I think I've heard every argument ever dreamed up about how the 'now' generation demands unprecedented trust, confidence and a blank check. Horse feathers. What every new generation needs is adult concern, supervision and a good, firm 'No' every once in a while.

"Every school kid I ever knew who got into trouble did so because his parents didn't know—or possibly care—what he was doing when he was getting into that same trouble. It's usually as simple as that.

"3. Do you know Junior's friends? Do they look reasonably clean, and talk the same way? Or do they look and talk as though they had crawled out quite recently from under some particularly noisome rock? If the latter description rings the bell, look out for squalls ahead. It's only a question of time until Junior joins them under the same rock.

"4. While we're at it, are you acquainted with the parents of Junior's friends? Have you taken the time to get together with these similarly harassed human beings and plan mutual strategy, if only for sheer self-defense? In case it hasn't occurred to you, it's a lot easier to enforce things like midnight curfews, dress codes and rules of conduct if Junior's gang is operating under identical home regulations.

"Here are a few heretical but delightful premises which I would like to propose:

"1. Since Mom and Pop are older, wiser and make more money to pay the grocery bills than does Junior, the latter should therefore keep a civil tongue in his head, obey orders and maybe even do a little work now and then around the house.

"2. A parent who pays his son's college bills without checking periodically to see whether Junior is rioting, foulmouthing or patronizing the campus LSD supplier with the old man's money is guiltier of contributing to our current mess in higher education than his kid is.

"3. All statements characterizing the younger generation as being more sensitive, aware, concerned, intelligent, worried, belligerent or sexy than previous generations are a lot of bilge. The kids today are just richer, that's all.

"4. Parents who let their adolescent offspring go around unshod, unshorn, unbathed, uncouth and unspeakable ought to be locked up or psychoanalyzed. Or maybe both.

"5. Parents who are too busy, tired, lazy, egocentric or indifferent to ride herd on their kids every minute of every day ought to have those same kids taken out of their custody. As a matter of fact, they should never have had children in the first place. They guarantee delinquency through sheer inertia."

If parents take to heart this kind of advice, they will find some badly needed order coming into the lives of their children and their homes. Yet at the same time they must be on guard lest they fall into the opposite danger—an overabundance of rules.

"Many laws, many transgressions." This is akin to a government which draws all things under its guardianship. It trains people for utter dependence rather than responsible independence. The result of this is, that the greater number of laws that are given, the fewer are kept. And a worse result in government, education, or family can scarcely be imagined than a decreasing respect for law altogether. The man who could bring us to live under few laws, but would see them fairly administered from above, and willingly obeyed for conscience' sake from beneath, would be the greatest possible benefactor of the state ... the school ... the family.*

One help in simplifying rules is to use the principle of absolute time-limitation. In other words, some activities may not be harmful in themselves, but children tend to carry them to excess. Typical of this would be movies, television, and comic books. Providing that the material is suitable, this can be a fun way for the child to spend a few hours in fantasy. However, if the child spends an inordinate amount of time sitting passively in front of the television screen, or if his room is constantly littered with comic books, these things begin to exert an undue influence over his life. The parent should set limits to the sheer amount of time devoted to this sort of activity. During the normal school year we allow the children two hours a week of television and one day on which they may read their comic books. On special occasions, or during vacations, we usually give them some extra TV watching, or an occasional movie. By thus limiting the amount of time spent in these activities, we give them a chance to develop and pursue other interests and with one basic rule we have set aside a dozen petty and never-quite-definite regulations.

However fixed and unchangeable the course of the household routine and the children's round of duties, yet they must be allowed some hours of the freest action, and of self-chosen pursuits. The parent must exercise oversight. But he must guard against a continual nagging, repressing, warning, and forbidding—and then allow it in the end anyway, but grudgingly. We may never leave the children in a situation where there is likelihood of danger. But it is wise to bring them into situations where they may begin to act for themselves. Observing from a distance, as it were, we can still hold the reins in our hands, and draw them tight at the proper moment. *

During summer vacation, Wednesday is "free day" in our family. The children can sleep as late as they like, have no household or yard chores, and can choose their own things to do. This makes for a pleasant variation of routine, and then the times of work and family activity become far more productive.

It seems that a special word needs to be said about rules for that person who is in transition between childhood and adulthood—the much-maligned teenager. Ideally, a person should be given increasing amounts of freedom during these years, so that he is ready to step out of the home as a responsible, self-disciplined young adult. What the parent must continually keep in mind, however, is the fact that a child's *desire* for freedom runs ahead of his *capacity* for freedom. The parent, and not the child, must finally determine the amount and kind of freedom which his maturing son or daughter should have.

This is especially true in relationships with the opposite sex. Our culture thrusts an intolerable burden upon young people at this stage in life. They have no real experience of the power of the sexual forces that are awakening within them. They have little grasp of the seriousness and scope of the relationship between a man and a woman. Yet we allow them to keep company with one another, under little or no supervision, without having given them even the most elementary instructions. Just at the time when they desperately need clear-cut rules and guidelines we turn them loose with almost no rules at all.

When students in a midwestern college campaigned for open dorms—boys and girls free to visit each other in their dormitory rooms—they raised a storm of protest from parents and alumni, as well as some understandable objections from the administration. A boy and girl cornered the dean of the college one day, and threw the standard rhetorical question at him. "Don't you think you can trust us?"

"No," he replied.

They had ready arguments for the lengthy circumlocutions and evasions which they had come to expect, but were a little taken aback by this untypically brief retort.

"Why not?" they queried.

"Because one of you is a male and one of you is a female." That ended the conversation. It's a pity more parents do not have the sensible candor of this college dean. It is astonishing to find how many otherwise intelligent parents operate on the naive notion that they must 'trust' their children. They do not seem to realize the extent to which they have been intimidated by this shallow appeal to a noble virtue. When a young lady chafes at restrictions—how late she can be out, with whom, under such-and-such conditions—she puts on her Most Crushed Expression and says, with imperious dismay, "You don't trust me!" To which the intimidated parent should reply, "Of course I don't trust you, honey." Trust is not something you dispense freely, like pink lemonade, to spread a feeling of togetherness. Trust is built on solid experience, not emotion. You would not think of 'trusting' your son—who has just finished a course in freshman chemistry, and wants to be a doctor—to perform an operation. Your trust would be premature and altogether misplaced. To 'trust' young people with the explosive potentials of sex—throw them completely on their own, with no safeguards, rules, or restraints—is as foolish as thrusting a surgeon's knife into the hands of a pre-med student. This is not trust, but foolish and dangerous irresponsibility.

Earlier cultures took a more realistic view of things. They recognized the power of the sexual urge, and they did not naively suppose that young people could or would control it all by themselves. They allowed relationship between the sexes to take place only under severely limited conditions—when necessary they provided chaperones. They did not allow a boy and girl to be together, alone, for prolonged periods of time. In other words, they did not ask of young people the impossible. They provided a framework of rules and restraints within which young people could be protected from forces they were not yet equipped to handle.

This business of establishing sensible rules for young people has grown to the point where it begins to pose problems not only in the high school and college years, but down into the junior high and elementary levels as well.

Parents in Charlotte, North Carolina, became alarmed at some of the things that were going on with their sons and daughters. Eleven-year-old girls were regularly going to school with lipstick. Seventh graders were seriously going steady. Thirteen-year-old girls went out alone on dates with boys in cars. At one time thirty-five married students were enrolled in Charlotte's Central High School. A seventeen-year-old girl had been married, divorced, and was the mother of a child.

"I was bored sick with dances, steady-dating, car dating," she explained. "Getting married seemed the only thing left to do."

One evening a sixth-grade girl was waiting for her date to take her to her first dance. Her father looked up at his daughter over the evening paper; in her long dress, wearing lipstick and make-up, she looked poised and serene. But when he stood up to leave the room she flew to his side and clutched his arm. "Daddy, don't leave me!" she cried. Suddenly the father saw that under the make-up, his sophisticated daughter was just a frightened eleven-year-old child.

This incident provided the impetus which resulted in the forming of a Parents' League in Charlotte. The League set up rules on parties, dating, social activities, cars. Teenagers were no longer left on their own. Their parents provided a framework within which they could grow up in a more relaxed atmosphere.

One fourteen-year-old girl said, "Since my parents joined the League, they've begun telling me what I can do and what I can't do. Frankly, it's a big load off my mind. And anyway, isn't that what parents are for?" [4]

Sensible rules and restraints, set up by the adult community, are a necessary protection for young people. If the community will not do it, then Christian parents must at least do it for their own children—even when this imposes on the child standards different from those in the surrounding community. The issues involved during these years of growing into adulthood are too serious and far-reaching to be subject to the whim of a teenage sub-culture.

Be an Example

Be that yourself which you would bring others to be. Be it with your whole being. If your demands stand in contradiction to that which you yourself are in secret, then expect no success, no blessing. Expect, instead, that your work as a parent will be brought to shame. [*]

The Apostle Paul could say, "Imitate me, as I imitate Christ" (1 Corinthians 11:1). Parents must be such in their moral behavior that they can invite their children to imitate them.

There are many who wish to give their children religion without themselves being religious. They are like the politicians who find religion an excellent thing for the people, but lay claim to another law for themselves. Let us pity such parents, and their children, but hope for them we cannot.

---

[4] Reported by Booton Herndon in *This Week Magazine.*

They have themselves undercut their whole mission as parents.*

When we were growing up, our father was the director of a summer camp for underprivileged children. My brother and sister and I entered into all of the camp activities. "Camp" was a household word with us, and conjured up images of swimming, fishing, boating, treasure hunts, marshmallow roasts—a seemingly inexhaustible round of activities which children delight in. As summer approached, all our talk around the house turned to camp—the fish we were going to catch, the ghost stories we'd hear from Dag Petersen, one of the counselors, the old friends we would be seeing again—we could hardly wait for another camping season to begin.

My parents had one problem with me, however. The language that some of the campers brought with them was not what they had learned in Sunday School! I heard words that I'd never heard before—didn't even know their meaning, though somehow I sensed that they were not altogether proper. Like a sponge, I soaked up these vulgarities, so the first three weeks back home my parents had to keep me in isolation while they fumigated my vocabulary.

Still vivid in my mind is a passing incident with my father. He was just leaving for early football practice (he was a coach), and as he was about to get into the car he turned to me and said, "You know that I don't swear—and I don't want you to swear either." No lecture. No threats. Just the power of his own example. Even though I did not follow that example as well as I might wish in my growing-up years, I never forgot it. The example of a father who had learned to discipline his speech was an inspiration to me.

Lutheran Youth Research, an office for research and statistical analysis among Lutheran young people, set out to discover the factors which determine a youth's involvement or lack of involvement in the church following confirmation. They discovered what should have been no surprise to anyone. The young people who remained active in the fellowship of the church were not necessarily those who had shown up in Confirmation Instruction as the brightest or most promising. The highest factor of correlation was *the involvement of the parents*. In other words, the power of example in a parent does more to train a child than any other single thing.

"Allow yourself to be trained by God, if you will train others." This is a basic principle; without it no one may expect his efforts with his children to bear fruit. Yet nothing is more frequent than this expectation—as foolish as it is audacious.*

It is unreasonable to expect moral success with our children, without submitting ourselves to the laws of morality. As soon as the children conceive only a suspicion of this kind, the effect of a hundred rules, precepts, and exhortations is lost. And let no man think that it is an easy matter to conceal from children his transgressions against the commandments of God. They cast many a look upon that which goes on behind the scenes. If reflection is not yet active, still there is early awakened a feeling that something is going on which is not right.*

Yet this attempt is not only foolish, it is audacious. For suppose we succeeded in keeping all impression of the hidden untruth and unrighteousness from the children; we might indeed deceive them, even if only for a time, but we cannot deceive God for a single moment. We are presuming to create moral masterpieces of our children without having the Founder of all morality on our side. We are acting as though the source of blessing were in ourselves, rather than in God. We are working as though we could dispense with Him, who alone can work upon the sinful heart of man, and as if the laws with which He rules the moral world were given into our hand. If we had purposely worked for the destruction of the works of our own hands, we could not have struck on a surer course.*

Men wish to have obedient children, but are not themselves obedient to God. Ernest the Pious, Duke of Gotha, used to say, "Let a prince be obedient to God, if he wishes to have obedient subjects." But just as there are rulers who expect faithful allegiance from their subjects and renounce their own allegiance to the King of kings, so there are innumerable parents who presume in the same way. Such a manner of ruling undermines all obedience, loosens all bonds, and prepares certainly for revolution. And so, too, such a method of raising children lays the groundwork for continually increasing disorder.*

We cannot help seeing ourselves reflected in the faults of our children. The sad experiences which we gain in them are appointed to humble us. God often places the most hidden thing, which He alone knows, before us in our children. Thus He gives us a reprimand which cuts more deeply into our conscience, because no one understands it but ourselves. Scripture shows us a connection between the secret actions of the parents and the behavior and fortunes of the children. It is written in the history of David. He had destroyed the family of Uriah. Therefore confusion broke into his own family, which up until then had been blessed by God. By his double sin of adultery and murder, he had destroyed honor and life. His sons committed sins of like character against themselves and against him. He had done it secretly; the retribution came upon him before the eyes of the world.*

In the face of such experiences, one will read soberly the words of Scripture which say that "God will visit the sins of the fathers upon the children." A father will tremble before such proofs of divine justice. God so orders things. It is His law for this world, that the sons should bear the faults of their fathers, as the individual bears the fault of his rank or nation. In the new age, that is, in the Kingdom of God, a new law will prevail: There every one will receive according to his own works, and no one will suffer for the fault of anyone but himself.*

Christ speaks of a man who built his house upon the sand (Matthew 7:24-27). Quickly and easily the house rose, but when the rain and the winds came, the house fell, and the fall of that house was great. So it is with him who hears the commandments of Christ, but does not keep them. So, too, must it be with him who teaches them, but does not keep them. Be not deceived by apparent success. Those who try to command others to keep the commandments, yet do not themselves obey, have a day of reckoning appointed for them. But the time comes when God will show upon what foundation the whole thing is built.°

Nothing is more important in establishing a parent's authority with the children than the example which the parent sets with his own life. Indeed, this goes right to the heart of the nature of authority itself. An 'authority' must sum up in himself all that his community stands for. He must be the living embodiment of the principles which he administers to his community—whether this be a nation, a military establishment, a church, a family.

The high affection accorded the late Dwight Eisenhower by the American People stemmed precisely from his fulfillment of this role. He embodied the dignity which springs from the soil of homely virtue. Whatever political blunders his opponents might accuse him of, they could not shake the simple conviction of the people that here was a good man, whom they could trust. They accepted his authority because he himself was the living symbol of that which they believed America was, or should be. Parents must themselves be the embodiment of their teaching, if they want their authority to be established. For no person can establish his own authority. It is established by the one who stands in authority over him. The authority of a parent is established by God, who has created this family, and to whom the father of the family is ultimately responsible. God asks no less of the parents than they, on His behalf, ask of the children.

DISCIPLINE

Here is the fact which Christian parents must see clearly: *God holds you accountable for the discipline of your children.* If you discipline and bring up your children according to His Word, you will have His approval and blessing. If you fail to do so, you will incur His wrath.

God punished the house of Eli, the priest, for the very reason that he failed to discipline his sons. "I am about to punish his house forever, for the iniquity which he knew, because his sons were blaspheming God, *and he did not restrain them.* Therefore I swear to the house of Eli that the iniquity of Eli's house shall not be expiated by sacrifice or offering forever" (I Samuel 3:13-14).

The Word of God holds the father responsible for the discipline of the children. "Hear, O sons, a father's instructions . . . when I was a son with my father, tender, the only one in the sight of my mother, he taught me. . ." (Proverbs 4:1, 3). The father is to instruct and discipline the child, enforcing both his own and his wife's commands. The wife, in this, as in other things, is the helpmate of her husband, and disciplines the children under his delegated authority, e.g., in his absence.

The point for both parents and children to realize is this: The child's obedience is not merely desirable or preferable. It is in no sense optional. It is required. It is required of the parent by God, and therefore must be required of the child by the parent.

The Apostle Paul writes to the Romans, "Consider yourselves dead to sin and alive to God in Christ Jesus" (Romans 6:11). This is a truth which we must hold fast for ourselves and for our children. We are building on the right foundation when we reverence our children as indeed children of God.*

But to what end then is discipline? Whence does sin still proceed, by which Christian discipline is rendered necessary? Christian discipline is rendered necessary in order still to hold down in death the old man which has been put to death by an act of God. For it has only been put to death and laid at our feet in such a manner that we, if we are unbelieving, can call it back again into life. We can yield to sin a fresh dominion over us, which will be harder and heavier than before. That which Christ has with bitter sufferings overcome, and put to death, we should not again awaken and bring up from the grave. But since we are, although new creatures, yet fallible instruments, there is need for watchfulness and discipline. This is the true meaning of all self-discipline and restraint, to practice and confirm ourselves in the continual victory over the old man. This is the goal of all discipline which God lays upon us; this is the goal of all that which we lay upon others. And our discipline is as necessary for our children, as the discipline which comes from God is for us.*

Therefore those persons do not deserve to be listened to who will hear nothing in education of punishment, or at least of corporal punishment. Discipline and punishment are two ideas closely allied, so that in truth all discipline is also punishment, though indeed all punishment is not also discipline. Retribution and declaration of righteousness lie in both, yet with this distinction: By discipline we are immediately reminded of the fatherly purpose to save, to purify, and to heal; but punishment can also be thought of without such a purpose, as a purely judicial act of righteous recompense.*

Back Up Teaching With Discipline

Discipline should begin when the child is in the cradle. An infant knows whether or not he can manipulate his parents, and if he can, he will. The baby who discovers that crying or holding his breath or being a feeding problem will make him the star attraction in the family, will cry, hold his breath, or be a feeding problem.

Don't be afraid to be boss. Children need to know there is someone stronger and wiser in the family. When the situation demands it, stand up and say, "No, you cannot go" or "No, you cannot have it." Your child may protest bitterly but deep down he will be pleased that you love him enough to risk his wrath, and that you have the good judgment and the strength to protect him against his own folly and lack of experience.

The child who has everything done for him, everything given to him, and nothing required of him is a deprived child. An M.D., writing in the *National Observer,* said that it is like serving the child a diet without the essential vitamins and minerals . . . and he will shortly show signs of nutritional deficiency: "A home that has no taboos, that makes no demands, that requires no politeness or conformity, that sets no firm rules and limits, is a home that the city sanitary inspector ought to serve a ticket to," he continued. "It's an unhealthy place, a breeding ground for trouble. And trouble there will be. A child's character needs adequate structure, and to begin with these controls must come from without. Only when the external controls have been adequate can the child take them into himself, make them part of himself, and thus have the necessary internal structure to allow growth to proceed fully and well."

The parent who tries to please the child by giving in to him and expecting nothing from him ends up by pleasing no one, least of all the child. For in the end, when trouble results, the child will blame the parent for his gutlessness.

Lt. Robert L. Vernon, officer in charge of the Los Angeles Police Department's Youth Service Unit, speaks from experience when he says that children actually want discipline, whether they realize it consciously or not. He maintains that neither parents nor the courts are doing youngsters a favor by being too lenient. He tells of interviewing a third-time offender who was arrested for grand theft. The boy was confused because he had not been punished. Lt. Vernon concludes that young people want to know how far they can go.

Continued threats, and angry exclamations followed by no acts (the habit with most mothers) are worthless. They produce in children indifference, and cause their respect to their mother to decline; thus she prepares for herself endless trouble and annoyance, which she might have spared herself. Her maternal heart sinks from inflicting severe punishment, and she therefore leaves her threats unfulfilled. A very small punishment precisely carried out, and repeated in case of the recurrence of the fault has an effect which can be attained by no threats.*

When discipline is necessary, it should be administered promptly. "Because sentence against an evil deed is not executed speedily, the heart of the sons of men is fully set to do evil" (Ecclesiastes 8:11).

A Basic Misconception

Since the time of the French Revolution, the idea has gained wide acceptance that human nature is basically good.

The 'evil' that crops out from time to time is due to lack of education and understanding, or perhaps from psychological patterns inflicted by one's background and environment. What is needed, we are told, is education and perhaps some adjustment in one's environment—economic, social, political, psychological. Once a person 'understands,' and once artificial restrictions have been removed, the innate goodness of human nature will burst into flower.

Two World Wars, followed by a generation of cold-and-hot wars, have somewhat tempered this naive optimism regarding human nature. Yet many of our unconscious pre-suppositions and judgments are still based on the idea that human nature is basically good, for this idea has penetrated every area of our culture and thinking. And not least the area of child raising! Much of the grief in parent-child relationships is rooted in this false understanding of human nature. Parents look upon their children as basically "good." When they show up "bad" in a particular situation, the parent begins to search frantically for the reason: "What *is* hampering and restricting my little angel, that he should *do* such a thing?"

First, reason is employed. Of course he simply does not understand. Once he understands, his innate goodness and reasonableness will show itself.

"Darling, you must not bang your head on the floor when I take the iron away from you. Mama needs the iron to keep your clothes looking nice. Beside, sometimes the iron is *hot*, and darling could get hurt!"

Darling only cries louder and continues to bang his head on the floor in a fit of temper. Obviously this is more serious than a mere lack of understanding. The iron must symbolize security and a sense of well-being for the child. Why not buy a second-hand iron so he can have one of his very own? The problem is solved! Darling is happy with his new iron. He pulls happily on the cord, oozing goodness.

But the next time Mama goes to the store, and he must stay at home with Older Sister, Darling throws himself headlong on the living room carpet and begins banging his head on the floor.

"Darling, don't *do* that. Why, you know that Mama will be back before you know it. Here, let's turn on the TV and see some of your favorite cartoons." (In emergencies, the "distraction technique" must be used, since one does not have time to search out that which is hindering Darling's innate goodness from expressing itself.)

Obviously Darling has a deep-seated feeling of insecurity. Mama and Daddy must be depriving him of something. (If they only knew what!) Perhaps they should both go to a psychiatrist and see what they are doing wrong. In the meantime, they must seek in every way to reassure Darling of their love and affection. If the situation does not improve, Darling himself will probably need psychiatric treatment.

The situation, however, does not improve. Darling is developing a thoroughly ingrained habit of throwing temper tantrums. Mama and Daddy cast about wildly for something to pacify him, certain that he is going to give himself a concussion one of these days.

One day, when Darling not only throws himself on the floor, but also fires Daddy's bowling trophy into the corner, breaking off the right arm, Daddy forgets himself. In a fit of anger and retaliation he turns Darling over his knee and soundly spanks him. Complexes or no complexes, that's more than Daddy can take.

Of course the whole scientific procedure of child raising has suffered a major setback by this outburst of uncontrolled irrationality and rage. This will erect such a barrier in little Darling's psyche that his innate goodness may be *years* in finding a way to express itself.

Indeed, Darling goes into a virtual psychological eclipse. Two full weeks go by before his damaged little ego can even summon enough to strength to throw another temper tantrum.

If the illustration is somewhat overdrawn, this basic approach to child raising is nevertheless widespread. In other words, parents widely accept the idea that human nature is basically good. Given this premise, the techniques of discipline are bound to follow the pattern suggested above: Heavy emphasis on reason, and adjustment of the environment to the child.

This approach has had a pretty thorough testing over the period of a couple of generations. The results have not been gratifying.

Yet, despite widespread concern over the breakdown of discipline, in the family and in society at large, it is astonishing to see how tenaciously people cling to the idea of the innate goodness of human personality. A joint committee of the Head Masters Association and the Association of Head Mistresses in London published a report on the relationship of teens to adults. The Introduction stated: "We are convinced that among the vast majority of teen-agers of all levels of ability, from every kind of social background, there is immense potentiality for good—their own and that of society at large.

"They increasingly take advantage of opportunities for formal education and for acquiring knowledge and experience of more informal kinds. They are, as young people should be, avid for experiment and adventure; they are critical yet compassionate, prepared to work hard in freely chosen causes, thoughtful, and realistic in outlook, friendly and responsible. Their quality is one of the most important assets of our society.

"Yet some conditions of our society today seriously threaten the full development of these assets...

"A rapid and intensive progress of scientific knowledge on all fronts has presented us with a number of powerful gadgets—the motorbike, the transistor radio, the pill, the TV screen—which we have not yet learned fully to understand or control.

"It has also weakened (temporarily, we believe) the once powerful sanction of religious authority. For large numbers of people religion is no longer the unquestionable basis for moral behavior.

"With this decline has come an uncertainty of moral standards among adults, and a disinclination to dictate to or exercise authority upon the young.

"While the older generation, teachers as well as parents, may be quite as deeply concerned as in the past for the welfare of the younger, their confidence as to how best to guide them has been undermined and so they sometimes contract out of the responsibility altogether."

In spite of admitted bafflement, there is a blind-faith clinging to the notion that "some conditions of our society" are really to blame. The problem is simply that "we have not yet learned fully to understand or control . . . the motorbike, the transistor radio, the pill, the TV screen." How about trying to understand and control the *children who ride the motorbike and stare at the TV screen?*

The problem lies in the presupposition. The Bible comes at the business of child-raising from a fundamentally different point of view. The Bible does not look upon a child as basically good! "Behold, I was brought forth in iniquity, and in sin did my mother conceive me" (Psalm 51:5). The Bible does not view a child as one who essentially wants to do the wise and right thing. Its understanding of the child's nature is different and therefore its approach to discipline is different. "Folly is bound up in the heart of a child, but the rod of discipline drives it from him" (Proverbs 22:15).

The Scriptural method of discipline is simple and unequivocal: *the rod.* Before we dismiss this as old-fashioned, barbaric, lacking in understanding and love, and hopelessly out of touch with modern psychological insight, let us consider what the Bible says about the discipline of the rod.

The Rod: The Way of Love

"He who spares the rod *hates* his son, but he who loves him is diligent to discipline him" (Proverbs 13:24). It is sentimentality, not love, that withholds the rod. Indeed, the Bible uses stronger language, and calls it *hate.* Teaching which is not backed up with Biblical discipline does not convey love and understanding to a child. What it does convey is a *lack of concern.*

A psychiatrist once told a group of people in our church about a seven-year-old girl whom he had treated as an outpatient. At one point in the treatment the girl made a statement that struck him as astonishingly perceptive.

"My mommy doesn't love me," she said. "She never spanks me..."

The Bible uses the strongest expressions with respect to the necessity of the rod of discipline. What then is the meaning of that softness and laxity which demands an upbringing without the rod? It can only be explained by an inward rebellion against discipline and law, which believes in no judgment, and in no eternal Judge, which preaches nothing about the wrath of God, which refuses to the government the duty of retribution, strips all judicial punishment of judicial earnestness, and then by a necessary consequence denies the father's power of punishment, and would also get rid of earnestness and wholesome severity in discipline.*

Some allege that by bodily punishment no moral effect is produced, it works only upon the senses. They maintain that in the future a person will shun evil only out of fear of corporal punishment. Thus the child is led by this very means of discipline to act from physical and not from higher motives, the opposite of all morality—the opposite of all that which should be the effect of our training.*

It is only against the rudest method of punishment that this objection is valid. It regards, so to speak, only the child and the paddle, as though nothing else existed. It forgets the person who punishes, and the relation in which he stands to the object of punishment. If the punishment is of the right kind it not only takes effect physically, but also through physical terror and pain, it awakens and sharpens the consciousness that there is a moral power over us, a righteous judge, and a law which cannot be broken. It does not dissolve, but rather strengthens the moral bond which binds the child to the father. And the extent to which severe fathers are loved by their children is a confirmation of this. It does not confirm a child in the false maxim of acting merely so as to avoid what is physically unpleasant. When the physical pain of a spanking is past, a serious impression remains, and this will help him in meeting the next temptation which arises.*

A spanking combines the twin aspects of love and fear, and in this it is patterned after our relationship to the Heavenly Father. Some people have trouble with the idea of *fearing* God because a certain brand of sentimental humanism has crept into our thinking. We think that love and fear cannot exist together. The Bible, however, consistently views love and fear as inseparable twins.

Israel's great confession of faith, which has sustained them as a people down to the present day, links together the twin commandments to *love* and *fear* God: "Hear, O Israel: The Lord our God is one Lord; and you shall *love* the Lord your God with all your heart, and with all your soul, and with all your might . . . you shall *fear* the Lord your God; you shall serve him, and swear by his name" (Deuteronomy 6:4, 5, 13).

A Pharisee once asked Jesus a question, 'to test Him,' i.e., to try to trip Him up:

"Teacher, which is the great commandment in the law?"

Jesus answered him by quoting part of the passage from Deuteronomy cited above: "You shall love the Lord your God with all your heart, and with all your soul, and with all your mind . . ." (Matthew 22:36, 37).

This was the "correct" answer, the one which satisfied the Pharisee's theology. It is clear from the context, however, that Jesus was not content to let the matter rest with a formal command to 'love God.' He goes on for the entire next chapter to pronounce His famed sevenfold 'Woes' on the Pharisees. It is completely contrary to the character of Jesus simply to 'let off steam,' i.e., to vent His spleen with no purpose other than to express His own feelings. The scathing woes which He pronounced upon the Pharisees were calculated to inspire in them a healthy *fear* of God. Their love toward God had grown cold, formal, and inflexibly self-willed precisely because the element of fear was lacking.

The New Testament recognizes this intimate relationship between love and fear; it is replete with admonitions not only to love God, but also to fear Him—

"Men of Israel, and you that *fear* God . . ." (Acts 13:16).

"Cornelius . . . a devout man who *feared* God . . ." (Acts 10:1, 2).

"Slaves, obey in everything those who are your earthly masters . . . in singleness of heart, *fearing* the Lord" (Colossians 3:22).

Some interpreters try to tone down passages like this by saying that the word actually means "awe" or "reverence." But the word used in the above passages is the same as the one used in the following:

"And when he (Paul) came to Jerusalem he attempted to join the disciples; and they were all *afraid* of him, for they did not believe that he was a disciple" (Acts 9:26).

"The police reported these words to the magistrates, and they were *afraid* when they heard that they were Roman citizens . . ." (Acts 16:38).

"They sounded and found twenty fathoms . . . and he said, 'Do not be *afraid*, Paul . . . .'" (Acts 27:23, 24).

The word is *phobeo,* from which our English word phobia is derived, certainly no mild term!

God's discipline of us, His human children, is calculated to inspire fear. And this does not signify a failure or withdrawal of love. Fear acts as a catalyst for love. He who fears God most will love Him best. If God, the perfect Father, so disciplines His children as to inspire fear, then we should follow the same pattern in dealing with our children.

Parents need to be delivered of phony guilt complexes when it comes to disciplining their children. This one simple realization changed the atmosphere in our family overnight: *God expects you to spank your children when they rebel or disobey.* I realized that my spanking of the children had been the imposition of my own will upon them. Therefore it had tended to be inconsistent, plagued with ill-will, and used only as a last resort. When I saw that it was not my anger but God's Word which determined a spanking, I came to it in an entirely different spirit. Not in anger against the child, but in obedience to God. The whole atmosphere was different —and the children sensed it at once. The spankings were surer, harder—and fewer. (Children established in a pattern

of Divine Order require few spankings; the word of authority suffices.) Out of this grew a new feeling of love which
touched not only the area of obedience and discipline, but
spread throughout the whole life of our family.

It is no doubt true that every parent feels angry and hostile
toward his children at one time or another. Jean Kerr puts it
humorously, "Our children will never have to pay a psychiatrist twenty-five dollars an hour to find out why we rejected
them. We'll tell them why we rejected them. Because they're
impossible, that's why." [5] While this kind of thing is true, however, it is also true that every normal parent loves his children
and this is by far the determinative factor.

The Bible contains few if any exhortations to love one's
children, for this is natural. They are our own flesh and blood,
and "no man ever hates his own flesh" (Ephesians 5:29).
On the other hand, the Bible contains many exhortations to
discipline our children. Parents should not withhold discipline from a child for fear that they may be venting 'hidden
hostilities' upon the child. It is an abnormal parent who hates
an obedient child. What we hate is a child who has not been
brought up properly—a rebellious, unruly child. A child disciplined in obedience to God will be a child disciplined in
love. Discipline does not militate against love. It is a channel
through which love flows.

The Rod: The First Response, Not the Last Resort

Most parents make the mistake of using a spanking as a
"last resort." When reason, pleading, cajoling, sarcasm, and
threats have failed, an irate and desperate parent finally gives
up and spanks his child. God did not intend spanking to be
the last line of defense for an embattled parent. It is the *first*
action which a parent takes, *in obedience to God,* to correct
disobedience in a child. It is the positive, corrective means
appointed by God to deliver and protect a child from the
clutches of his own willfulness. "The rod of reproof gives
wisdom, but a child left to himself brings shame to his mother"
(Proverbs 29:15).

---

[5] In *Please Don't Eat the Daisies.*

Parents must remember this simple fact: *You are an authority to your child*. God has made you that. You do not plead with your child for obedience. Neither do you threaten—"Do this or you'll get a spanking!" *No, you speak a word of authority.* A right word, a well-considered word, a word which the child understands and can carry out, a word which God can approve of and back up.

If a child refuses to obey, you must take him aside and administer thorough scriptural discipline, then lead him back and repeat the word. When this is done early in life and consistently, a child will soon learn that his parents' authority is not to be trifled with. A child so disciplined will rarely require a spanking. He will be a happy, secure, obedient child —living under the protection of his father's authority, living in accord with God's Divine Order.

The respect for order and authority which a child learns at this age is relatively painless. The sting of a spanking lasts but a few minutes. If the lesson is not learned at this stage of life, then it has to be learned at a later stage, in other ways and at much greater pain. Sooner or later—when he applies for college entrance with a lazy-C average, when he is laid off a job because he constantly challenges his boss' authority, when he misses a promotion because of his sloppy work habits—sooner or later, he has to learn what a responsible parent should have taught him before he was twelve years old. In the first twelve years of life a child can learn through the seat of his pants what he must otherwise learn at great cost and suffering.

No amount of psychologizing will get a child to have a cheerful and positive attitude toward a spanking. "For the moment all discipline seems painful rather than pleasant; later it yields the peaceful fruit of righteousness to those who have been trained by it" (Hebrews 12:11). Parents should have their eye trained upon the future, and quit trying to win a popularity contest with their children. What your child may think about you in the immediate context of discipline is relatively unimportant. What your child will think about you twenty years from now is the thing to take more seriously.

"I had the meanest mother in the world," writes a housewife, who is now raising a family of her own. "While other kids ate candy for breakfast, I had to have cereal, eggs or toast. When others had Cokes and candy for lunch, I had to eat a sandwich. As you can guess, my supper was different than the other kids' also.

"But at least, I wasn't alone in my sufferings. My sister and two brothers had the same mean mother as I did.

"My mother insisted upon knowing where we were at all times. You'd think we were on a chain gang. She had to know who our friends were and what we were doing. She insisted if we said we'd be gone an hour, that we be gone one hour or less—not one hour and one minute. I am nearly ashamed to admit it, but she actually struck us. Not once, but each time we had a mind of our own and did as we pleased. That poor belt was used more on our seats than it was to hold up Daddy's pants. Can you imagine someone actually hitting a child just because he disobeyed? Now you can see how mean she really was.

"We had to wear clean clothes and take a bath. The other kids always wore their clothes for days. We reached the heights of insults because she made our clothes herself, just to save money. Why, oh why, did we have to have a mother who made us feel different from our friends?

"The worst is yet to come. We had to be in bed by nine each night and up at eight the next morning. We couldn't sleep till noon like our friends. So while they slept—my mother actually had the nerve to break the child-labor law. She made us work. We had to wash dishes, make beds, learn to cook and all sorts of cruel things. I believe she lay awake at night thinking up mean things to do to us.

"She always insisted upon our telling the truth, the whole truth and nothing but the truth, even if it killed us—and it nearly did.

"By the time we were teen-agers, she was much wiser, and our life became even more unbearable. None of this tooting the horn of a car for us to come running. She embarrassed us to no end by making our dates and friends come to the door to get us. If I spent the night with a girl friend, can you imagine she checked on me to see if I were really there. I never had the chance to elope to Mexico. That is if I'd had a boy friend to elope with. I forgot to mention, while my friends were dating at the mature age of 12 and 13, my old-fashioned mother refused to let me date until the age of 15 and 16. Fifteen, that is if you dated only to go to a school function.

"Through the years, things didn't improve a bit. We could not lie in bed, 'sick,' like our friends did, and miss school. If our friends had a toe-ache, a hang nail or other serious ailment, they could stay home from school. Our marks in school had to be up to par. Our friends' report cards had beautiful colors on them, black for passing, red for failing. My mother, being as different as she was, would settle for nothing less than ugly black marks.

"As the years rolled by, first one and then the other of us was put to shame. We were graduated from high school. With our mother behind us, talking, hitting and demanding respect, none of us was allowed the pleasure of being a drop-out.

"My mother was a complete failure as a mother. Out of four children, a couple of us attained some higher education. None of us has ever been arrested, divorced or beaten his mate. Each of my brothers served his time in the service of this country. And whom do we blame for the terrible way we turned out? You're right, our mean mother. Look at all the things we missed. We never got to march in a protest parade, nor to take part in a riot, burn draft cards, and a million and one other things that our friends did. She forced us to grow up into God-fearing, educated, honest adults.

"Using this as a background, I am trying to raise my three children. I stand a little taller and I am filled with pride when my children call me mean.

"Because, you see, I thank God, He gave me the meanest mother in the world."

The Rod: It Works

David Wilkerson, of *Cross and Switchblade* fame, speaks approvingly of the firm discipline he received from his father.

"Spanking is out of style today," he says. "It is considered harmful to the child's development patterns. Spanking is called 'child beating'; scolding is 'brow beating'; old-fashioned discipline is called 'parental temper tantrums.' My parents had a different name for it—they called it *woodshed therapy*. Parents used to believe that the best way to keep children from becoming delinquents was to spank the devil out of their nature.

"There were five children in our family and each of us had a holy respect for Dad's razor strap that hung on a big nail on the way downstairs to the coal bin. Dad conducted all his 'counseling sessions' in that coal bin. He would never spank me when he was angry, but he waited until I thought he had forgotten all about my disobedience. Then, with a soft voice, 'All right, David, let's go downstairs and learn another lesson on obedience.' He would turn me over his knee and before he laid a single stripe on me, I'd wiggle like a snake, scream like I was being murdered, and cry like I was about to die. My crying never seemed to frighten or impress him. I got it—hard! Then I had to kneel and ask God to forgive my stubbornness, and after making it right with heaven, I had to put my arms around him and tell him how much I loved him. That is why that stubborn, foolish, disobedient little child grew up to be a minister of the gospel instead of a gang leader! I believe it's time for a woodshed revival!"

Many parents make the mistake of failing to carry through with a really hard spanking. We think of the scriptural admonition, "Do not provoke your children to anger," and we hold back. But what is it that provokes a child to anger? It is discipline which merely irritates, a nagging, indecisive, half-hearted discipline. If you spank your child only enough to make him angry and rebellious, you have not carried out thorough, scriptural discipline. The spanking must go beyond the point of anger. It must evoke a wholesome fear in the child. When an honest fear of his father's authority and discipline occupies the child's mind, he will have no room left for anger. This, again, is nothing but an accurate reflection of the way in which God Himself deals with us, His children. "It is a fearful thing to fall into the hands of the living God" (Hebrews 10:31).

If our chastisement is to resemble the chastisement of Christ, it must be righteous. Firmness and uniformity must prevail in it. There must not be harshness at one time and then indulgence at another, in the same case. It must be proportioned to the importance of the fault. The money's worth of damage cannot be our measure. We must look to the moral issue. When something is unintentionally broken, a word of admonition should suffice. If a child remains indifferent when an actual sin has been committed, such as lying or cruelty to animals, it should be treated with corresponding severity.*

As Christians, we live under the discipline of Christ. He disciplines us severely as often as we need it. His object is not to spare us pain, but to surely slay the will of the flesh. Yet He disciplines us with moderation. He does not afflict us willingly. And as soon as He sees that we bow down and acknowledge our faults, He comes to us with consolation; He lets us feel how great is His kindness! So he deals with us, and so we ought to deal with our children. "Fathers, do not provoke your children to anger, but bring them up in the discipline and instruction of the Lord" (Ephesians 6:4). This means, "Discipline them as Christ disciplines you. Admonish them as Christ admonishes you. Allow yourselves to be educated by Him. Learn both the severity and the kindness of true discipline. Imitate Him, give yourselves as instruments to Him. He Himself will by you educate your children!"*

Chastise sharply when chastisement is necessary, but not with passion or bitterness. "The anger of man does not work the righteousness of God" (James 1:20). The indignation of the natural man, though it appears to be a genuine moral feeling, does not produce the moral fruit which it aims at. Wrath awakens wrath, and bitterness begets bitterness. All the profit of the punishment is lost when it ceases to be the application of a superior holy law, and becomes the outbreak of a sinful disposition. Let anger die, and the fear of God rule within you. It is only then that you can be His instrument, and that there can be blessing through your punishment.*

Little David had been difficult all day despite his mother's efforts to attend to him. Now he was getting under her feet while she was catching up on her ironing.

"Now it's time to play by yourself," she said, "Mama is busy."

A few minutes later he was back under her feet. This time she implemented her words with a swat across the bottom. David scampered off, but a few minutes later he was back under her feet, whining and complaining.

"David, Mama is busy! Now go away!" Two swats.

Three minutes later, repeat performance. On it went.

Grandpa was sitting by, watching all this. Finally he spoke up and said, "Sandra, a spanking is an *event*. You're simply abusing that child!"

Sandra got the idea. The next time David came back, she took him by the hand, led him into the bedroom, where they had an "event." That was the end of it. No more whining and complaining; no more nagging, scolding, and swatting. One spanking, soundly administered, will render unnecessary hours of nagging, shouting, arguing, threatening.

Furthermore, a firm stand by a parent with one child will usually have a salutary effect on the other children in the family, for it brings a spirit of authority into the house. Estelle Carver tells the story of a mother whose children were carrying on at sixes and sevens. She became so upset that she poured the orange juice into the pancake batter by mistake. She felt she couldn't throw the good batter away, so she went ahead and baked the pancakes anyway.

The teenage daughter took one bite, wrinkled up her nose and said, "Ugh! These taste terrible—like sour oranges!"

The father said, somewhat sternly, "Thank you for your opinion, Mary Sue. This is a new recipe your mother is trying out."

The twelve-year-old son bit into one and spit it out onto his fork, "Hey, they do taste like oranges. I'm not going to eat them!"

The father looked him squarely in the eye. "Son," he said, "there comes a time in every man's life when he must choose whether he will act like a man or like a cad. This is one of those times. You kids were carrying on so before breakfast that you got your mother all upset, and she poured the orange juice into the pancake batter. Now either you're going to eat those pancakes, or you and I are going outside to have this out."

The five-year-old boy sat by, taking all this in. He gulped down a bite of pancake, and managed a cheery, "Yum, yum!"

This incident also illustrates a basic principle of discipline in the family, and that is the cooperation between father and mother. Father and mother must appear before the children as having one will in a given matter. If they have disagreements, they should work them out privately. Unless it is a serious matter, it is generally better for one partner to go along with something the other has started than to challenge it in the presence of the children. This establishes a spirit of authority in the household. Where the children suspect that they can play one parent off against the other, they will do so.

If we find a house full of disobedient children, we may suspect that the mother is accustomed to contradict the father, to despise his authority, or to make it void behind his back. She then has to pay the penalty that her children are disobedient to her, as she is to her husband. She hankered after authority which did not belong to her, and so she forfeits that which rightfully belongs to her. While she wishes to make her authority prevail in a perverted manner, she in turn loses it where it should prevail without contradiction. A wife cannot weaken the authority of the father without undermining her own, for her authority rests upon his. The mother, therefore, must consider it a fundamental law of the family not to contradict the father in the presence of the children.*

Just as a husband expects his wife not to undermine his authority, so it is the sacred duty of a husband to leave the authority of his wife unassailed in the presence of the children. If he is obliged to overrule her objections in a serious matter, he must do so in a tender and kindly manner. If he turns to her with roughness and harshness, jealous of his own authority, it is not only the heart of his wife which will be estranged. The children, too, will feel a weakening of the moral power which rules over them. If, in their presence, their mother is blamed as being foolish or obstinate—is lowered to the grade of a child or a maid-servant—then the sanctity immediately vanishes which in the eyes of the children surrounds the heads of both father and mother in common.*

The primary responsibility for administering discipline rests with the father. When he is in the house, it is his responsibility to take care of the discipline of the children. The wife here, as elsewhere, is the helpmate. When she disciplines the children it is on his delegated authority, e.g., in his absence or in minor matters. The child should be raised to recognize this fact, for it is a basic principle of Divine Order. Intuitively, children have greater respect and fear for the authority of the father than that of the mother, and that is as it should be. The father who abdicates this responsibility—or the wife who usurps it—has entered upon a dangerous tinkering with Divine Order.

In little matters the mother must act herself, immediately. More important cases she must reserve for the father. She ought not to conceal from him such occurrences with a view to sparing him. He ought to bear the burden. His is the power and the duty from which he may not withdraw himself. Let him have no fear that he will thus become a bugbear and tyrant to his children. If he lives as he should, a father in the midst of his family, he will share not only in the sorrow of punishment, but also in the joy of their good conduct.*

If ever a severe punishment is necessary, it must be carried out so far as possible to spare the child's self-respect. Spankings should not be given in the presence of brothers or sisters, and certainly not in the presence of strangers. For the other children in the family, it is enough if they perceive at a distance something of that which happens. But if they see the punishment, as at all public punishments, the devilish pleasure of looking at it can be too easily awakened. And where the least degree of mockery arises, bitterness and a loss of self-respect are the consequences to the punished child. [*]

The Rod: God's Appointed Means of Discipline

Parents will never have a clear-cut approach to the discipline of their children until they accept the rod as God's appointed means of discipline. It is the choice of His wisdom and His fatherly love. When a parent finds himself shirking the responsibility which God gives him at this point, shrinking from it because of his own feelings or reasonings, let him set God's Word above his own feelings and reason: "Do not withhold discipline from a child, if you beat him with a rod, he will not die. If you beat him with a rod you will save his life from hell!" (Proverbs 23:13-14).

Consider. One day we must stand before the judgment seat of Christ (2 Corinthians 5:10), and answer for the way in which we have raised our children.

"What did you do with the children I entrusted to your care? Did you raise them according to My Word?"

God has ordained issues of the greatest importance to hinge upon the discipline of the rod—even involving the child's eternal salvation.

"Do not be afraid to use your authority," writes one mother. "One would think, to hear some parents talk of their relations with their children, that they did not possess an iota of God-given right over them. All they dare to do is to reason, to persuade, to coax. There is no command, no firmness, no decision, no authority, and the child knows it by its instincts, just as an animal would. Men are much wiser in breaking in and training their horses than their sons, hence they generally get much better served by the former than the latter." [6]

Being a parent is an awesome responsibility. That is why God has provided clear instructions to help us accomplish His purposes. Only the unwise would leave the safety of this "ark" which God has provided, and follow instead the

---

[6] From the article "The Training of Children," courtesy of Loizeaux Bros.

prescription of a sick and dying world. Yet that is precisely what two generations of parents have done. They have left the clear and time-tested wisdom of the Bible, and entrusted the destiny of their children to a slapdash of contrived opinion. The veneer of intellectual sophistication in the so-called 'modern approach to child-raising' (it was going on in Bible times, too, and was dismissed as the way of the fool) has ensnared many a parent, but it hasn't fooled the children one bit. They caught onto it right away, and have run circles around their befuddled parents.

"Child guidance has taken on a new meaning," says columnist Ann Landers. "Parents are being guided by children. Those of us who are past 40 have witnessed a dazzling historical triple pass. In our growing-up years Father was the undisputed head of the house. With the advent of World War II, Mother displaced Father. And now, in far too many families, the children are calling the signals. They are clearly in control."

One example. The Public Affairs Committee, a non-profit educational organization founded "to develop new techniques to educate the American public on vital economic and social problems and to issue concise and interesting pamphlets dealing with such problems," published a booklet entitled "How to Discipline Your Children" by Dorothy Baruch. The underlying presupposition of the entire booklet is the weary old dogma that "human nature is basically good." In rhymed-couplet, even:

> As the bad feelings come out
> The good feelings sprout!

One of the biggest steps in helping a child get rid of "bad" feelings is enabling him to bring them out to you. Sometimes this, of itself, works like magic.

"I hate you, you old witch," shouts ten-year-old Sheila.

What do you answer? The old way would have been to grow indignant. "You're a bad girl. That's no way to talk to your mother. Go to your room." But wouldn't this only have made Sheila hate all the more?

Sheila's mother tried the new way. She said back Sheila's feelings with understanding acceptance. "You do hate me sometimes. I know how it feels."

From Sheila, astonished. "Did you ever hate grandma?"

"Of course," venturing bravely to be honest. "But I guess I got so ashamed of it, it's hard to admit even now."

Sheila's eyes were enormous. "Did you want to run away too when she sent you to your room? Did you think, 'Then, she'll be sorry'?"

"To get even, sort of."

"Gee, Mom. I do that. I keep my mouth locked, but you can't lock up your thoughts, can you?"

"No, darling, you can't," with a gulp.

"Oh, Mom. You're the most understanding mother." A far cry from her original expression of hate.

Obviously the bad feelings can't come out any old way. Neither for the child's good nor for ours. There are certain action-pathways along which it is safe for the bad feelings to travel and others that must be marked "Forbidden."

"And yet, how are you going to stop them?" asked Martin's father, raising his eyebrows. "It won't stop Martin from kicking me or his mother simply by saying, 'You can't.' We've done plenty of forbidding and it's no more effective than a puff of wind."

"You haven't tried it, though, in combination with providing other action-pathways along which to bring the anger out." That's the point. The secret of success lies in the combination. Alone the forbiddings don't do a thing. But when a child has been shown that there are acceptable ways of letting out anger, then he is far more willing to give up the unacceptable ways.

"You can't throw your spinach all over the carpet because daddy didn't stay to play with you. But you may tell me all about not liking daddy to go away."

"I can't let you pinch the baby. But you can show me how mean you feel toward him because he takes so much of my time. Here's a baby doll to pinch instead."

"No dear. I can't let you hit me. But I do know you think I'm an old meany. Let's get the pillow—that old green ugly one—and call it Mommy. You can show me how you feel on that mommy but not on me."

In short, you can say mean things and get them off your chest by "saying." You can play out mean things and get them off your chest by "playing." You can talk about them all you wish. The words won't do actual physical harm to anybody. You can take a rag doll and pinch and kick and bend it till you've vented your anger on it. You can dance a dance of vengeance. You can splash paint over paper. You can pound and pummel and pull and decapitate mothers and fathers and sisters and brothers that you've shaped out of clay. But you can't do any actual physical hurt or harm.

What this writer fails to recognize is that little Martin has an inexhaustible supply of meanness to draw upon—and the more freely he is allowed to express it, the more powerful an influence it will gain over his life. When you act on a given idea, belief, or feeling you intensify its power over you. Act on a negative feeling, and you increase its power. A child who is encouraged to pommel a pillow named "Mommy" may spend his hostility for the moment. But it will only be in-

creased in intensity the next time around. And along the way
he has lost a precious cargo that will not be easily regained:
respect for his mother.

The writer draws us along this way of thinking by posing a
false set of alternatives at the outset. When little Sheila cries
out, "I hate you, you old witch," we are not limited to—

a) growing indignant, scolding, sending the child to her room;
b) putting your arm around her and helping her to express her
'bad' feelings.

Neither of these ways would be the Bible way. The Bible
way would go something like this—

The father would drop his evening paper, and speak to
his daughter.

"Sheila, we don't talk to your mother that way. You know
that. Go into Daddy's bedroom."

The father would follow her then into the bedroom, and he
might say something like this: "Sheila, I don't allow any of
the children to speak disrespectfully to your mother. You
know that. You may feel that way inside yourself, but you
cannot speak that way." Then would follow a sound spanking with a paddle (the Bible's consistent use of the term
"rod" suggest a neutral object, rather than the bare hand),
the object being to cause the child enough pain to rouse a
wholesome fear.

At this point should follow an important step which we
will skip and come back to presently. And then the father
would take his daughter back to the living room with the
instruction to apologize and be reconciled with the mother.

It takes a little more time and effort. Initially, it is not so
pleasant to take as a syrupy discussion about one's 'bad feelings.' But it is far easier to live with in the long run. For it
instills into a child a respect for authority, one of the chief
assets he needs to acquire for a useful and meaningful life.
*It maintains an atmosphere of stability and mutual regard in
the home, which is far more important to a child's emotional
development than the license to express himself freely.* A
child so dealt with is not likely to turn up at the age of nineteen in a line of placard-toting disgruntleds, shouting ob-

scenities at a college president. He will have learned to express himself in more acceptable and effective ways.

It should be noted that a spanking is normally reserved for dealing with *disobedience, rebellion,* and *stubbornness* (usually a not-so-subtle form of rebellion). "Beware of stubbornness in your child," says David Wilkerson, who has demonstrated more love and compassion toward rebellious teenagers than most of us. "Stubbornness is one of the most dangerous of all human traits. It is the one trait I find in every addict and gang member I have worked with. Either lazy or unconcerned, our parents today are too soft. Like the priest Eli in the Bible, they allow their children to be neglected by a lack of stern discipline . . . God will bless parents who restrain their children, and judge those who neglect them."

To pass over clear-cut disobedience and rebellion in your child without punishing it is to set your own will and wisdom above God's. The same, however, does not apply in the area of blunders or honest mistakes, even costly ones. Here an admonition should suffice. For our primary concern is to mold the character of our children; personal inconvenience or the accidental damage of material things should be a secondary consideration. Of course, if a 'mistake' or 'accident' becomes habitual with a child, it then enters into the area of disobedience. A child who occasionally spills a glass of milk should be told to be more careful, to set the glass more toward the center of the table, etc. A child who does this at three or four meals running should be spanked, for then he is not heeding the admonition. In other words, a spanking should be directed against the self-will of the child, which overtly or covertly sets itself against authority. He should not be punished for the mistakes which are a part of the normal learning and growing-up process.

A few paragraphs back we skipped over a step in the discipline process which we now want to mention. This is the step of *forgiveness,* and it touches on a point which is important for our understanding of the essential purpose and effect of discipline.

After a child has been spanked, the father should kneel

down with him and have the child ask God's forgiveness
for the specific sin committed. ("Dear God, please forgive me
for sassing Mommy.") The father may then want to pray
also, thanking God for the forgiveness which He gives
through the blood of Christ. If we take seriously the father's
priestly role in the family, it would not be at all out of place
then to lay your hand upon the child and declare to him the
forgiveness which God has given through Christ. And then
your own forgiveness should also be expressed—most
effectively with a hug and a kiss. For this is the goal of all
discipline: forgiveness and reconciliation.

A child who has just received a sound spanking will not all
at once be the soul of broken repentance. That is not the important thing at this point. The important thing is that the
child make a clear-cut identification, namely, that sin must
be forgiven by God. No amount of spanking will take away
sin, but only the blood of Jesus. A child who has learned this
has learned a profound spiritual truth.

One of our boys had been sent to the bedroom for disobedience. When I came in, he was already on his knees,
praying up a storm. When I took him in hand for the spanking
he began to argue that he had already asked God to forgive
him, and therefore he shouldn't get a spanking! I explained
to him that punishment and forgiveness were two different
things. Forgiveness is something which indeed we must settle with God, for He *is* the only one who can forgive
sin. Punishment is given because that same God who forgives
sin also says that disobedience must be punished. Without
this, 'asking forgiveness' could very quickly degenerate into
an empty ritual, a vehicle of self-interest, which our son was
attempting to make it. But properly understood and used,
the movement from punishment to forgiveness can be one
of the most significant aspects of all our discipline.

More important even than the punishment itself is the suc-
ceeding quarter of an hour, and the transition of forgiveness.
After the storm, the seed finds the soil warm and softened.
The terror and hatred of the punishment are now past. Before the child had resisted and struggled against the word.

Now gentle instruction finds its way, and brings healing with it, as honey assuages the sting of bees, and oil the pain of a wound. In this hour we can say much, if we use the utmost gentleness of voice, and by the evidence of our own pain soothe that of the child. But every continuance of wintry anger is poisonous. Mothers easily fall into the prolongation of punishment. This continuance of anger, this would-be punishment of pretending to hold back love fails on one of three counts. Either the child fails to comprehend it, because he is wholly immersed in the present, and so misses its effect. Or he becomes satisfied with the absence of the signs of love, and learns to do without it. Or he is embittered by the continuance of punishment for a sin which he has already buried. Through this prolongation of harshness we lose that beautiful and touching transition into forgiveness, which by coming slowly and after a long period only loses its power.*

This distinction between forgiveness and punishment touches on a basic aspect of discipline which we must understand: A spanking is aimed at controlling *outward behavior*. It does not, of itself, change the inner life of the child. It merely creates a better atmosphere in which that inner life can be developed. Forgiveness, on the other hand, deals directly with the inner life. And the point is this: God alone can effect a change in the inner life. My spanking will change a child's actions; only the Holy Spirit can change his heart.

If parents understand this essential purpose—and limitation—of discipline, they will avoid many problems. They will recognize that discipline has a limited function—the control of outward behavior—and they will not introduce a harsh, strident note by attempting to force an inner attitude.

A father can tell his child to sit up and eat. He cannot tell him that he must enjoy the food. He can tell the child to sit quietly beside him in church. He cannot say, "and you're going to *like* it." He can demand respectful behavior, but he can only pray for the inner attitude of love and respect.

It is important to convey this distinction to a child. He needs to know that the sacred boundary of his inner life is not being transgressed. We may surely let him know how we feel or believe, but we cannot in any way apply pressure to make him believe as we do—for this is simply impossible. "A person convinced against his will is of the same opinion still." Once a child knows that his parents are not trying to force an attitude or belief upon him, he has no one to deal with but himself and God.

When children rebel against their parents' standard of faith and life it is usually because they have never been permitted to express an idea or opinon of their own, or their ideas were never listened to seriously or sympathetically. So long as the child is serious in his opinions and respectful in his manner, he should be allowed freedom to express himself. Mere frivolous contrariness, of course, should be no more allowed than any other form of rebellion. But the expression of doubt or difference should be given serious hearing.

This does not mean that the child should be allowed to dominate the mood or discussions of the family, nor even that his ideas, once expressed, should be allowed further expression if they are utterly contrary to the standard of the family. The point is that he has a right to *hold* these ideas or beliefs. He knows that his parents are making no attempt to force his inner attitude or belief. Dr. Harry Goldsmith, a clinical psychologist, puts it thus: "You should expect your children to *obey* you, but you cannot force them to *agree* with you."

Of course parents *can* do much to influence the ideas and beliefs of their children. But this influence is more indirect than direct. It is the work of prayer. It is the power of example. It is, ultimately, the working of the Holy Spirit.

It is my fond hope and prayer—indeed, my expectant faith —that my children will grow up to be faithful Christians. But I cannot force this faith upon them by any kind of discipline. I can only be to and for them the kind of father that Jesus wants me to be; can only present them before the throne of His grace daily in prayer; can only share with them the knowledge of this faith in family worship, discussion, and teaching. Each one must make his own personal decision whether or not he will become a true follower of Jesus.

LOVE

Sometimes children have to be naughty to be noticed. Too many parents are more quickly aroused by bad behavior than by good. Children want the companionship of their parents, just to *be* together. Playing games together, rough-housing with Dad, baking with Mother, just sitting close together in front of the fire, reading a story or watching a good television program together . . . and really *listening* when your child tells you something. There are so many ways to let your child know you love him. It takes a little time, that's all. You put down the newspaper, or make that phone call *after* the children are in bed. Children shouldn't have priority in all things; but neither should their needs come in last place.

Comfort and happiness in the home are as necessary as the pain of fatherly discipline. A child who is not surrounded by any pleasures in the home will never attain to any true home feelings. If a sullen, unhealthy spirit prevails at home, he will seek elsewhere for that recreation which the youthful mind requires. He will escape from the protecting barrier of the family, and find outside his comforters, friends, teach-ers, and models which become everything to him which father, mother, brothers, and sisters should be. And these will pull down with careless ease that which has been built up with so much toil at home. Parents should strive with all their power to make their home the center of the child's hap-piness, and of pleasant recollections for his whole lifetime. It is not so very much which is required to make a child happy, if he has been brought up in an orderly manner. If this be neglected, the cause of the neglect may sometimes indeed be the poverty of the parents. But more frequently it is their irritable, quarrelsome, and worldly spirit.*

Just as punishment demands physical expression, so does love. The sense of touch can convey love as nothing else can. It is the first way we have of communicating love to our chil-dren as babies; cuddling a child tells him more than words ever could. The father's and mother's lap should be a familiar place for the child. Our love should be unshamedly "hugging love," as one child put it. Paradoxically, firm, even stern discipline goes hand-in-hand with tender, hugging love. For in both, the child senses the concern and love of the parent.

Saturday morning is "cuddle time" in our family, because it's the one day we can stay in bed a little later. Our youngest is an early riser, and as early as he dares, he comes tip-toeing in to see whether we are awake. When he detects one half-open eye he flies into bed with us and announces, "Time for cuddling!"

These moments pass by all too quickly. We need to make the most of them. In a Father's Day message, John Dresches observes wisely that "*Now* is the time to love. Tomorrow the baby won't be rocked, the toddler won't be asking, 'Why?,' the schoolboy won't need help with his lessons, nor will he bring his school friends home for some fun. Tomorrow the teenager will have made his major decisions."

It is said of Susanna Wesley that she spent one hour alone every week with each of her nineteen children. This points up perhaps the key factor in expressing love toward our children: *time*. We can love our children without spending a lot of money, without elaborate preparations, without a lot of paraphernalia. But we cannot express our love without spending time at it. Not sporadically, according to mood, nor fitfully with one distracted eye on the clock, but regularly and naturally. Parents today are far too ready to give their children virtually unlimited claim upon their pocketbook, but they give of their time grudgingly. Fathers, especially, fall into this error, in their pursuit of success, status, career.

What is to be said of a father who shirks his duty in the moral and spiritual training of his children, in order to acquire wealth, or positions of honor, to which he is not called by duty? Who has bidden him to choose a condition in life which hinders him from caring for the spiritual welfare of his children? Who can justify him in going after gain and worldly success in such a way that he has no time remaining which he can give to his family? He knows nothing of his duty and dignity as a father, who is not ready to make every sacrifice of money and time in order to fulfill his responsibility as father and head of his house. The Christian sets aside the Lord's day for rest from worldly activity; he knows that God will therefore bless the labor of the six working days. So too, a father must every day relax a while from his work, in order to serve God in his children. The fruits of such toil will be sweeter reward than all other gain. In giving himself up to such obligations, he may expect with greater confidence the help and protection which comes from above.*

To give time to your children does not mean that you must put yourself at their disposal, and enter into their activities, although one may do this on occasion. But it is equally effective—and usually more exciting for the child—to be included in some activity of the parent. My father liked to hunt and fish, and we spent hours with him tramping through the woods or sitting in a boat. We did not get the feeling that he was now going into a belabored process of "spending time with the children." He was just doing something he liked—and included us in it.

"Hey son, want to go downtown with me?" Maybe it's just to pick up a garden rake. You have to go anyway. Why not spend the time with your child while you're doing it? These little moments—these natural and spontaneous ways of including the child in your activities—bind parent and child together in love. We often go to the drugstore for ice cream cones after supper. We could get a carton of ice cream and serve it at the table. But the drive to the drugstore, each picking out his own flavor, and the talk we have along the way is a fun family time. It isn't a mere dutiful "giving some time to the children." It's something we all enjoy.

Most parents would never think of denying their children the necessities of life—good food, clothing, adequate medical attention, education. In fact, the tendency today is to go far beyond mere necessities. Today parents tend to err on the side of giving their children too much of personal material possessions, too many things that are "theirs," and this often as a guilt-payment for not truly giving themselves. The nat-

ural greed in a child must be subjected to restraint and discipline. He must be taught that prosperity is a cause
for thankfulness, generosity to the work of God, and for the
help of those less fortunate, but not for ostentation or indulgence of our every whim. If the child sees ostentation in
the parents, of course, the force of such teaching is utterly
lost. But parents who live simply will have little trouble in
saying 'No,' when the requests of their children need to be.
curbed.

Children in a Christian family need to learn that whether
or not we can afford something is not the ultimate consideration. The more fundamental question is whether the Lord
authorizes such an expense, for He is the Lord also of the
family finances. Even if a parent is well-off financially, he
should not give his children an undue amount of personal
material possessions. This too easily becomes a cheap substitute for yourself, and then is it any wonder that our children grow up with an inordinate attachment to things, but
stunted personal relationships? A half-hour spent listening
to your child, or a dinner out with the whole family, will do
more to express real love than adding to the pile of toys in
the child's closet.

A sense of humor is an indispensable ingredient for a successful family life. The nature of humor is to set things in
perspective, and sometimes we become so engrossed in the
details and snarls of family life that we need a touch of
humor to see ourselves and our situation from a new point
of view.

One evening our youngest son was called in from play by
his mother, to take a bath and get ready for bed. He grum-
bled that the other children were still outside having fun,
and why couldn't he play a little longer too? He went to his
room in a none-too-happy mood. The next thing we heard,
he was standing up on a chair like a circus barker—

"Hey, hey, come in and see the big show, 'The Great
Spoiler of Fun,' starring Mommy!" It was pretty hard to
sustain a somber atmosphere after a performance like that!

A child should be treated with due courtesy: "Please"

and "Thank you" are as much in place with one's child as with one's friends. Sincere compliments are like summer rain to a growing child. Parents need to listen to their own voices as they speak to their children. When nagging and barking out orders like a First Sergeant fail, a polite but firm approach will usually evoke a more positive response.

These suggestions are not normative or exhaustive; they merely illustrate the fact that love is made up of many little things. It's a moment shared, it's a hug-on-the-run, it's a ride out in the country, it's an afternoon at the beach, it's a song at the supper table, it's a compliment on the new boy friend, it's praying for a better day in school tomorrow, it's dropping a magazine to listen, it's ruffling up the hair, it's wiping away a tear, it's a blessing at bedtime.

Being a parent is an awesome responsibility. That is why God has provided clear instructions to help us do the job.

Parents! Teach. Discipline. Love. So you will bring blessing upon your children. So they will grow up to be a blessing to others and an honor to their Lord.

CHAPTER FIVE

God's Order for Husbands

Ask the average husband, "Do you love your wife?" and he will reply with a ready, "Certainly! Of course I do!"

In saying this, he means what he *feels* toward her; or perhaps what he *does* for her, by way of care and consideration. But the love which the Apostle Paul speaks about . . . "Husbands, love your wives, as Christ loved the Church and gave Himself up for her . . . husbands, love your wives, and do not be harsh with them" (Ephesians 5:25a, Colossians 3:20) . . . this kind of love is measured not by what one feels nor even by what one directly does. Rather, it is measured *by the sacrifice of one's self*.

Husband, love your wife—
sacrifice yourself for her

The original language of the New Testament was Greek. Three different and distinct words in Greek are all translated by the single English word, "love." *Eros* means love in the sense of passion, feeling, desire; our word "erotic" comes from this. This word never appears in the New Testament, yet it is tl.e primary meaning given to our word "love" in common usage! *Phileo* means love in the sense of human affection and concern; our word "philanthropy" comes from this. This word is used sparingly in the New Testament. *Agape* means *love which is measured by sacrifice*. This is the word which is overwhelmingly used in the New Testament to describe the love of God and the love which He engenders in men. This is the "love" of John 3:16, Romans 5:5, and I Corinthians 13. It is this word *agape* which the Apostle Paul uses when he says, "Husbands, *love* your wives." And he clearly means a love-ready-to-sacrifice, for he continues, "As Christ loved the Church and gave Himself up for her" (Ephesians 5:26b).

Here we touch on the spiritual tap root of God's order for the family. At first glance one sees the husband and father set as authority over his wife and children, and this seems like a fine perch for the man: "I'm the lord of my castle, the sovereign, the liege." . . . But one must look deeper. For the divine authority vested in a husband and father is modeled upon Christ. And Christ's authority was rooted in the sacrifice of Himself. Only when Calvary was behind Him did He come to His disciples and say, "All authority in heaven and on earth has been given to me" (Matthew 28:18). The authority of Christ, and therefore the authority of a husband and father, is not a human, 'fleshy' authority. It is not one person lording it over others. *It is a divine and spiritual authority which is rooted in the sacrifice of one's self.*

The basic and most obvious expression of this is seen in the husband's support of the family. A sign of the moral breakdown of our times is the ease with which husbands visit this responsibility upon their wives. "Working wives" and "working mothers" have become so much a part of our culture that we scarcely stop to consider what a departure this is from Divine Order, or the deleterious effect it has upon family life.

The burden of caring for the support of the family lies upon the man. The woman is glad to draw this burden to herself, for her character always tends toward watchfulness in material things. But the burden is too heavy for her. Stronger shoulders are given to the man; he has a greater natural strength of mind to enable him to stand up under the pressure of these cares. The heart of a woman is more easily discouraged and dejected. God has made her that way. Therefore, also, he has spared her the responsibility for supporting the family.*

Careful and faithful management of material goods benefits the woman; the great toil and care of acquiring these goods befits the man alone. Economy, thrift, and faithfulness in caring for material things are the domestic virtues of the woman; restless activity for the maintenance of the family's economic well-being is the task of the man. The burden of the children and the management of the household is a task laid upon the wife, and it is task enough. Let the husband fulfill his responsibility of providing for the family, so that the wife shall have no excuse for taking upon herself more than is allotted to her. *

Nowhere does our enslavement to materialistic goals show itself more brazenly than in the naive notion that the wife must work in order to maintain a decent standard of living for the family. That cases of genuine necessity exist no sensible person would deny. But it is also evident that in many, perhaps the great majority of cases, the income of the wife goes toward luxuries which a family could do without. A working wife also tends to employ fewer habits of thrift in her management of the household, thus narrowing the actual margin of economic advantage which her income provides. And no amount of income can counter-balance the loss to the family in having the wife and mother spend her energies outside the home.

If the husband enters into a calling for which he is fit, and earns a modest income, it is no disgrace in the eyes of God to live simply, within that income. But it is a disgrace to let the lust for material things set aside the Divine Order which God has established for the well-being of the family. As the Church looks to Christ alone for all her good and welfare, so should the wife and children receive their material needs through the faithful service of the husband. If the husband must give up a measure of ease or prestige in the eyes of his friends, in limiting his standard of living to that which he himself can provide for his family, that is no less than God calls him to. This is but one illustration of the role of a husband, which is to deny himself—that is, to express his love in yielding up his ego, his pride, his comfort, in order to serve his family.

A husband and father who takes seriously his role in God's order for the family must therefore bring to reality the word of Jesus, "If any man would come after me, let him deny himself and take up his cross and follow me" (Matthew 16:24). God says that the husband should love his wife. But this love is *agape*, which is more than even the finest natural love of a man for a woman; the rare and divine flower which grows only where the 'self' is denied, sacrificed, given up to death. Thus God's Word to husbands—"love your wives"—has imbedded within it a call to the radical fellowship of Christ's sufferings, the fellowship of the Cross.

Now this begins to look like a 'love' so rarefied and spiritual that it could hardly offer a woman the warmth and comfort and security and encouragement which she needs in the everyday encounters of life and marriage. But let us see how sound and realistic it actually is.

Husband, love your wife— care for her spiritual welfare

A husband who loves his wife, according to this word of Scripture, gives first priority to her spiritual need. His first concern is that she be rightly related to the Lord. He recognizes that any real happiness and fulfillment for her as a woman, wife, and mother must be built upon the solid foundation of a relationship to Jesus. This is no mere pious nod to one's 'need for religion' or a 'spiritual outlook.' This is a practical, thoroughgoing recognition of the primary significance and absolute Lordship of Jesus Christ. If the Lord provides that a husband shall implement and enhance his wife's relationship to Jesus, is that not cause for them both to rejoice? How better could he show his love for her than by doing this?

The highest duty of the Christian husband is to care for the sanctification of his wife. His model is Christ, who has sacrificed Himself for His Church, in order to sanctify it. He ought not only to lead her in a Christian life and walk, he ought also do everything in his power to make the full blessing of God accessible to her in the Church. At home, by prayer and word, he must sustain her in spirit, strengthen her feeling for high and heavenly things, and forward her in Christian knowledge. No minister has any right of spiritual counsel or authority over a woman against her husband's will. Even the regular pastor of the family—that one recognized by the head of the house—must be on his guard against taking upon himself that oversight and care for the spiritual health of the wife which belongs to the husband. If he intrudes into it, the husband has the right to repel him. He should leave to the husband the share of the responsibility which rests upon him for the spiritual health of all the members of the family. But let the husband feel the heavy burden of the responsibility. As the head of a congregation has to give an account for the condition of all those under his charge, so the head of a family has to give an account for the state of his household. Both men and God expect it of him. The praise or blame which falls upon his wife—her virtues or her faults—touch him directly.*

It is neither possible nor right that anyone else upon earth should have a more decisive influence upon the spiritual health of a wife than does her husband. Whether he thinks it or not, the consequences of his behavior toward her are immeasurable, for good or for evil. The effect will be produced upon the inmost part of her being. A clergyman who is a hypocrite might still be the cause of good for a time; but for a husband this is impossible. He cannot hide from his wife that which he in reality is. In a man's own house, hypocrisy cannot keep its ground. If in secret his conduct is unjust toward his wife, there is nothing in the world which can counterbalance this demoralizing influence. Let him not load himself with the guilt of causing her a secret, even a life-long sorrow, which she can share with no one on earth. Let him not harden his heart against the tender being who is so completely entrusted to him. Let him deny himself that he may be able to spare and cherish her.*

The husband should care for the sanctification of his wife. He will rightly care for it if he believes her to be holy. She is so, for she is a Christian. She is entrusted to him as a holy

.hing. It is his duty to do everything possible that she may not only be preserved holy, but confirmed and perfected in holiness. No one can be such a hindrance to a woman in spiritual things as her husband. But also no one can so encourage her advance in all that is good as he can. He is set of God to be to her a channel of blessing which comes from above. From his mouth should she learn what he has received in the Chruch for their spiritual welfare (see I Corinthians 14:35). Perhaps she is behind him in Christian knowledge. There may yet be a resistance to the way of salvation. The husband has already trod upon these paths in his own experience. Let him not be discouraged, or disheartened, or suspicious towards his wife. With all the greater firmness and gentleness, let him hold fast to that which is good. Through him, God will enlighten his wife, change her mind, and guide her rightly. The devil causes differences to rise up between Christians. Let the husband be on his guard that such differences do not bring any estrangement of heart from his wife. He must not regard her as standing at a great distance from him in the main issue of faith. He should acknowledge in baptism a Divine bond of unity. Beside this, all that which might stand between them is of secondary importance. Let him look upon his wife with this happy thought: "I am appointed to bless her. Not only to make her happy here below. I should sacrifice myself to her everlasting welfare. I should love her, as Christ loved His Church."*

A husband who takes seriously his role in God's order for the family does not take for granted his wife's relationship to Jesus. Nor does he evade his responsibility by saying piously, "That's between her and God." He recognizes his call under God to be a spiritual 'head' to his wife. As Christ is responsible for the care and growth of the Church, the husband is responsible for the spiritual care and growth of his wife and family. This parallel is unmistakable in Ephesians 5:25-33.

> *Husband, love your wife—*
> *go the way of the Cross before her*

And *how* does the husband exercise this responsibility? By

lecturing her on spiritual life and principles? No, he *gives himself up for her.* That is, he goes the way of the Cross before her. He shows by example what it means to die to self. And he does that not only for his own sanctification, but on her behalf. In short, he does not 'drive' her, nor does he even 'lead' her in the conventional sense. Rather he draws her into Christ, as he himself allows the Cross to do its work in his own life.

How does this work out in practice? Consider an everyday example: When an argument flares up in a marriage, it is the husband's place first to humble himself and beg forgiveness for whatever was wrong in his behavior. This is death to the ego. It may be that the wife's guilt is as great or greater. No matter. His call is to 'love his wife *as Christ loved the Church.*' Jesus humbled Himself under the guilt of sin "while we were yet sinners" (Romans 5:8).

In this situation a husband does not judge his wife's sin, and above all does not calculate what effect *his* repentance might have upon *her.* He simply goes the way of the Cross— denying self, giving up his own rights, because this is God's call to him as a husband. The gateway to all spiritual life and blessing is repentance. As the spiritual head of the family, the husband and father must be the first to repent.

It may be, in the example above, that a wife will take her husband's apology as a vindication of her own righteousness. At this point a husband would be tempted to rise and say, "Now, I confessed *my* sin, and you ought to confess *yours!*" No, a husband cannot go the way of the Cross with any ulterior motives. He goes the way of the Cross—and goes that way first, ahead of his family—because God calls him to it, because the Holy Spirit has given him true remorse for his own sin and he knows that repentance and forgiveness is the only answer.

A husband who falls to lecturing his wife on her duty to be submissive to his authority has already yielded up the ground of his authority. His call under God is to fulfill *his* role in the family, not to harangue the wife concerning hers.

Moses was one of the greatest leaders of all time. God invested him with great authority. Yet he was, according to the Bible, 'the meekest man on the face of the earth' (Numbers 12:3). When the people of Israel rebelled against him, Moses would flee to the Tabernacle and plead with *God* about it. Then God would deal with the rebels (Numbers 12:10, 16:33). But when Moses sought to deal with the people in his own strength, venting his pique upon them, God dealt with Moses in utmost severity—even denying him the privilege of leading Israel into the Promised Land (Numbers 20:2-12).

The authority which a husband exercises over his wife and children is not his own authority. It is an authority which God vests in him. The husband must exercise that authority both with firmness and wisdom, but it is God who establishes and maintains the authority.

If a husband finds his wife and children rebellious under his authority, his first recourse must be to God. And his mood must be one of repentance—

"Why are You not able to establish my authority in this family? What is it *in me* that makes me an unfit instrument for Your purposes?"

"The head of every man is Christ, the head of a woman is her husband" (I Corinthians 11:3). If a wife is unsubmissive to her husband, it may well be that the man is secretly or openly rebellious against Christ. Only those who live under authority are fit to wield authority. A man with a rebellious household must look first to his own relationship with *his* authority—Christ. This may well be a humbling experience. Yet out of it can come a broken and contrite spirit, repentance, a new gentleness and meekness toward his family and, amazingly, a new measure of authority—authority which he must no longer strive for, but which is yielded gladly, for he has 'died to self,' and therefore God has been able to establish his authority in the family.

Whether and when and how his 'death' will draw his family after him is the prerogative of the Holy Spirit. A husband's life and love is meant to be a daily 'burnt offering,' a sacrifice of the ego, which the Holy Spirit may use according to His own infinite wisdom. To so offer oneself for his family will mean inevitable suffering for a husband and father. But this is the will and the call of God. And the over-arching promise of the Lord is this: "Unless a grain of wheat falls into the earth and dies, it remains alone; *but if it dies, it bears much fruit*" (John 12:24).

Thus when the Bible says "husbands, love your wives," it is saying far more than that he should entertain fond and affectionate feelings toward her. It is saying that he should *die* for her, as Christ died for the Church. Out of such 'death,' the Holy Spirit will bring forth His fruit in the entire family: love, joy, peace, patience, kindness, goodness, faithfulness, gentleness, self-control (Galatians 5:22).

Husband, love your wife— exercise authority in humility

With the husband should the authority remain, which has been given to him. But he should feel it not as his right, but as his duty. He should never think of the power entrusted to him without remembering the responsibility which is thereby laid upon him. He should recognize the rule to be a burden, and bear the weight of it as a burden. Let whatever is done in his house be done according to his will, for the responsibility of it rests upon him. Let him not hide this responsibility from himself, or seek from weakness to put it away, for this is impossible. He may from a false good nature sacrifice that which he knows to be right and salutary. He is not thereby freed from the account which he must give of whatever, with his knowledge, is done in his family. If he bears with that which is foolish, injurious, and offensive in those that are his, there is no excuse for him. In vain will he plead that he allowed the helm to slip from his hands for love of peace; he dare not yield up his responsibility on the excuse that he is trying to avoid the evil of domestic discord. For this responsibility was not put into his hand by men, but by God. He must refrain from an annoying display of authority. Yet, in all matters of importance, he must gently and wisely maintain his standing as head of the house, with firmness.*

A wife writes, "Don't yield your leadership, that's the main thing. Don't hand us the reins. We would consider this an abdication on your part. It would confuse us, it would alarm us, it would make us draw back. Quicker than anything else, it will fog the clear vision that made us love you in the first place. Oh, we will try to get you to give up your position as Number One in the house. That is the terrible contradiction in us. We will seem to be fighting you to the last ditch for final authority, but in the obscure recesses of our hearts we want you to win. You have to win, for we aren't made for leadership. It's a pose."

Though he has authority and responsibility over all that takes place within the family, the husband must fully respect his wife's sphere of duty and competence. In this sphere it is his place to provide broad oversight, leaving the immediate responsibility and authority in her hands. It is no diminution of his authority openly to refer certain questions to her for opinion or decision. It is simply common sense, since this is the area of her special competence—just as the president of a corporation will refer certain things to his department heads for decision.

Everyone has an inclination to shine in that which is not within his border, and to show his wisdom where no charge has been committed to him. Into this error the woman falls, who is eager to put in her word with her husband in his higher duties. Into this error the man falls when he mixes himself up with all the little matters of housekeeping, and fancies that he understands them better than his wife.*

The wife should look with respect upon the husband's sphere of action and authority. And let not the husband despise the unpretending activity of his wife. It is with great injustice that he fancies that what she has to do are mere trifles. Let him remember that he is not only bound to support his wife; he is also bound to cherish her, and to treat her feelings with delicacy. If he depreciates her work and responsibility, he causes her great hurt, which is not easily mended.*

A housewife in our church shared this wise word concerning a husband's attitude toward his wife: There is a special 'vitamin' that a wife needs for her well-being. Even in Christian homes this is sometimes lacking. A man works and earns money. His salary check and his employer's commendation are a recognition of his worth. A housewife has no such criterion. Yet she, too, needs appreciation and motivation. Many husbands don't realize the depth of this need. They brush it off with, "Well, I married you, didn't I?" Or, "You don't keep on running after you have caught the bus."

In Proverbs 31:10 a good wife is described as "far more precious than jewels. Her husband . . . praises her: 'Many women have done excellently, but you surpass them all.'"

Husband, consider your wife a treasure given to you by a bountiful God. Love her. Honor her. Recognize her talents. Appreciate her efforts. Be considerate of her feelings. With tenderness and sincerity express your love for her in some way every day. This daily 'vitamin' will make married life far more rewarding for your wife—and for you.

"Husbands, love your wives, and do not be harsh with them" (Colossians 3:19). In these words, St. Paul mentions one fault in husbands which outweighs all others—harshness. Harshness undermines the finest marriage, which seemed to stand firmly as a rock. The husband comes to trust too much to the fidelity which lies at the bottom of his heart. He does not watch over his manner of expression in the 'little things.' He allows himself to be careless where he ought to show the greatest tenderness and respect. He behaves respectfully to every stranger. For them he puts on his Sunday clothes. But at home he is quite another man. It would be better to injure any other person in the world than this one person who has altogether given herself to him. It is his duty to gladden her heart daily, to continually bind her to himself by his tender attention and noble behavior. If he has grounds for dissatisfaction, let him speak out so as to hurt her feelings as little as possible, when they are alone together. All blame in the presence of her children, all complaint in front of outsiders, is a bitter pain to his wife. Moreover, to do so lowers his own dignity.*

Marriage is founded on mutual esteem. Courtesy is a support for this esteem. Of course this must spring from a deep inward source. It must not be a hollow ceremony. And yet the outward forms are helpful, and no one should despise good manners in the daily life of married people. They are not a matter of indifference, burdensome, or ridiculous. Carelessness in our dress and speech at home borders upon disrespect. We know that there is a connection between cleanliness of body and purity of soul. Likewise, a disregard of the outward forms of respect easily brings with it a contempt for personal dignity in oneself, and in others.*

When Scripture demands that wives be treated tenderly, and honored as joint-heirs of the grace of life, it adds the warning to the husband, "That your prayers be not hindered" (I Peter 3:7). The feelings and dignity of a wife may carry a secret wound inflicted by the husband; perhaps she can share it with no person on earth. Yet a higher Judge looks upon her sorrows and takes up her cause. In times of holy meditation, and in the necessities of life, the husband looks upward in prayer. Then it is that God makes him feel how he has acted toward his wife. Has he ill-treated and injured her? Then his prayer cannot rise to heaven. He finds the heavens closed against him. His words fall back to him, and die upon his lips. Something has stepped in between him and God, which hinders his approach to the throne of blessing; it is his wife's sorrow, which he has caused. God closes his heart against him, because he has closed his own heart against his wife. He has been hard with her, now he has to learn that God is hard with him. He has, perhaps, grieved the Spirit of God in her, and now God in all justice makes him taste of heavy grief. As he was to her who was put under him, so will God be to him. He cannot reconcile himself to God until with gentleness and self-sacrifice he has reconciled himself with his injured wife.*

Spiritual authority is rooted in a paradox. Jesus said, "If any one would be first, he must be last of all and servant of all." He Himself demonstrated this principle when He washed His disciples' feet. It is of surpassing significance that this act of Jesus is prefaced with the words, *"Jesus, knowing that the Father had given all things into his hands . . . girded himself with a towel."* (John 13:3, 4). In full consciousness of his spiritual authority, Jesus washes His disciples' feet. This is the prototype of spiritual authority properly exercised. Not pride nor power nor self-assuredness, but humility is the wellspring of spiritual authority. The authority of a husband over his wife and children is an authority ordained by God, a spiritual authority. Its principle of operation is therefore rooted in this same paradox which Jesus exemplifies in the foot-washing, and eventually the crucifixion. 'He who would exercise spiritual authority must be the servant of all . . . must go even to the death on behalf of those for whom he is responsible.'

Husbands: love your wives! Give up your pride, your ego, your 'rights.' Follow your Lord Jesus to the Cross, and the transforming love of Calvary shall flower in your home!

PART TWO:

Practicing the Presence of Jesus

We said at the beginning that the secret of good family life is simply this: *To cultivate the family's relationship with Jesus.* We began with a consideration of Divine Order. But Divine Order alone is not enough. As God's Order begins to shape the outward form of a family's life, the presence of Jesus must be given full sway to transform its inner life. And here is where we face a fundamental problem.

Precisely what do we mean by "the presence of Jesus"? Just how *does* a family "live together with Jesus Christ"?

Our little niece, Martha, was about three years old when she reported a simple and profound discovery to her grandmother. She pointed to a picture of Jesus on the wall and said, "That's Jesus. I say 'Hi' to Him, but He doesn't say 'Hi' back to me." Her sister, Nancy, younger by a year, picked up the thought and declaimed at the table one day, "Je'thuth, Je'thuth, Je'thuth! Dat's all I hear 'round here, but He don't say nothin'!"

With the innocent candor of childhood, they put their finger on a deep mystery and paradox of the Christian Faith: Christian faith is a personal relationship with Jesus, *but Jesus does not behave like an ordinary person.* He doesn't come around so I can see Him. He doesn't speak to me, He doesn't write me any letters, He doesn't call me up on the telephone. A 'person' is someone I can talk to and be with, but 'He don't say nothin'!

It is not that the child is a skeptic. He is simply a realist. He hears Jesus talked about as a person. In prayers he hears Jesus addressed as a person. So he expects Jesus to behave like a person. But time after time this does not take place. So as the child grows older, he begins to accommodate his thinking to his actual experience: Jesus *was* a person on earth long ago; one day we *will* meet Him in heaven as a person; but in the meantime, 'He don't say nothin'! A personal relationship with Jesus alternates between nostalgia and hope, but does not touch down in the here and now.

It is no wonder that Jemima Luke's Sunday School hymn is such a favorite with children. It expresses precisely their attitude and understanding.—

> I think when I read that sweet story of old,
> When Jesus was here among men,
> How he called little children as lambs to his fold,
> I should like to have been with him *then*.
>
> I wish that his hands *had been* placed on my head,
> That his arm *had been* thrown around me,
> And that I might *have seen* his kind look when he said,
> "Let the little ones come unto me."
>
> I *long for* the joy of that glorious time,
> The sweetest and brightest and best,
> *When* the dear little children of every clime
> *Shall* crowd to his arms and be blest.

If the truth were known, many adults would confess the same sense of puzzlement and frustration voiced by children. They know about Jesus and they truly believe in Him. Yet the experience of a distinct personal relationship is vague or lacking.

Why is it, for instance, that so few Christians can speak simply and confidently of having experienced clear guidance from the Lord in a matter of their own life? Many even protest piously that it is presumptuous to think one can know the specific will of God. If a child were sent to the store by his father, he would state it as a matter of simple fact to anyone who inquired as to the purpose of his trip. How many Christians can say with childlike directness that they are where they are—that they do what they do—because they have received a command from their heavenly Father?

Theological textbooks and evangelical tracts are fond of distinctions like this: "It isn't enough to know *about* Jesus—

you must enter into a *personal relationship* with Him." We may nod agreement to this, but what do we actually understand such a phrase to mean? A personal relationship implies a definite encounter and exchange between persons. Suppose a husband and wife have a long talk over the supper table. They do not come away from the table wondering whether they have spoken with one another. They are not plagued with uncertainty as to whether there actually has been a personal encounter and exchange. Yet, for many Christians, the sense of personal relationship with Jesus is plagued with a sense of uncertainty and vagueness.

The problem is this same one discovered by our little nieces: *Jesus does not behave like an ordinary person.* How can you have a personal relationship with Someone who doesn't say 'Hi' back to you?

An American was traveling in Germany and needed directions for getting to a certain town. He saw a Shell service station—a comfortably familiar sign—and stopped to inquire. He came back crestfallen to those waiting in the car, and reported, "He can't talk." What he meant was "The attendant can't speak English." In America, a Shell service station is a place where one can speak to an attendant and get clear directions. But in Germany, even though Shell attendants make noises, 'They can't talk.' 'They don't say nothin'!

This is the experience of many Christians. The outward symbols of personal relationship—words like 'see,' 'speak,' 'know'—are familiar. But when they try to enter into the experience of these words in another realm, the realm of the Spirit, they meet with disappointment and frustration.

At this point, of course, we can offer the standard theological tranquilizers prescribed for quieting down this kind of raucous realism: We 'see' Him with the eyes of faith; He 'speaks' to us in the Bible; we 'meet' Him as we encounter human need; we 'know' Him in our heart. All of this is true. But for many Christians this becomes only a pious circumlocution for 'He can't talk.' They may take the pill, and quiet down, but their longing for a truly personal relationship with their Lord remains unsatisfied.

It is not enough merely to say, we see Him with the eyes of faith, we hear Him speak in the Scripture, we encounter Him in our involvement with people, we know Him in the depth of our hearts. Just as it would not be helpful merely to tell the American, "You must speak to the Shell attendant *in German*"—if one does not also tell him *how* to speak German. As a matter of fact, one can enter into a fine conversation with German Shell attendants, *once one has learned the language of that country!* And one can enter into a dynamic personal relationship with Jesus, *if one is willing to learn how personal relationship is established and maintained IN THE REALM OF THE SPIRIT.*

To draw out the point of the illustration: A person who is a Shell attendant in Germany does not speak like an American for the simple reason that he is a German-person, not an American-person: The Lord does not communicate with us like a human-person for the reason that He is a Spirit-Person.[7]

In trying to convey to our children an understanding of a personal God, we have given far too little attention to this simple fact. Jesus said, "God is Spirit, and those who worship him must worship in spirit and truth" (John 4:24). This fact must occupy a more prominent place in our thinking whenever we speak about a personal relationship with God. The reality of Jesus' presence in our families will be greatly effected by it. For the kind of relationship one has with a Spirit-Person is significantly different from the kind of relationship one has with human-persons. The neglect of this basic fact has led to vagueness and confusion across a wide theological spectrum.

The evangelical speaks warmly of a personal relationship

---

[7] By His incarnation, of course, Jesus became a human-person in the fullest sense. Furthermore, He remains forever 'the Son of man,' as well as the Son of God (Daniel 7:13, Revelation 1:13). The point here is that Jesus and the Father are now communicated to us through the Holy Spirit (John 16:14, 14:23), and therefore the believer's personal relationship with God is established and maintained after the manner of a Spirit-Person not a human-person. Thus the Apostle Paul writes, "Even though we knew Christ as a man, we do not know him like that any longer" (2 Corinthians 5:16, Phillips).

with the Lord. But the fact that this relationship is with a Spirit-Person has been all but passed over. Instead of teaching plainly what a relationship with a Spirit-Person involves, we have let it rest, unexplained, on the analogy of a human relationship. Thus it has been all too easy for people to come away thinking that the characteristic of a genuine relationship with God is that it stirs the feelings and imagination much like a relationship with a human-person. The danger here is that one begins to look too much within himself for the authenticating marks of a relationship with God.

Those with acute social concern speak about personal encounter with God through involvement with other people. But again the fact has been glossed over that the relationship with God is a relationship with a Spirit-Person. The distinctive characteristics of this relationship have not been spelled out. Now a genuine encounter with God will lead to encounters also with people. The encounter with God and the encounter with men are deeply identified. *But they are not identical.* And precisely here lies the danger. In the theology of social concern, the encounter with God and the encounter with men have become vaguely synonymous. Involvement with people is meant to be an out-growth and expression of a genuine encounter with God. Instead, it has become a substitute for it.

Those with strong literary or intellectual or ecclesiastical leanings also use the language of personal relationship in speaking of God. They will express with great precision the *idea* of a personal relationship with God. But once again the simple, rudimentary fact is scarcely mentioned: This is a relationship with a Spirit-Person.

Of course we must use language or other appropriate symbols (pictures, actions, artifacts) in order to convey to another person this theme of a personal relationship with God. But essentially this should be a description of experience, not the mere projection of an idea. The danger here is that one may become deeply committed to the language or religious forms (e.g., worship, confession, commitment) of personal relationship without entering deeply into the experience of it.

And here the danger is particularly subtle, for an idea has a certain reality and existence of its own. We say that a person 'holds an idea,' but we also say that an idea 'gets hold of a person.'

As a matter of fact, without much conscious reflection upon the phenomenon of it, all of us carry on considerable inner dialogue with our own ideas. The whole stream-of-consciousness literary technique is posited on this common experience. In a limited sense we could be said to have a personal relationship with our own ideas. And this relationship with our own ideas has certain superficial similarities to a relationship with a Spirit-Person, e.g., intangibility, continuous availability, intimacy. The danger is that one may get an *idea* of a personal relationship with God, and then enter into a relationship with the idea itself, thinking it is the real thing. The number of people who are related to an *idea* of God rather than God Himself is perhaps far greater than we would care to imagine.

Thus the task in this second part of our book comes to a focus: *As simply and clearly as possible, we want to portray the relationship which our families may have with our God, Who has revealed Himself to us as Father, Son, and Holy Spirit.* And throughout we shall keep in mind the fact that this relationship is with a Spirit-Person; indeed, with 'the *Father* of (all) spirits' (Hebrews 12:9). Therefore we should expect that this relationship will be unique in many regards.

Before our families can enter into this relationship, we must give up some of our notions about what constitutes a 'relationship.' One's relationship with God will have certain similarities to other relationships. But in many respects it will be altogether different—even frustratingly different. We must accommodate ourselves to manners of communication and modes of experience which are appropriate to a relationship with a Spirit-Person.

God supremely accommodated Himself to the level of human relationship in sending His Son to become a human being, the man Jesus. But His ultimate purpose in this was not a permanent accommodation. Rather, it was the means by which we might be so transformed that we could enter into a relationship with Him on His level—the level of Spirit. In other words, Jesus comes to us where we are, but He does not leave us where we are. His becoming like us was a means to an end—that we might become like Him (1 John 3:2).

While He was on earth, Jesus had a personal relationship with His followers as a human-person. When His work on earth was finished, and He prepared to return to the Father in heaven, He promised His disciples that He would be with them always (Matthew 28:20); the personal relationship would continue. But the nature of the relationship would change, for now it would be no longer with a human-person, but with a Spirit-Person (John 14:16).

The initial response of the disciples was sadness. They could not imagine anything beyond the human relationship. Jesus' going away seemed to spell the end of their personal relationship with Him. But Jesus said, "It is to your *advantage* that I go away, for if I do not go away, the Counselor (Holy Spirit) will not come to you" (John 16:6, 7).

Jesus foresaw for His followers, not the severing of their personal relationship with Him, but a progression of that relationship into a new and yet more rewarding dimension. And it is worth noting in this regard, that after Jesus returned to the Father in heaven, you find no trace amongst the disciples of hankering for the 'good old days' when Jesus walked and talked with them. A young man leaves childhood behind —not perhaps without a touch of nostalgia. But the adventure of entering into adult life soon absorbs him in a challenge and reality which goes beyond anything he knew in childhood. To return to childhood would be a retreat from reality. Just so, the disciples progressed from the reality of a relationship with a human-person into the greater and wider-ranging reality of a relationship with a Spirit-Person.

We have said that our task in this book is to *portray this relationship*. But for what purpose? What should you, the reader, expect to receive from reading this book?

Our purpose is not merely to describe the relationship which families may have with God. The spectator stands in the arena of Christian experience are already overcrowded —men and women trying to live vicariously off the experience of others, because they have not learned themselves how to maneuver on the field of spiritual relationship. Nor do we want to analyze and explain, merely with a view to giving a measure of understanding about this relationship with God. Rather, our prayer would be that we might offer some practical suggestions to encourage families actually to *enter into* this relationship in a fuller and deeper way. Knowledge and understanding will help make that entering-in more precise and effective. But one cannot content himself merely with knowledge and understanding of these things. For unless the Christian Faith becomes a definite and deepening encounter with the Lord, God's purpose is not achieved. And there is no better place in which this encounter can take place than in the Christian family.

CHAPTER SIX

Jesus, the Family's Savior and Lord

It has been said that God saves *families*. There is some biblical ground for this, too: The example of Noah, who constructed an ark for the saving of his household (Genesis 7:1, Hebrews 11:7), the jailer in Philippi who was saved, together with his household (Acts 16:31). The instructions for the Passover—the great type of salvation-deliverance in the Old Testament—stipulated "a lamb for a *household*" (Exodus 12:3).

Parents should take seriously these biblical types, and claim their households for God. St. Augustine attributes his conversion to the faithful prayers of his mother, Monica. Through long years he kept God at arm's length. He said, "Yes, I want to be a Christian, I want to serve you, Lord— but not yet." Persistently and patiently Monica prayed, until finally his heart was melted and he was won to Christ. And he became a fountainhead of blessing for the Church to this day. Only eternity will disclose how many children have been brought home to the Father through the believing prayers of parents.

This is the beginning point for Christian family living. Each member, at his own level of understanding and appropriation, needs to experience the forgiveness, love, and acceptance which God offers us in Christ. Each one must know Jesus as the *Savior* of this family.

The Bible leaves no doubt that even small children can enter into this experience. Jesus spoke of a child as "one of these little ones *who believe in me*" (Matthew 18:6). The parallel passage in Mark indicates that the child was still small enough to be held in Jesus' arms (Mark 9:36). When the Apostle Paul addresses the 'saints' in Ephesus and Collossae (Ephesians 1:1, Colossians 1:2), he clearly includes the children, for he addresses them directly later on in the letter, admonishing them to obey their parents *in the Lord* (Ephesians 6:1-3; Colossians 3:20). To do anything 'in the Lord' is only possible for a believer.

The Bible knows nothing of the rationalism which supposes that a tiny child cannot 'believe.' Such a notion is the product of an over-intellectualization of the biblical concept of faith. It is true that the conscious, intellectual aspect of faith comes with maturing understanding. But the essential element of faith—the personal trust-resulting-in-spiritual-life-union—this depends upon the gracious condescension of God, not upon a person's mental grasp of the process. Faith is the gift of God, not the work of man. And the Bible leaves no doubt that God shows this grace not only to adults who can respond to it at the level of intellectual understanding, but also to little ones who receive it at the level of feeling and intuitive response. "You are He Who took me out of the womb; You made me hope and trust when I was on my mother's breasts" (Psalm 22:9, Amplified Bible).

A nursing infant does not respond to God at the level of intellectual understanding. Its hope and trust is expressed at a more elemental level. But it is nonetheless *real*. It is not some kind of 'provisional faith,' awaiting the day when he attains to an intellectual grasp of it. God's access to our heart is not limited by our understanding. (Else what would we be forced to say concerning the chances of salvation for those who suffer brain damage or mental retardation?) We can respond to God in faith long before we can understand or describe the process in intellectual terms.

John the Baptist had a clear-cut response to the Lord Jesus before either of them were born! "When Elizabeth heard the greeting of Mary, the babe leaped in her womb . . . she exclaimed . . . 'When the voice of your greeting came to my ears, the babe in my womb leaped for joy' " (Luke 1:44).

Indeed, the Bible sees the problem from exactly the opposite point-of-view. It is not the child's intellectual immaturity, but the adult's intellectual sophistication, which is the real barrier to faith. "Now they were bringing even *infants* to him that he might touch them . . . Jesus called them to him, saying, 'Let the children come to me, and do not hinder them; for to such belongs the kingdom of God. Truly, I say to you, whoever does not receive the kingdom of God like a child shall not enter it'" (Luke 18:15-17). Since it is by *faith* that we receive the Kingdom, we have here the unmistakable authority of Jesus to assure us that children—'even infants'—can indeed receive His saving grace. This is absolutely fundamental to Christian family living. We must have the faith that the Holy Spirit works in even the very small child, bringing him into personal relationship with Jesus.

Missing this fundamental teaching of the Bible, we have often misconstrued our problem and responsibility as parents. On the one hand, we teach our children to sing, "Jesus loves me." Yet on the other hand, we half-accept the rationalistic notion that children 'can't believe,' and await the day when our child will grow up and be able to 'receive Christ.' If only we believed the Bible, and realized how unreservedly the child *believes* what he sings! There is not the slightest thought in his heart but that Jesus indeed *does* love him. His problem is not a lack of faith, but a lack of experience. The job of the parent is to let that faith become a doorway to experience. In concrete and practical ways the parent must help the child to recognize the love of Jesus in the everyday affairs of life.

Even sophisticated theologians are wont to contrast faith and experience, as though when you have faith you neither require nor desire experience. Nothing could be further from the thought-world of the Bible, where faith always *leads to* experience. New Testament faith is not a faith which 'seeks signs' but it is unmistakably a faith with 'signs following' (Mark 16:17). In other words, you do not seek an experience in order to believe, but your belief most certainly leads to confirming experience. Without experience faith becomes cold, dead, formal, legalistic. We must not only teach our children to believe that God is, but also go the second step which the Bible calls for, and help them to experience that 'he rewards those who seek him' (Hebrews 11:6).

This will have an immediate effect on the way we pray with our children. It will lead us beyond the "God bless Mommy and Daddy . . ." bedtime offering—a prayer more-or-less impervious to defeat or disappointment—into real prayers of *faith,* prayers that ask for and expect a definite answer.

Our youngest son once lost an honor pin which he had won at school. He was supposed to wear it on his tie, and to have lost it was looked on as a great disgrace. We ransacked his room looking for the pin, but couldn't find it anywhere. So in our morning prayers, he prayed that he would be able to find his honor pin. Two days later, when I came home for supper, he met me at the door all abeam: "We found my honor pin—*just like I prayed!*" A dozen sober and theologically correct pronouncements could never have conveyed so convincingly the love of God to that six-year-old boy as this one simple answer to prayer.

A child whose faith consists solely of a learned doctrine may have that faith badly shaken when it collides with rival doctrines in high school and college years. But a child who carries about within him the memory of countless encounters with the reality of God will not have to worry about holding his faith. His faith will hold him.

All too often we fail to lead our children into simple ventures of faith because we are afraid to lay our own faith on the line. Behind our pious pretensions lurks the fear, "What if nothing happens?" Well, what if nothing *does* happen? If God is not a prayer-answering God, aren't we better off to find it out right now, and have done with this pious nonsense? If God can't be approached with our everyday needs, aren't we better off to discover it right now, so that our children can be spared the hypocrisy and futility of believing in an all-powerful God who never lifts a finger?

A professor who would refuse to carry out an experiment involving a given element, for fear his students might lose faith in that element, would sacrifice his standing as a scientist. Whereas the professor who experimented freely and openly would lead his students into a precise and confident knowledge of just how that element reacts under varying conditions.

Oftentimes prayers are *not* answered. And let us not take refuge in the pious assertion that He *always* answers, but sometimes the answer is 'No' or 'Wait.' This little pat on the head is intended to hold faith unshaken. But actually it reduces prayer to an impersonal exercise in doctrine, rather than a living encounter with God. It is altogether true that sometimes God *does* say 'No.' But that 'No' is not simply the logical inference which we draw when our prayer goes unanswered. It is an actual experience which yields to us the assurance that God has spoken—just as blessed, in its own way, as a resounding 'Yes.' But often we experience neither a 'Yes' nor a 'No'—just a silence, as though God weren't even listening to our prayers. We must have the courage to venture with our children into these waters that test our faith. For it is here that we learn how to pray aright. It is here that we wrestle with God until He blesses us. It is here that the encounter with God becomes real. Unanswered prayer is like an unsuccessful experiment—a spur to further research.

Faith is not a lofty citadel in which we sit secure, raised up above the petty conflicts and trials of life. Faith is a weapon with which we enter into all the warfare and ambiguity of life. We suffer blows and defeats, we become mired down in uncertainties and doubts. Yet we battle on. And we prevail, because we have dared to use our faith. Faith does not raise us above the need for experience, where we behold the reality of God in a kind of detached splendor. Rather, faith operates right down in the kitchen and office and playground. It does not take us away from life, but brings God into life.

Children are capable of exercising this kind of faith. They are well able to take the disappointments and defeats by which faith is tempered and matured, if they but see their parents engaged in the same bold venture. For God will not allow them to be tested beyond their strength. (See 1 Corinthians 10:13). And in this venture their faith will grow, for they will come to know Jesus as the Living One. Faith isn't built by reason and argument. It is built on an encounter with Jesus. It may begin by accepting the testimony of another person, but it moves from that to a personal encounter, like the people of Samaria who heard and believed the woman's testimony, but then met Jesus themselves (see John 4:39-42): "No longer do I believe that Jesus loves me only because my parents told me so, but I have experienced for myself . . . that He is indeed my Savior."

Hand in hand with the family's experience of Jesus as *Savior*, goes the family's commitment to Him as *Lord*. Jesus does not occupy the guest room in the home, but the throne room. Every discussion, activity, decision has as its background the fact that this thing involves not only family members, but involves also Jesus—and He is our *Lord*.

It is at this point, the point of His Lordship, that many people draw back from their relationship with Jesus. There is no more certain way to stifle the sense of reality in one's faith than by disobedience. And conversely, there is no other single factor which so keeps us alive to Jesus' Presence as obedience to His Lordship. The family which wants to live together with Jesus must acknowledge His Lordship over every aspect of their life.

Two aspects of family life serve as helpful keys, opening the way for Jesus to exercise His Lordship over the breadth of the family's life and activity. They involve a commitment of two basic ingredients of our life: time and money.

Time means a set time each day for family worship. In the next chapter we will offer specific suggestions on how to make this a meaningful experience in the family. Here we simply note the necessity of making a specific commitment of time for this purpose. If Jesus is truly alive, if He is truly the Lord of our families, then it is unthinkable that a period of time should not be set aside each day exclusively for Him.

Families sometimes discover with great surprise that as simple a thing as this, a specific commitment of time for family worship, can have a transforming effect on everything that happens within the home. The reason is not hard to find. When you commit time to anything at all, you set up a reaction-situation between yourself and that to which you commit yourself. You commit time to eating breakfast: your body acts upon the food you eat, and the food has an inevitable effect upon your body. You take time to telephone a friend and make an appointment for lunch: your day is affected, his schedule is affected, the day of the parking attendant, the waitress, the cook at the restaurant are all affected to the extent of your visit. When a family commits significant time exclusively to Jesus, they set up a reaction-situation between themselves and Him, the Lord of heaven and earth. They open the door to all the creative potential which Jesus would bring into that family.

The second basic commitment of the family is money. Money means at least one-tenth of the family income given to the Lord. Money, as one man has said, is congealed sweat. It is an affidavit of the time and skill we have put out, which gives us claim on certain material necessities. Ever since the curse in the Garden of Eden, man has squinted at the material necessities of life through the twin emotions of fear and greed . . . anxious lest after all his toil and sweat he still come up short. When a family commits the first tenth of its income to the Lord, it links its material destiny to God. Though it offends the altruistic pretensions of the effete humanist, the Bible clearly speaks of the tithe as an *investment*. "Bring the full tithes in . . . and thereby put me to the test, says the Lord of hosts, if I will not open the windows of heaven for you and pour down for you an overflowing blessing" (Malachi 3:10). When God asks for the tithe, He invites a family to set aside fear and greed and let Him have the first tenth of its income. He promises, in return, to bless them materially. And, indeed, families who have trusted Him for this have learned that He is so able to bless our labor, so able to protect us from unnecessary outlays that we experience no lack.

Tithing has so often been presented as a solemn duty that we have missed its deeper significance: God *wants* to bless us in material possessions. He wants a family to know security at this point. But He wants the security to be rooted in *Him,* not in a job or in a comfortable accumulation of assets—for these can be wiped out overnight. So He asks us to give the first tenth of our income to Him, an investment with no other security than His good word. The family which learns to trust the Lord at this point experiences a security which no portfolio of blue chip stocks can rival.

These two basic commitments of time and money establish a foundation for the Lordship of Christ in a family. They tie us to Jesus at the point of our highest aspiration, communion with God—and at the point of our most elemental need, our daily bread.

CHAPTER SEVEN

The Priesthood of Parents

Writing to Christians in general, St. Peter says, "You are a royal *priesthood* . . ." (I Peter 2:9). This was one of the doctrines recovered by Martin Luther during the Reformation, 'the priesthood of all believers.' Protestants have usually emphasized the fact that this gives every believer personal access to God, without any intermediary; a person may act as his own priest.

This is true enough, as far as it goes. The tradition of the priesthood provides for a ministry of the priest to himself (See Leviticus 9:7). But both in the Old Testament type, and in the New Testament application, the primary emphasis is upon the priesthood's ministry to others. Whatever ministry a priest does on his own behalf is a preparation for his ministry to others. We are called into the priesthood of all believers not merely that we might have our own private line to God, but in order to 'declare the wonderful deeds of him who called us out of darkness into his marvelous light' (I Peter 2:9)—in other words, to minister God's grace to others. The Priesthood of all Believers means that a believer has personal access to God. But, more important, it means that a believer may act as priest for another believer. What a field of service the Christian home affords for this privileged ministry. Parents—called and ordained by God as priests unto their children.

PRESENTING GOD TO YOUR CHILDREN

In liturgical worship, a minister or priest sometimes faces the people, and sometimes faces the altar. The significance of the two stances is this: he faces the people when he speaks to the people on behalf of God; he faces the altar when he speaks to God on behalf of the people. These two stances symbolize the two basic functions of a priest: *to represent God to the people, and to represent the people to God.*

The priesthood of parents involves these two basic stances. First, parents are called to present God to their children. This they do through example, through teaching, through leading in various forms of family worship. Then, secondly, parents are called to present their children to God. This they do primarily through the ministry of prayer.

Deuteronomy 6:4-9 offers a helpful guide for the parent-priest, in the stance where he faces his child. It outlines three basic steps for presenting God to your children.

Presenting God to Your Children—Through Example

"Hear, O Israel, the Lord our God is one Lord; and you shall love the Lord your God with all your heart, and with all your soul, and with all your might."

This familiar passage of Scripture is actually the beginning of an instruction to parents. Note that it begins by describing the attitude which the parents themselves must have toward God. The Lord knew that without a fundamental love toward God on the part of parents, their teaching of the children would be hollow and base. The starting point for the priest-hood of parents is the parents' own love and devotion to God.

If parents do not have a living relationship with Jesus, they cannot hope to convey such a relationship to their children. Is the parents' relationship to the Lord one of dry rules and regulations? A stern moralism, and nothing more? A dreary round of religious duties and exercises, evoking little excitement, and nothing of real joy? A thin veneer that is tacked on the outside mainly for show? Children are far more perceptive in spiritual matters than adults sometimes realize. They do not respond merely to the words and formal beliefs of their parents. They sense the inner *spirit* of the faith, and that is what they react to. Oftentimes young people who rebel against the Christian Faith are not rebelling against God at all. They have never had an actual encounter with the Living God. They are rebelling against a religious formalism which imposed upon them a set of rules or rituals.

Parents who want their children to know God must cultivate their own relationship with God. First and foremost this means a life of *prayer*. No amount of moral instruction, firm discipline, religious instruction, or church-going can make up for the lack of a praying parent. For it is pre-eminently in and through prayer that we pass from the realm of theory into the realm of reality and personal experience.

How can we convince our children that God is important, if we never give Him any of our time? How can we pretend to love Him, when we scarcely spend a minute with Him alone? Our children may dutifully learn their rituals, and chant their mealtime grace, "God is great, God is good, and we thank Him for this food." But down in the heart, where the real attitudes are formed, our prayerless lives have taught another message: "God is great but He can wait; gotta hurry or I'll be late."

Happy the child who happens in upon his parent from time to time to see him on his knees, who sees mother and father rising early, or going aside regularly, to keep times with the Lord. That child has learned a lesson no lecture could impart. He has seen that God matters—He's important enough to take up our *time*; and He is *personal*—you don't just obey His rules, you actually communicate with Him.

A personal prayer life is not something you enter into merely out of a sense of duty. Nor do you take it up just so you can set a proper example for your children. You do it *because it's important*. Prayer is not a pious exercise. It is doing serious and significant business with God.

I first began to take prayer seriously when I was in my last semester at seminary. I was just six months away from going out to tell people how to follow the Lord and be good Christians, yet I had never taken prayer seriously. Oh, I had 'prayed,' I had gone through the motions. I had said the words. But if a prayer of mine had ever been answered, I would have been the most surprised person in the world.

One evening, during the first year of seminary, I had a cup of coffee with two former classmates, from college. "I don't know how much longer I can take the seminary," I said glumly. "Pray, pray pray! Before every class. It's driving me crazy! Once a day, or once a week, would be plenty!" To me, it was just a routine to get over with, and get on with the important business of educating our minds.

I didn't take prayer seriously. Had I analyzed my thinking, I would have made another discovery: I really didn't take the Bible seriously either. I didn't take the supernatural realm seriously. Prayer, therefore, was nothing more than a kind of a psychological litany, or a respectable routine that people go through as a kind of religious duty or exercise. But the God who opens the eyes of the blind had a plan for opening my eyes.

During my years at the seminary, I had a job at our church's publishing house. One part of the job was to review Christian literature on a radio program. A book came across my desk one day called *The Healing Light* by Agnes Sanford. I began to read it. Here, I discovered, was a thoroughly modern individual, living in our own time, who took prayer seriously. She prayed and saw things happen. She was so objective about prayer that it almost made my skin crawl. She wrote about prayer the way a scientist would write about natural laws and forces. She sounded like a research chemist who would say, "Our experiment didn't work—let's try a different mixture." That's the kind of approach she took to prayer. She said, "If you plug your iron in and it doesn't get hot, you don't sit there and say, 'Oh, dear iron, please get hot!' And then, if it doesn't get hot, 'Well, I guess it isn't God's will for that iron to get hot.'" That's ridiculous—you go and check the connection, you find out where the short is, and what's wrong with the thing. It's supposed to get hot. That's what irons are for. And prayers are supposed to be answered. That's what you pray for—in order to get an answer. A prayer that only goes out and never comes back with an answer isn't a prayer—it's only half a prayer. The prayer is never complete until the answer comes back. The answer, of course, will depend upon the nature of the prayer. But there should be a response, because prayer involves the pray-er and the One to whom we pray.

This was a new realm to me. The thing which I couldn't escape was that this woman wasn't talking theory. She was reporting what she had actually experienced. This excited me tremendously. I began to go back into the Bible, to all of the things that I had mentally scissored out. Slowly the thought began to dawn: "Maybe those things *could* happen. Maybe they could happen *today*—praying for the sick and expecting them to get well, praying for real miracles and seeing them come to pass."

I began with a search of the Scriptures. Then I went into the history of the Church. One thing becomes clear as you go into the study of these things: *Every great man of God is always a great man of prayer*. There appear to be no exceptions to that rule. Think of Moses, Elijah, Nehemiah, Daniel, the Apostles. A great man of God is inevitably a great man of prayer; the two are ever related to one another.

Consider our Lord Jesus Himself. What did His disciples ask Him to teach them? Did they ask Him to teach them how to cast out devils, how to raise the sick off their sick beds, how to still the storm, how to change water into wine, how to work miracles? No, they never asked Jesus to teach them any of these things. The one thing they asked of Jesus was: "Lord, teach us to *pray!*" They discerned, in watching Jesus, that His life of power rose out of His life of prayer. He spent whole nights in prayer. Then He came back in the power of the Spirit. They saw that there was a relationship between that life of prayer and what happened in Jesus' ministry.

Go to the Old Testament and see a man like Samuel. What tremendous evidence of the power of prayer—and how highly regarded was the prayer of Samuel. In I Samuel 7:4 we read about the idolatry of the Israelites. Then Samuel says to them, "Gather all Israel at Mizpah, and I will pray to the Lord for you." In other words, "I'll see if I can get this thing straightened out for you." In I Samuel 8:5, the Israelites come to Samuel, asking him to appoint and anoint for them a king.

Samuel was opposed to this. As far as he was concerned, this was a rejection of God's rule. They wanted a human king rather than to be under the direct rule of God. So he told them the dangers that they were getting into, some of the calamities that would come upon them because of this unwise action. So the people begged Samuel (I Samuel 12:19), "Pray for your servants to the Lord their God that we may not die, for we have added to all our sins this evil to ask for ourselves a king."

Because God had spoken to him about this, and had said to go ahead and give them a king, Samuel said to the people, "Fear not, you have done all this evil, yet do not turn aside from following the Lord, but serve the Lord with all your heart; and do not turn aside after vain things which cannot profit or save, for they are vain. For the Lord will not cast away his people, for his great name's sake, because it has pleased the Lord to make you a people for himself. Moreover as for me, *far be it from me that I should sin against the Lord by ceasing to pray for you;* and I will instruct you in the good and the right way" (vss. 20-23).

This was no pious exercise. We sometimes say to a person, "Pray for so and so," or "Pray for me." Often they go home and forget about it and that's the end of it. We would never know whether they prayed or not, because nothing every happens anyway! When Samuel prayed, things happened. That's the way prayer ought to be.

Martin Luther was a great man of prayer. He said that when he was busy he had to get up early because then he needed extra prayer. He didn't alibi, "Oh, I'm too busy to pray." When Luther was busy, he felt the need to have four hours in prayer instead of the normal two. And he was the head of a family with six children.

It was said that the Queen of England trembled when John Knox went to his knees; he prayed with such power that all Scotland was awakened. "Lord, give me Scotland or I'll die!" he cried. And he prayed with such intensity that the Lord answered. What would happen in our families if we began to take prayer seriously as some of these great men of God?

Coming to a more recent time, we find the story of a little Negro boy, whose name was Samuel Morris. He was converted to Christianity from rank paganism in 1888. He came to a mission station from the African jungle, and was converted at the age of sixteen. A year later he went to America, and he died at the age of twenty-one. Yet in that time he became the fountainhead for a whole missionary movement out of a particular branch of the Protestant Church in the United States.

While attending Taylor University in Indiana, Samuel Morris visited a congregation there. He asked permission to speak. The pastor had hardly sat down after giving young Sammy the pulpit, when he heard a commotion. He looked up in amazement to see the whole congregation on their knees, weeping and praying and shouting for joy. Sammy was in the pulpit—not preaching, but praying. As he said, he was "talking to my Father." Afterward, the minister said of this occasion, "I did not listen to hear what he was saying. I was seized with an overpowering desire to pray. What I said and what Sammy said, I do not remember, but I know my soul was on fire as never before." No such visitation of the Holy Spirit had ever before been witnessed by that congregation.

The question naturally arises: "How much time should I spend in prayer?" Let me suggest that you set one-half hour a day as a goal, later one hour. But start out from where you are. If you have not been praying at all, start with five minutes a day. Later increase it to ten minutes, then fifteen, then more. You can't move suddenly into strenuous spiritual exercise any more than you could into a program of physical exercise. But by entering in by stages, you will be able to work up to an hour a day.

The idea of spending a whole hour in prayer may shake you up at first. "That's a lot of time! I have to go to work . . . I have so many things to do!" Yet if you were suddenly stricken with a serious disease, and your doctor told you, "You must spend one hour a day in therapy," you would do it without question. Isn't your family's welfare worth as much? Furthermore, if you are a member of the Body of Christ, it also needs your time in prayer. For the health of the Body of Christ, the Church, depends upon the health and vigor of its component parts—the individuals and families which together make up the church.

If the President of the United States were to say to you, "You have talent which I need to help run the government of the United States. I want to call you up and speak to you personally one hour a day"—you'd be so excited that you would tell all your friends about it. There would be nothing that would interfere with that hour, for you would surely consider it a great honor to spend that time talking with the President.

When the Lord of the Universe says to you, "I want to speak with you one hour a day," dare we settle for less? When God finds parents who are willing to take time apart for prayer, He is going to have families through whom He can work, a people prepared.

Hold out before yourself the initial goal of one-half hour a day of solid prayer. Devote yourself during this time exclusively to prayer. Take the telephone off the hook, if necessary. Inform your family and friends that you are not available during that hour of the day. This is the key to God's working in our families, that parents learn to pray.

When we consider the God-ward stance of the parent, in which he presents his children to God, we will give some specific helps in prayer. Here we simply underscore the *im-. portance* of prayer. It is the workshop in which the life of a parent-priest is hammered and shaped into an instrument which God can use to bless the children which He places in the home.

Out of this life of prayer will flow a *godly* life, in the true sense of that word: The life will be formed and shaped by God's direct dealing. You will be able to speak to your children about God in a natural way. Without embarrassment, without any phony pretense, you will be able to bring the Lord into the many aspects of family life. Jesus' presence in the family will become real to the children because it is real to you. Happy the child who has such godly parents!

Presenting God to Your Children—Through the Word

"And these words which I command you this day shall be upon your heart; and you shall teach them diligently to your children, and you shall talk of them when you sit in your house, and when you walk by the way, and when you lie down, and when you rise."

The religious training which God here commands us to give to our children is no lick-and-a-promise. It is a *diligent* teaching. Diligent, in this context means *pervasive*. It is not a harsh, oppressive schoolmaster spirit. Rather, it is a quiet threading of God's Word through the warp and woof of family life— 'when you sit in the house, when you're out for a walk, when you go to bed, when you get up.' God's Word becomes a natural point-of-reference for anything that may come up in the family. And through the Word, Jesus takes up His dwelling in the family—as naturally as the sunlight streams through the window when the shade is pulled aside.

It is this presence of Jesus which is the goal of our teaching. The teaching is diligent because His presence in the family is important, surpassingly important. We live in an age when a thousand sirens beckon for the ears and the minds of our children. It is not enough to teach them a code of ethics. It is not enough to teach them a few rote prayers. Our homes must be so filled with the presence of Jesus that they encounter Him at every turn; come to know Him and love Him as effortlessly as they come to know their parents. In such a setting, Jesus can engage their loyalty and fire their imagination. And this is the only antidote to the powers of darkness and corruption which are loose in the world today. The time is past when parents can give their children a pleasant surface-coating of religion. Our children are either going to be filled with Jesus and excited about Him, or filled with sin and excited about it. All that we can bring our children will be worthless unless we can bring them Jesus.

We said in the previous chapter that an essential of the family's relationship to Jesus is a commitment of time for family worship. In many other areas of family life we will speak *about* Jesus. Here we speak *with* Him. Jesus' presence in the family comes to its sharpest focus as the family gathers in His presence to worship. For worship is communion with God *par excellence*. In worship we gather in His presence; we assemble under His Lordship; we reach out to receive His grace; we listen to His Word; we submit ourselves to His will. Our trouble as human beings is that we are ec-centric: we make ourselves, our family, our interests, our concerns the center rather than God. In family worship we daily reorient ourselves around our true center which is Christ.

The keynote to family worship is a Holy Spirit-inspired variety. Our life together with Jesus can't be expressed in static forms. There is no one set pattern for all families, nor a set pattern for one family at all times. The way in which we worship will vary with the age of our children, with our cultural and educational heritage, with our particular church affiliation—the essential thing is that it be a living encounter with God in which every member of the family participates. The suggestions which follow are just that—suggestions. As your family enters into a disciplined pattern of worship, the Holy Spirit will add to it a creative variety tailor-made to your own family.

Singing. A modest investment in song books—one for each member of the family—will pay rich dividends. In our family we pick a new song at the beginning of the week and sing it every day as an opening to family worship. Each member of the family takes his turn at choosing the song for the week. The children will tend to pick "favorites." The parents can introduce a new song every so often. In this way the family deposits in the heart of each member a rich treasury of Christian music.

Where a family has some musical talent, they can use some accompaniment. Sing-a-long records offer another avenue for musical expression.

It is no accident that the Old Testament book of worship, the Psalms, contains a number of psalms with the exhortation, "Sing unto the Lord! Sing unto the Lord a new song!" Singing has a unique capacity for releasing our emotions, setting us free from our inhibitions, so we can enter freely into a time of worship.

Invocation. This is a step which is often skipped in family worship. Yet it can add a note of reality which enhances all that follows. It means simply what the word implies: we 'invoke' or ask the Spirit of God to be present with us. This, again, can pass around the family circle. On occasion it can be formal: "In the Name of the Father and of the Son and of the Holy Ghost." This will tend to link the family's worship to the worship of its larger family, the Church. At other times it can be informal and spontaneous: "Lord Jesus, here we are, gathered together so we can hear your Word. Be with us, Lord Jesus!" From the four-year-old we may even get a spontaneous, "Hi, Jesus. Let's get started!" (As long as it does not pass over into silliness, we should not fear the element of spontaneous humor which will crop up in family worship. If we look at it closely, we will probably discover that the humor arises from the child's vivid sense of *reality.* Jesus is so real to him that he speaks out just as he would to another member of the family.)

Memory Verses. Many programs of Bible study emphasize the value of learning parts of the Scripture by heart. "I have laid up thy word in my heart, that I might not sin against three" (Psalm 119:11). I remember once hearing a man speak who had learned whole chapters of the Bible by heart. As he spoke, he picked up a theme from the fifth chapter of *Revelation.* Then, almost without our realizing it, he was delivering the words of that chapter by heart. I had read that chapter of the Bible many times, yet never had its power—its sheer cadence and melody, its awesome sense of worship—so struck me. And according to this man's own testimony, the value of memorization to his own life and faith was incalculable. The memorized word can have an impact and staying power that will remain with a person all his life.

Family worship offers an ideal setting for memorizing Scripture. The secret of memorization is repetition. Most children have an astonishing capacity for rote learning. (How many television commercials do they know by heart—without any effort at learning them?) A family can memorize a short passage of Scripture each week. In a few years' time the whole family will have laid into their hearts a rich treasure of God's Word.

Sometimes it is helpful to have some kind of simple scheme to follow, when one begins to memorize Scripture. We have arranged some of the great themes of the Bible in alphabetical order. This makes it easy to review what you have learned:

Atonement, I Peter 1:18-19
Believe, Romans 10:9
Confession, I John 1:9
Deliverance, Colossians 1:13-14
Enemies, Ezra 8:31
Father, 2 Corinthians 6:18
Guilt, Romans 3:23
Holiness, Hebrews 12:14
Inspired, 2 Timothy 3:16-17
Joy, Nehemiah 8:10
Kingdom, Revelation 11:15
Lord, Acts 2:36
Mercy, Lamentations 3:22-23
New, 2 Corinthians 5:17
Offering, Psalm 50:14
Prayer, Mark 11:24
Quietness, Isaiah 30:15
Righteousness, Matthew 5:6
Salvation, Romans 1:16
Tithe, Malachi 3:10
Understanding, Psalm 119:104
Victory, I Corinthians 15:57
Witness, Acts 1:8
Youth, Ecclesiastes 12:1

As a family gets into the habit of memorization, they will be led into some challenging adventures, even memorizing whole chapters together. The children can be asked to say the memory verses in their own words from time to time, to keep it from becoming purely mechanical. But where it occupies a small time in family worship, there is not great danger that memorization will become sterile.

Reading. Through the written word we can invite into our homes the saints of God in all ages. The apostles of the New Testament, the prophets of the Old Testament, as well as modern-day saints can sit down in our family circle and share their faith with us.

During the first ten years of our marriage, family devotions were a total flop. We tried first one thing, then another. Nothing lasted for more than a few days or weeks. We couldn't seem to get off the ground. The missing element was a lively sense of sharing the witness of a fellow believer, through the written word. We seemed to be "doing" the daily devotion, rather than *receiving* it.

One day we sort of relaxed and read the children a story out of *Egermeier's* Bible Storybook. The next day came the enthusiastic request, "Let's read another Bible story!" And so it began. Day by day we invited this gifted storyteller into our home, to share her love of God and of His Word. Bible stories wear well! When we were nearly finished with *Egermeier's,* I remembered that we had a copy of *Hurlbut's* Bible Storybook, which my mother had given me for my tenth birthday. Its vocabulary and choice of material are slightly more advanced than Egermeier's, so it is suitable as the children get older.

Jesse Lyman Hurlbut was a masterful storyteller. "One of the earliest recollections of my childhood," writes Charles Hurlbut, "is sitting with a group of other children, with my father in the center and a huge Bible on the table in front of us. The Bible was unusual, for it had a full-page woodcut on alternate pages. From the Creation to the Last Judgment, it was all there—the greatest picture book that any child could ask for.

"Nothing thrilled us more than to sit on his knees to hear him tell the stories as he turned the pages. Not only his own children, but all their friends flocked to these little gatherings, so that 'hearing Bible stories' became a standard diversion in the neighborhood.

"The old Bible was completely worn out before the story-telling period ended, for it extended over two complete generations of children. In the process, by long practice, my father learned the language that holds a child's attention and the way to make a story real to him. . . ."

So here was another one of God's people whom we could invite into our home each morning. *Hurlbut's* Bible Storybook is particularly good because it is designed to lead the reader to the Bible itself; the language of the Bible, or a language similar to the Bible, is used. Far from becoming bored as we went through the stories a second and then a third time, on many days the children would beg us to go on and read the next story—they knew what was coming and they couldn't wait.

We invited John Bunyan into our home to tell us his great allegory, *Pilgrim's Progress.* Dr. D. Vaughan Rees, an Anglican missionary, told us the inspiring story of *The Jesus Family in Communist China.* One of our most delightful guests was *Billy Bray,* the Cornish coal miner whose story has been compiled by F. W. Bourne. Billy's stirring conversion experience, his lively faith, and his tangles with "old smutty face," the devil, filled our household with Billy's own infectious joy in the Lord.

As the children grew older, we read from the Bible itself. Matthew, John, Luke, and the chroniclers of the Old Testament came one by one to share their faith with our family. We didn't rush this encounter, but took it slowly, savoring it, a few verses each day. For these guests sometimes speak a great deal in just a few words, and it takes some pondering. We would go around the family circle, each one reading a verse. After each verse, the person sitting one away would paraphrase the verse, saying it in his own words. In this way even the youngest child will stay abreast of the reading.

David Wilkerson visited our family devotions for a month or so, and told us about his experiences with teenagers who were hung up on dope—in his book, *The Cross and the Switchblade.* This is pretty strong medicine for children, but it is the world they live in. Dope traffic is becoming a problem down into the junior high and even the elementary school level. Children need to know its fearful consequences. But even more important, from the standpoint of our family worship, David Wilkerson shared with us his own vibrant faith that 'the power of Jesus can break every chain.'

We have found that our reading of the Bible itself is enlivened when we intersperse it from time to time with these visits from Christians, past and present. They serve to illustrate and apply the truth of Scripture, so we see more clearly its relevance and reality.

Dramatization. Study the instructions which God laid down for worship in the Old Testament—observe the modes of worship which surround the throne of God in the *Revelation*—it is a *highly ritualistic* worship. It involves more than an edifying discourse for the mind. It calls for ritual into which the whole person enters with his body, with actions, and with his mind also. Simple ritual and dramatization heightens the sense of *encounter* during worship.

Bible stories lend themselves to spontaneous dramatization. After the story has been read, let the whole family act it out. Look for the element of conflict in the story, and build the dramatization around that point, for conflict is the essence of drama. Set up the scene quickly and simply, and enter into it spontaneously. The aim is not dramatic excellence, but participation.

It was no meaningless form that God commanded, when He told the children of Israel to re-enact the great events of their deliverance out of Egypt through a stylized ritual (Exodus 13:5-10). Through re-enactment the truth and reality of the word is conveyed with double force. A little girl who in family worship plays the part of Mary Magdalene at the tomb on Easter morning will capture something of Mary's own awe at encountering the Risen Lord. The boy who plays the lame beggar at the Beautiful Gate of the Temple (Acts 3:1-10), will enter into that mysterious world of faith where miracles really do happen.

Families can develop their own meaningful rituals, to sharpen the awareness of Jesus' presence in their midst. A simple but meaningful ritual is joining hands around the table as the grace is spoken. It symbolizes the family's unity before the Lord, and it enables the smallest child to participate. Or the family may join hands just after the grace is spoken, and greet one another with an appropriate word, such as "Blessed mealtime," "The Lord is with us," or "Blessed are those who are invited to the marriage supper of the Lamb."

Families can also have special times of "celebration." One time we had a "Heavenly Festival." What was the object? To enter into the promise which God holds out for every Christian—that we may enter into the Kingdom, that we may come to the Marriage Supper of the Lamb. Two members of the Mary Sisterhood, from Darmstadt, Germany, were visiting with us, and they prepared this symbolic festival for us in a grove of trees behind our house.

The time for the festival came, and we all lined up. The rules were that we must have the right "password" to get into heaven. Being the first in line, I said with authority, "I'm a Lutheran minister." "That won't get you into heaven," came the reply. "I taught Sunday School for three years," I said, a little more meekly. But no, that answer didn't satisfy either. Then I came with the sure clincher: "I've always lived a good life! I always lived by the Golden Rule!" At that, the Sister sent me to the end of the line! Our youngest son, who was four at the time, could no longer contain himself, "I know the password!" he blurted out. He ran up and whispered to the Sister, "Jesus took my sins away!" The Sister smiled and ushered him into the Heavenly City. (Then he tried to whisper the answer back across the line, so I could get in too!) This was an experience which he will never forget—that we get into heaven not because we live a good life, but because Jesus takes our sins away.

The Festival proceeded according to the Book of Revelation. One of the Sisters took a napkin, enacting the part which says, "He shall wipe away every tear from their eyes—." God's grace flowed down, touching adults who had known real sorrow. The Lord ministered to all of us through that simple childlike festival, in a way which the most eloquent discourse could not have done.

Prayer. Through prayer, preeminently, we present our children to God; we will say something of that a little further on. But in teaching our children to pray, prayer also becomes a vehicle by which we present God to our children. Through prayer they come to know Him as the One who listens and speaks and acts.

How can we teach our children truly to pray? Is there some secret formula which will open up to them the reality of prayer, so it does not become a dull rote? Yes there is: It is the secret prayer life of the parents which stands behind the family prayer time. This, and this alone, will give life and reality to family prayer.

It is good to introduce a note of variety into family prayer. For instance, each day of the week you can concentrate on a different prayer project. At one time our prayer-week ran something like this—

Monday: *The Prayer of Faith.* Each member of the family picks out a prayer project with the objective of obtaining an answer before the week is out. It is important to distinguish between the different kinds of prayer because each prayer has a different objective, and a different approach. If we come to prayer in a vague way, we may pray well enough, but we may pray the wrong kind of prayer for that particular situation. A prayer of faith has as its objective getting a job done. A more detailed descripton of the prayer of faith follows in the next section.

It is a basic prayer. You will incorporate many of its principles into the other prayers that come up during the week.

Tuesday: Prayer for family, far or near. Each one picks a relative or a member of the immediate family, and prays for some specific need which that person may have.

Wednesday: The Lord's Prayer. Here you can introduce interesting variations. The Father can pray the Prayer a sentence at a time. Then the members of the family can offer petitions which make specific each thing the Lord's Prayer deals with. Under "Thy Kingdom come" may come a prayer for the peace of His Kingdom to come in our own home, or in our nation. Under "Forgive us our trespasses, as we forgive those who trespass against us" may come the confession of a resentful and unforgiving attitude toward a playmate.

Thursday: Prayer for missionaries. Each one picks a missionary and prays for him. This helps project the family's concern for Christ's Kingdom 'to the ends of the earth.'

Sometimes it is fun to introduce a note of variety by first praying *silently* for one's particular prayer project. Afterwards, each one can act out his missionary or family member or prayer of faith as a charade, while the others try to guess who or what he prayed for.

Friday: Prayers of confession. Each member openly confesses one sin which has disturbed the peace and harmony of the family. To begin with, this may well be more difficult for the parents than for the children. Children are used to being corrected and chastened within the family, but not the parents. Yet parents, too, stand in need of forgiveness. Here is a setting in which irritations and resentments can be dealt with, not in the context of anger and recrimination, but in the healing light of forgiveness.

One Friday one of our children seemed at a loss to recall anything to confess, and said, "Well, I'm open for bombardment . . ." Brothers and sisters make fine auxiliary consciences! Parents, too, can both give and receive suggestions, in order that genuine sins and hurts are brought out. Of course the parents must watch closely the way in which this kind of thing is done, that no spirit of impudence or bitter accusation enter in. Where it is done in love, it can beget genuine and even deep repentance.

Saturday: Prayers for our church. Each one picks out some aspect of the Sunday services to pray about—Choir, Sunday

School, Sermon, Holy Communion, particular individuals in the congregation—whatever has to do with our common life and worship in the Body of Christ.

On Sundays our worship in the congregation usually takes the place of our regular family devotions, unless it be a special time of song and praise around the dinner table, or by the fireplace in the evening.

Presenting God to Your Children—Through Symbols

"And you shall bind them as a sign upon your hand, and they shall be as frontlets between your eyes. And you shall write them on the doorposts of your house and on your gates."

The way in which we decorate our homes can either dull or intensify our awareness of Jesus. The deep truths of God often go beyond the limits of human language. A symbol can express the truth more simply and more profoundly than mere words. Christian symbols are spiritual windows through which God's truth can shine. If Jesus is the center of our family life, then why should not the decor of our homes reflect that—tastefully, artistically—but outspokenly? A cross, a lamb, the Alpha and Omega, three intertwined circles, a nativity scene—all relate an aspect of God. Through pictures, wall hangings, plaques, tableaux, we can surround our everyday life with a silent heavenly language—a quiet reminder of Jesus' presence in our midst.

The story is told of a woman whose three sons, to her great disappointment, all took up the life of seafaring men. She was relating this to a visitor in the home one day, saying that she could not understand why they had all chosen to go to sea.

"How long have you had that picture?" The visitor inquired, pointing to a large painting that hung in the dining room?

"Oh, for years," the woman replied, "ever since the children were small."

"There is your answer," the visitor said. For hanging on the dining-room wall was the painting of a large sailing vessel cutting smartly through the waves, its sails at full billow, the captain standing straddle-legged on the quarter-deck, his spy-glass in hand, scanning the horizon. Morning, noon, and night—with every meal—the boys had taken into their inner consciousness the sense of high adventure portrayed in that picture. Effortlessly, with never a word being spoken, it had planted in them a hankering for the sea.

The surroundings in the home make a tremendous impact upon the growing child. We want our children to cultivate an awareness of spiritual realities. With little effort and expense, we can surround them with subtle reminders of those realities, so that they will grow up "looking not to the things that are seen, but to the things that are unseen" (2 Corinthians 4:18). Silently, effortlessly, Jesus will convey Himself to the whole family, through the symbols and representations that decorate our homes.

PRESENTING YOUR CHILDREN TO GOD

Hebrews 7:25 portrays the high-priestly role of Jesus. His stance is God-ward. It indicates the basic way in which a priest presents his people unto God—

"He always lives *to make intercession for them.*"

Through prayers of intercession, the parent-priest presents his children to God. Here it is important to recognize the *spiritual authority* which God invests in one called to be a 'priest.' His prayers have power because God has charged him with certain responsibility. He dare not evade this responsibility through any feelings of false modesty. The primary responsibility rests with the father, then with the mother, should the father be absent from the home. Called to be a priest unto his family, the father must come reverently yet boldly before God, and present each one before His presence. The father who undergirds and surrounds his family with his powerful intercessions, has established the family's well-being upon immovable granite.

Family prayer is not merely a beautiful human custom, it is the condition to which God has bound the prosperity of the Christian household. Without it it is impossible to fulfill the solemn obligations of the Christian husband and father. With the help of family prayer he may be successful, but not without it. Outward and inward hindrances may pile themselves up against us, but the man who does not break through them all has never acknowledged his responsibility; he does not know his own dignity nor the blessing which should come through him; he has no idea of the mighty help of Christ, which is assured to him in his office as a father.*

The prayers which we teach our children are integral to Christian family life; they bring the child into personal contact with God. But they cannot become a substitute or replacement for the father's priestly prayers. His prayers are invested with special authority for the provision and protection of his family.

Prayers read from books are like cistern water, in comparison with the living spring, compared to the prayer which rises from the fullness of a father's heart, and brings the wants and thanksgivings of all his house before God the Father Almighty.*

The role of priestly intercessor requires a *disciplined prayer life*. Like a marksman with a rusty rifle, like an archer with an unstrung bow is the parent-priest with a slipshod prayer life. He who has little intimacy with God will secure few blessings for his family.

Presenting Your Children to God—Through Prayer

In the previous section we considered some kinds of prayer that may be used in family worship. Now we want to look briefly, at some kinds of prayer which enrich the parent's personal communion with God, and so equip him to fulfill his priestly role in the family.

The Prayer of Faith

There are four steps in the prayer of faith:

1. *Choose your prayer objective.* There are some qualifications for choosing a prayer objective. First of all, the prayer objective should be one that is about your size.

The story is told about George Washington Carver going

out into the woods for his morning prayer—he was a great man of prayer—and he prayed a prayer for wisdom. He said, "Lord, why did you make the world?" The answer that came was, "Little man, that's too big for you. Ask something smaller." Then he said, "Lord, why did you make man?" And the answer came back, "Little man, that's still too big for you. Ask for something smaller." So he thought for a while and then he said, "Lord, why did you make the peanut?" And the answer came, "That's just your size." And he went, as a man of God, as a man of prayer, into his laboratory and discovered one hundred and fifty-three uses for the peanut, and transformed the agriculture of the South.

You must help the children pick a prayer objective that is about their size. It's ridiculous to pray for the conversion of all the Communists in the world when we can't even cure a common head cold. Prayer is not some kind of magic—prayer is a science, or an art. It is something we learn to do. We grow in it. We become more capable as we enter into it and practice it. We can learn to pray so that we begin to get more and more results. People who get answers to prayer have disciplined themselves and learned the art of prayer. We can teach our children to become such people if we will set ourselves to the job in earnest. But each one must begin where he is, and choose a prayer objective which is within his scope.

Another thing to consider in choosing the prayer objective is: *Does this accord with the will of God?* God won't contradict Himself. We can't twist God's arm to get Him to do something He doesn't want to do. We have to learn what God's will is and then pray according to God's will (I John 5:14). This is such an important point that we put it at the head of the list, not at the tail. If you put it at the tail of a prayer of faith, you ruin the prayer. Have you ever caught yourself doing this? You pray and pray, you put your heart and soul into it, and then you tack on at the end, "If it be Thy will." That sabotages a prayer of faith. Never end a prayer of faith with, "If it be Thy will," Jesus never did that. Before He spoke a prayer of faith He had already determined that it *was* God's will.

What if you don't know whether it is God's will? Then don't pray for it. If you don't know that something is God's will, you have no business praying for it. It would be better then to pray a prayer for guidance and determine what God's will is.

2. *Use your creative imagination.* Visualize that person or that situation the way it's going to be when God enters in. Why do we use the imagination at this point? For this reason: The doorway to faith is buried deep within us. It isn't in the conscious mind. The conscious mind directs us. It is like a steering wheel. But a steering wheel doesn't supply the motive power. That comes from far deeper recesses of our being. And those depths within us do not respond nearly so much to logic and reason as they do to pictured and symbolic representations.

A simple way to check this is to ask yourself: Do you dream in pictures or do you dream in intellectual concepts? You dream in pictures, in symbols. This is the language of the depths. So you impress an image upon the depths of your personality, your consciousness—an image of wholeness, completeness, something into which God has entered. That opens up the doorway of faith, so that God can move in *through you.*

For example, you have a person who is sick and you are praying for him to get well. Don't see him in the hospital bed with that broken leg up in a sling, or all yellow and under-nourished, or whatever else his condition might be. See him well. Or, if that's a little too difficult for you, see a picture of light around him and see a picture of Jesus standing by the bedside and ministering to that person, so that you are bringing the activity of God into the situation through your active imagination. *You see the answer—you don't see the problem.*

Children are good at this. Let them visualize their prayer, describe how it will be when God answers it. Get them into the game, so they are thinking God's thoughts of wholeness. You will be amazed how this can completely transform the situation, because it opens up the deep recesses of the personality to the inflow of God's power. When you have seen the thing with your creative imagination—seen it not as it is, but as it *will be* when God has entered into it—then you are ready for the third step.

3. *Speak the word.* Make the request. "Lord, let your healing power flow into my friend Johnnie and make him well . . . help me to be all quiet and confident inside when I take my science test on Thursday . . ." Speaking it out energizes the prayer, for the word is creative. (But before the word can be filled with power, you have to open the doorway of faith, and that's what the imagination does.)

When you speak something, and speak it confidently, you impress it at several different levels—at the level of your own consciousness, at the level of the consciousness of the other people with whom you are praying, and often with tremendous effect upon the world of unseen powers which surround us.

4. *Give thanks.* Someone comes to your door at Christmastime and says, "Here is a present." You don't know what is in it. You haven't opened it. Yet the only courteous thing to do is to say "thank you," even before you know what is in it. "Thank you" is the language of acceptance. When you have asked God to answer a prayer, and you say 'thank you,' that is the language which accepts the answer. You say, "Even though I don't see it, Lord, I thank you that that prayer is being answered now." Don't say more than you can genuinely believe. There is a difference between presumption and faith. We can be presumptuous with our words and say, "Lord, I know that this person is healed right now." But you look down and they are just as sick as ever. That is mere presumption. If you truly had the faith, they would be well.

But most of us can say without presumption, "Lord, I believe that your healing power is at work in this person now, bringing him toward wholeness . . . I believe that your power is at work to make Susan and Anita friends again . . ." In other words, we speak out to the absolute extent of our faith, and then we end with "Amen," which simply means, "It shall be so." Not, "If it be Thy will." If you have gone through all this and then say, "If it be Thy will," you are really saying,

"I don't know if this is your will or not, and I don't know if it is going to be answered or not"—which undermines faith. Faith is a venturing out 'into seventy fathoms of water,' as Kierkegaard said. It's a daring venture to trust God's Word, regardless of what out fears and potential doubts might be.

The Prayer for Guidance

Sometimes we don't know what God's will is, and so we have to pray that God will show us what His will is. We want to know what God's plan is in a particular matter; oftentimes we have to pray a prayer for guidance before we can pray a prayer of faith. "Make me to know Thy ways, O Lord; teach me Thy paths. Lead me in Thy truth, and teach me, for Thou art the God of my salvation; for Thee I wait all the day long . . . (Psalm 25:4ff). This is the concern of the Psalmist; He wants to know what God's will is. He wants to move in the stream of God's commandment. So he prays a prayer for guidance.

The prayer for guidance begins with a period of waiting. You come before the Lord, and are silent. There is no activity, but rather a passivity. You are trying to hear.

Have you ever been in a situation where there is just a faint sound? You say, "Is that a mouse scratching over there in the corner?" You even quit breathing so you can hear better.

We need to get quiet before God, inside and out. In our day and age that takes some doing. You will be astonished to discover how much noise there is in your mind and in your whole being. If you want to hear God's voice, you have to get quiet. Elijah heard a strong wind, an earthquake, a raging fire. But God wasn't in any of these things. Then, after all the noise, God began to speak to him in a still small voice.

After you have gotten quiet, you state your need: "I want to know Your will in this matter." Then you picture yourself opening up, without reservation. What you are really saying to God is, "Lord, as far as I am concerned, it can go any way, just so it's *Your* way. I am completely open to Your sugges-tions." *Don't pray a prayer for guidance unless you are will-ing to take God's answer*. If you come with a strong will, and say, "Now this is the answer I want to get, Lord, so You tell me if that's okay"—you won't get an answer to your prayer for guidance. *The pre-condition to receiving an answer to a prayer for guidance is absolute openness to God's way.*

His ways are so creative and unique that it will surprise you. A thought that never would have occurred to you will come when you are praying for guidance with absolute openness. In other words, you must be willing to say, "I'll go to the right, I'll go to the left, forward or backward, just so I know it's Your will." When you have that kind of openness, God can truly come and let you know what His will is.

As a final step, you thank Him, even before you may have received the answer. The answer to a prayer for guidance doesn't always come during the prayer time. Often it comes afterward. You have to be open to God's way of bringing answers. He'll bring them through an individual you meet who begins to speak to you about the very thing that you have been praying over. As this person begins to speak, it dawns upon you that this is really your answer, if you have an ear to hear. You may get it out of Scripture. Maybe the next Sunday's sermon deals with the very thing you have prayed about. Sometimes it will unfold through circumstances or it will come through your own inner impressions. God will come to you in various ways, and you must be open to hear it.

The Prayer of Adoration

This is the prayer that opens you to God. You will notice in a worship service that this comes near the beginning—prayers of praise and adoration—because it focuses you on God. Our tendency as human beings is to focus upon ourselves. When you focus on God, in a prayer of adoration, it opens you up to His presence. Here is where you can use songs, hymns—it is good to memorize them and sing them to yourself—or you can make up songs with simple words of praise and adoration.

The Prayer of Meditation

This is the quiet prayer, where you just abide in God's presence. Do you remember when you were first courting, and sometimes you just sat? You didn't talk much. You were just together. The prayer of meditation is somewhat like that —you are just being together with God. You may take a simple word or phrase, perhaps the name of Jesus. You focus upon it and maybe see it in your mind in block letters, or you just say it, over and over again. Or, you may have a specific thing you want to think through, and you are just thinking it through in God's presence—where the conscious mind is not completely in control, nor is it completely out of the situation. You just let the flow of God's ideas enter into the whole process.

The Prayer of Intercession

A prayer of intercession simply means to pray for someone else. One thing you discover in intercession is that often we pray *at* people rather than with people. One of the children, let us say, has a bad temper and you start to pray that bad temper away. It's usually not too successful, because there is a certain element of judgment which short-circuits prayer.

Here is a thought which may prove helpful: When you have a need that you want to pray about—somebody else's problem —visualize yourself taking that person into yourself before you begin to pray. You get a whole new feeling. You are no longer praying at that person. You have taken the person into your heart, and you are now *involved*. God is in you, and in your heart an interaction between that person and God is taking place. Instead of beaming a prayer out to them, you take them into your heart and let God, who is in you, begin to transform that situation. It's amazing how thoughts of judgment and criticism begin to melt away because you've taken that person so close to yourself. It's hard to judge a person who is within you! Holding them within yourself, you begin to pray. You have a much kinder attitude, a more loving attitude, and love is a transforming power. That is a simple mental habit which may help your prayers of intercession.

Arrow Prayers

You shoot off a quick prayer because you are in the midst of your daily work. You don't have time to take off a half-hour for prayer. You pray right now because a situation has come up.

Of course, arrow prayers are only successful, as a general rule, when they are well grounded in the life of prayer. It's the person who is schooled in prayer and praise as a regular thing, who can draw upon prayer in situations of immediate need.

In Nehemiah 2:4, we see Nehemiah coming as the cup-bearer to the king: "And the king said to me, 'What would you like to request?' So I prayed to the God of heaven." Now, Nehemiah didn't get down on his knees and have a half-hour prayer session there in front of the king. He shot off an arrow prayer to God right then, because he wanted God to be in his answer to the king. And God answered Nehemiah's arrow prayer.

You can't find God on the run. You have to be willing to take the time necessary to come into His presence. Arrow prayers, in the midst of daily activities, gain their power from the blocks of time set aside solely for prayer. People who live out of their pockets don't have an adequate diet. Neither do people find the power of God filling their prayers who try to exist spiritually on moments of prayer fleetingly flung toward heaven.

Prayer is a rich and varied experience. It takes time, effort, dedication, But no time is better spent, no dedication more wonderfully rewarded. The promises of God are as great as His boundless love: "*Whatsoever* you ask . . ." (Mark 11:24).

As you enter into a disciplined life of prayer, you will discover certain hindrances and certain helps to prayer—things that *keep* prayers from being answered, and things that *get* prayers answered.

Hindrances to Prayer

One great hindrance to prayer is resentment, or an unforgiving spirit.

The laws of prayer are just as inviolable as the laws of physics or chemistry. Certain things just can't occur until the conditions are right. Jesus says in Mark 11:24, "Therefore I tell you, whatever you ask in prayer, believe that you receive it, and you will." But then he goes on in verse 25 to say, "And whenever you stand praying, forgive, if you have anything against anyone; so that your Father also who is in heaven may forgive you your trespasses." It is a law: If you don't forgive, God can't forgive. It isn't that He doesn't want to forgive, that He is hard-hearted about the thing and expects you to do something before He does it. It's simply a law of forgiveness.

You cannot receive forgiveness if your heart is all clogged up with resentment. If you find yourself resenting a situation or a person, or if there are circumstances which seem to deal you hard blows, you must deal with that resentment.

A woman once told us of an experience which she had had with her daughter. Her daughter had gone off and gotten married without her permission. It filled the mother with resentment. She thought that she had every right to be resentful. She had raised the girl all alone, for the father had been killed in the war. And now the daughter was so thankless as to go off and get married, without even stopping to ask her mother.

The mother was perceptive enough to realize that she herself was out of contact with God, for she was a woman of prayer. She finally went to a priest of her church and said, "You've got to do something. I can't find God." She went for a time into the sanctuary of the church, and there a tremendous understanding unfolded before her inner vision, an understanding of the power of forgiveness in Christ, especially of the power of the blood of Christ to cleanse away sin. She said it was as though God came in with a big vacuum cleaner and sucked all resentment out of her.

In the wake of this experience of being cleansed from a terrible resentment, she came to a deeper knowledge of its nature. She saw, in the first place, that the resentment was sin on her part. What the daughter had done was between the daughter and God. But as far as she was concerned, her resentment of the daughter's action was sin. And then she received an astonishingly deep insight: "You do not lose your contact with God, you do not lose your peace with God, over somebody else's sin, but only over your own sin."

Think about that. If you are disturbed, if you lose your peace with God because of what somebody else did, look closer. *That other person cannot rob you of your peace. The only thing that can rob you of your peace is your own sin.* People did all sorts of things to Jesus, but He never lost His peace. He never lost His contact with God. It didn't get into Him and evoke from Him resentment.

Another thing which blocks prayer is sin or guilt. In Psalm 66:18 it says, "If I regard iniquity in my heart, he will not hear me." In other words, if we have a secret habit of life which we know to be contrary to the will of God, it is an absolute short circuit for faith. Why? Because deep within us, no matter how much we rationalize with our conscious mind, is the conviction that this thing is wrong. Our deep mind refuses to pay the slightest attention to our rationalizations. You may say, "Well, this is a very unusual circumstance." You may argue your conscious mind into accepting it. You may argue your friends into accepting it. It may all sound very nice. But your deep mind (we could also say your *spirit*) doesn't listen. Your deep mind knows what God says about sin and guilt. The door of prayer is slammed tight, and there is nothing that you can do to open it until that issue is dealt with.

Another thing which can block prayer is doubt. The whole basis for prayer is believing and trusting God's Word. The key is just this: *What has God said?* Not, what has man said, or what do I think, but what has God said? Martin Luther prayed like this: "Not the merits of my prayer but the certainty of Thy truth."

Here we have to re-educate the subconscious mind because that is where many of our doubts are rooted down. We may say with our conscious mind, "Oh, I believe! I have all the faith in the world!" But the subconscious mind says, "Oh yeah?" In the subconscious are buried all the fears, doubts, uncertainties that have been shoved down there from childhood. And they don't change overnight. You only change them through a process of re-education and re-experience.

This is where the whole school of so-called positive thinking has its proper place. The deep mind reacts to positive thoughts, positive suggestions. You begin telling yourself, through prayer, meditation, reading the Scripture (reading it out loud!) that "God can be trusted—you can bank on God!" If you keep feeding that into the computer of your subconscious mind, sooner of later it's going to begin feeding back answers of faith. It's just about as simple as that—but *it takes time!* It does not happen overnight. *Faith does not grow in a day.*

Psalm 16:7 has a wonderful promise for us when it comes to the activity of God upon the deeper levels of our consiousness. It says, "I bless the Lord who gives me counsel; in the night also my heart instructs me." Your conscious mind goes to sleep, but your subconscious mind never sleeps. If you go into this seriously, the way every Christian should—the way a scientist or any specialist spends time and dedicates himself to his specialty—you will find yourself waking up praying; you realize that you were in a state of prayer before you woke. That has been taking place in the depths of your mind, as you slept.

So faith must be learned, not only in our conscious mind where we say, "I believe." It must also be learned in the depths of our being. One man has said, "If we would believe the Apostles' Creed, every word of it, there would be miracles happening in every single worship service." That is literally true—if we believed the Creed from our toenails to the top of our head. But we do not. We have deep levels of doubt within us. That is not a word of condemnation, but simply of fact. To know that fact gives us a starting point, so that we can be aware of it and enter into a program of growth.

Another hindrance to prayer is praying for something that is not according to God's will. We stressed the importance of determining God's will in connection with the prayer of faith. Praying in accordance with God's will is a basic condition for answered-prayer (I John 5:14). On the other hand, it may be that something is simply not according to God's priority, or according to God's timing. Maybe it's basically God's will, but you are praying for "three" when you haven't yet prayed for "one." Or you are praying for something that God will bring to pass two months from now, but you want it right now. There may be a whole process that God wants to knit together.

Suppose you are praying for one of the children who has as serious kidney ailment. You want your child to be healed. It may be that God wants to use the whole situation in a redemptive way. In the family there are a whole series of relationships that are going to be knit together, and that will be a part of the healing. You are like a Junior Assistant Carpenter who wants to nail two boards together, but the Master Carpenter sees a whole house to be built. There are certain things that have to be put in order so that the whole job can be done. It doesn't always mean, when a prayer has been delayed, that God isn't going to answer it or doesn't want to answer it. It may mean that there are other factors which have to be taken into consideration.

A final hindrance to prayer is the opposition of Satan. Satan opposes everything that God does, and he is not without power. We have to reckon with that. Daniel prayed a prayer which was not immediately answered. When an angel of the Lord did come with the answer, the angel said, "Fear not, Daniel, for from the first day that you set your mind to understand and humbled yourself before God, your words have been heard, and I have come because of your words." What a wonderful commentary on our prayer-answering God! Then the angel tells Daniel why the answer was delayed: "The prince of the kingdom of Persia withstood me twenty-one days; but Michael, one of the chief princes, came to help me, so I left him there with the prince of the kingdom of Persia" (Daniel 10:13).

He is not talking about an earthly prince here. He is talking about a demonic power which had control over that particular part of the earth's surface. It's what St. Paul calls a "principality" (Ephesians 6:12). Michael is an angel, one of the chief angels of heaven. So here was a prayer answer 'on its way'; a demonic power came and opposed the power of God, and held it back for twenty-one days, until Michael came and made war on it and then the prayer got through. How many prayers are hanging up there 'half-way to earth,' waiting for faith to bring them through? For it is faith and prayer that stimulate God to action. That is why Jesus gives us two parables, urging us to *persist* in prayer for oftentimes prayers won't be answered right away. (See Luke 11:5-13, 18:1-8.)

Helps to Prayer

If you enter into prayer and make a serious business of it, make it a part of your everyday life, you will begin to live no longer out of your own human talents and resources. You will begin drawing on the power of God for your everyday life.

First of all, keep a *daily quiet time with God.* This is simply the discipline and training of the spiritual life which would be comparable to the training and practice of an athlete. When you see an athlete perform a perfectly executed maneuver on a field of contest, you are seeing him at an instant of action. Behind that instant of action is a whole program of discipline and training. He never would have had that instant of perfectly executed action if the discipline and training were not behind it. Nor will you have moments of real encounter with God and moments of answered prayer, if you don't go through the discipline of a daily quiet time with God. This is an absolute essential. If you are not willing to do this, then you might as well forget about prayer. Prayer for you will always be something that you hear about rather than something that you experience.

Anything that you want to do is going to require some of your time. There is no better way to find out what you really put value on than to look at the way your calendar is arranged. What you give time to is what you really consider significant. As you evaluate how much time you give to God, you can pretty well tell how important you really consider Him to be. And, again, your subconscious knows this. If you say, "Oh, I believe in God, and I'm going to serve God, but I'm just too busy for prayer," your subconscious says, "I get it. It's just a big cover-up. It doesn't mean a thing." When you really believe something is important, you make time for it. So that is the first rule, and if you keep that as faithfully as humanly possible, you will discover tremendous changes coming into your life.

Secondly, if at all possible, get into a group where you have the experience of group prayer. You learn from others. There is more power, and special promises, in connection with group prayer.

One last thing to consider is the power that has been invested in the *Name of Jesus*. Jesus said, "If you ask anything of the Father, he will give it to you in my name" (John 16:23). What does it mean to pray in the Name of Jesus? It means to speak to the Father, *not on the basis of who you are, but on the basis of who Jesus is.*

A policeman comes to the door and says, "Open up, in the name of the law!" If he came and said, "This is George Murphy!" you would say, "Who's George Murphy?" But if you hear, "Open up, in the name of the law!" you know what that means. It means that the whole legal system stands behind that uniformed man outside your door, and you have to open —not to him, the person, but to what he represents and stands for. When you say a prayer in the Name of Jesus, you are speaking to God and to all the powers of Heaven in the Name of the Son of God. It means that you are acting in His place, as His representative, in that prayer situation.

There is tremendous power in the Name of Jesus. If you recognize that it's always on the basis of who Jesus is that you come into the presence of God with your prayers, it opens the doorway of faith. Otherwise we fall too easily into the rut of thinking, "Well, things have gone pretty well today. I haven't popped off to the kids, and I didn't snarl at anybody in traffic. It's been a pretty good day." So you pray with a nice, light conscience. "God's well pleased with me today. I've had a pretty good day."

Well, God is pleased with you. There's nothing wrong with that. But that's not the reason He lets you into the Throne Room of Heaven. The reason He lets you into the Throne Room of Heaven is always and only because of who Jesus is, and that you are identifying yourself with Him. Jesus is the only access we have to God. Jesus said, "I am *the* Way." He didn't say "I am *a* Way," but "I am *the* Way." It's because of who Jesus is that I can also come to God when I've had a *rotten* day. "Here I am, God. I'm your child, your problem child, but I still know that what Jesus did is for me and therefore I come." And as you begin to meditate and as you begin to praise God, you discover that He accepts you *that* day, too! He accepts you on the same basis that He does on a good day—because of who Jesus is and because you are identified with Him.

A personal audience with the King of the Universe—that's what prayer is. And God wants us to avail ourselves of it, for ourselves, and for our families.

Presenting Your Children to God—Through Blessing

In addition to the secret work of prayer, a parent will also present his children to God through prayers of blessing which minister directly to the child.

A family in Germany shared with us their custom of blessing the children as they go to bed. The father placed his hands on the head of each child and said the benediction from the service of Evening Suffrages: "Our almighty and merciful Lord, Father, Son, and Holy Spirit, bless you and keep you." We began to do this when our own children were small—even before they could talk. I remember once forgetting to do it. Our little daughter began to jabber and carry on in a stream of baby sounds. When I stepped closer to the crib, she took hold of my hands, placed them firmly on her head, closed her eyes, and waited for the blessing. I knew then that this was no meaningless ritual. She was *receiving* something through that simple blessing. Is not this the very way that Jesus Himself chose to minister to children? "He blessed them, laying his hands upon them" (Mark 10:16).

Family devotions may well include times of blessing on occasion. At the beginning of a new school term, before leaving on a family vacation, in connection with some special event in a child's life, the great festivals of the Christian Church, the father may pray a special blessing upon the members of his family.

When a child is sick, the prayers of the parents should bring that child into the healing presence of Jesus. If a serious illness strikes, the parents may want to call upon others in the Body of Christ to join with them in prayer. But many of the normal ailments of childhood will yield to the believing prayers of a father and mother, for God has vested them with spiritual authority to be used on behalf of their children. This surely does not mean that a parent will not also avail himself of medical help when it is needed, for God brings healing along many avenues, medical as well as spiritual. But that point hardly needs to be stressed, for parents generally recognize the responsibility to care for their children along physical and material lines. What is less recognized is the responsibility —and authority, and power—which God has given parents in the spiritual realm. When parents come to see this priestly role as God sees it, the blessings which they will convey to their children will leave no area of the children's lives untouched.

Father! Mother! God has called you to be priests unto your children. Through that priesthood, Jesus will enter into the life and experience of your home. And already here upon earth, you and your children will experience a foretaste of heaven. "For this is eternal life, that they know thee the only true God, and Jesus Christ whom thou has sent" (John 17:3).

CHAPTER EIGHT

Our Family, a Witness for Jesus

A "witness" is someone who has *experienced* something. You see two cars collide in the intersection—you are a witness, by the very fact that you saw it happen. When a family experiences something of Jesus in their home, they become witnesses for Him. That experience, *and that experience alone,* qualifies them as witnesses. A preacher or a teacher may speak from theory or second-hand knowledge, and say some accurate and quite helpful things. But a witness, by definition, speaks out of first-hand experience.

It is families which are ready to become His *witnesses* that Jesus is looking for today. Around us we see the wholesale breakdown of family life. Our country has never before experienced such flagrant disregard for law and order. Teenagers have no respect for authority. They grew up sassing their parents, talking back to their teachers, and finally they run afoul of the law. Parents opt out of their responsibilities to their children, to society, and to one another. Divorce rates climb. A befuddled society staggers under first one blow and then another struck at the very foundation of its structure.

What our society needs is lived-out examples of good family life—Christian fathers, mothers, sons, and daughters—who quietly begin to live out the kind of family life which God calls us to. In and through these lived-out examples, Jesus will find access into many a heart and home.

Christian families have rarely had a better environment and setting in which to witness for Christ than they have today. We do not say the *easiest* setting. On the contrary, it is one of the most difficult which history has handed the Christian family. But for that very reason the opportunity is unparalleled.

The most hardened pagan will sit up and take notice of a family which has learned to live well together—a family where husband and wife show mutual love and respect, and the children are polite and well-behaved. Those who have not found a good family life nevertheless want to. Those who do not have satisfying relationships in their own homes nevertheless look with favor on those who do. Those who have not raised up their children well nevertheless admire those who have. Those whose families are barren of love and laughter and friendly interchange nevertheless look with undisguised envy at the family up the street which has such a good time together.

A spoken testimony for Jesus has its distinct place and purpose in God's scheme of things. But we live in a day when people have become wary of mere words. They have found it impossible to respond to the sheer volume of words spewed out upon them by modern technology—radio, television, film, press (who reads even a fraction of the items stuffed daily into his mailbox?). Furthermore, people have experienced that highly sophisticated methods of propaganda, employing words, have as often bilked them as blessed them—whether it be on the scale of a nation sucked into catastrophe by the mesmeric words of a dictator, or at the level of a housewife conned into buying a new appliance which she doesn't really need. In self-defense, people have raised up a shield of indifference to mere words.

What a person *sees working*, however, makes him stop and take notice. When he sees a change come into another person's life—a change for the better—he becomes interested: What caused the change? He becomes doubly interested if that change occurs in an area where he himself is experiencing difficulty. He wants to know what the secret is.

This is the opportunity which lies before us as Christian families—to so experience the reality and power of Christ in our homes, to so live according to His Divine Order, that those around us can *see* that something has happened. Then, when the opportunity to speak a word comes up, when we are able to tell something of our life in Christ, it will fall on ears that are ready to hear. Even where direct questions do not arise, the silent testimony of a family which has found the secret of life together with Jesus will say more than many an eloquent discourse.

The kind of witness which our families become for Jesus will depend upon many things, the kind of things we have considered together in this book. Yet there is a *key* to it all, and that key is *faith.*

We want our families to be a witness for Jesus. But we cannot simply decide to "be a witness." Rather, our prayer must be, "Lord, *make* us Your witness." The glory of man is not to do something for God, but to receive what God has for him. It is thus with our salvation, and it is thus no less with our sanctification. We must believe that God is as interested in this project as we are. We must confidently expect Him to reveal and share Himself in our family, and thus make us His witness. It is that very expectation which allows Him to come in and transform our family life. In our families, no less than in our individual lives, God's rule is, "according to your *faith* be it done to you" (See Matthew 9:29).

Christian family life, therefore, is not a simple human possibility. It is not just a matter of putting our mind and our will to it, and building a good family life. Perhaps, even as you have read some of the things in this book, you have thought, "That's just impossible!" And indeed, *humanly* speaking, it is an impossibility. It only becomes possible as we come to see that God is in charge of our families. If we amount to anything at all, it will be because of His doing.

The first step toward acquiring faith is a humble admission of need. A Sunday School teacher was teaching a class of sixth-graders the rudiments of prayer. After some brief instruction she prepared them to actually enter into a time of prayer.

"Get quiet inside yourself," she said, "think about the way things are in the world around you, the way things are in your own families, and then talk to God about it."

There followed some moments of silence, then one little boy called out, "Help!" That was his prayer, and it would be hard to improve on its eloquent brevity.

Family life *does* stand in need of help. The age-old institution of marriage would seem to have been struck a crippling blow amidships. She flounders in a heaving sea of difficulties. Some have begun to abandon ship—the intelligentsia of the West is already prophesying the demise of marriage and the family as we have known it, to be followed by 'a less rigid, more humane social structure.' What can a Christian do in times like these? Where can he turn?

A British film maker put out a movie depicting the ill-fated maiden voyage of the Titanic in 1912. The Titanic ran into an iceberg in the North Atlantic and sank, losing 1200 people. As the story unfolded in a dramatic way, more than once people were heard asking, "Who's in charge around here?" This was the crucial question: Who can direct us in this time of imminent disaster?

The story of the Titanic is not a bad example of the situation of family life today. The family is like an ill-fated vessel which has suffered a disastrous collision. We, also, might well ask: "Who's in charge around here?" Who can save marriage and the family from the disaster which threatens it?

Left to the wisdom and skill of man, marriage may well suffer the fate of the Titanic, its long and often proud history notwithstanding. The pride of man declared the Titanic 'unsinkable.' But man did not reckon upon the mighty forces of destruction submerged in the waters of the North Atlantic. Marriage has weathered many a stormy sea, but forces out of the deep now batter her hull. Hell itself has raised a tempest to cripple and destroy her. Those who close their eyes and ears to what is happening to marriage and the family in our day will be like the nearby ships which heard and saw the Titanic's distress signals, but simply would not believe or accept it . . . for she was unsinkable!

The Titanic went down. The captain, the man in charge, could do nothing to save her. He had the best that man's wisdom, skill, and technology could produce. It was not enough.

The Bible tells the story of another ship. It, too, was adrift on a turbulent, unfriendly sea. The skill and strength of men had done their best, but to no avail. "High waves began to break into the boat until it was nearly full of water and about to sink" (Mark 4:37, *The Living New Testament, Paraphrased*). In desperation the men in that boat turned to One who, curiously, was fast asleep on a cushion at the back of the boat. "Frantically they wakened Him, shouting, 'Teacher, don't you care that we are all about to drown?' Then He rebuked the wind and said to the sea, 'Quiet down!' And the wind fell, and there was a great calm. And He asked them, 'Why were you so fearful? Don't you even yet have confidence in me?'" (Mark 4:38-40).

That boat did not sink, for there was One aboard who had *authority* over the very forces which were threatening it with destruction. Before He left them to return to the Father, Jesus said to His Disciples, "*All authority* in heaven and on earth has been given to me" (Matthew 28:18). If the forces which threaten marriage and the family today were merely human forces, then conceivably man's wisdom could deal with them. But the human factors are only the visible dimension of the problem, like that small part of an iceberg which protrudes above the surface. The great danger—that which truly threatens—remains hidden from view. It is with these forces that we must ultimately reckon. "For we are not fighting against people made of flesh and blood, but against persons without bodies—the evil rulers of the unseen world, those mighty satanic beings and great evil princes of darkness who rule this world, and against huge numbers of wicked spirits in the spirit world" (Ephesians 6:12, LNT). In this field of encounter, human wisdom and human strength count for nothing. Here nothing prevails except *the authority of Christ*. When He takes charge, those forces which are threatening to swamp the Christian family will recede and withdraw. But if we let Him sleep on in the back of the boat, we may well be washed overboard.

This is the simple choice which faces the Christian family today. Will we call out to Jesus, and ask Him to take charge of our homes, or will we keep straining away at the oars of man-made schemes, while the waves around us mount higher and higher?

The first step toward faith, we said, was a humble admission of need. The next step is a humble acceptance of the help which is offered. It is this thing called *surrender*. It is letting God take charge. Writing to Christians in his day, who also faced perilous times, the Apostle Peter put it this way: "Humble yourselves under the mighty hand of God" (I Peter 5:6). Let Him come in and take charge of our families. Let our private wills and hopes and plans and opinions be surrendered to His sovereign presence.

What does it mean for Jesus to "take charge"? Assuming that we recognize the need, assuming that we raise the cry for help, assuming that we make this step of surrender—what may we expect to follow, in terms of practical results?

The Apostle Peter suggests that when we humble ourselves under the sovereign hand of God, He takes charge of three basic concerns of our life. He takes charge of our sense of personal *worth,* our quest for personal identity; He takes charge of our *worries,* the practical problems that press in on us in everyday life; He takes charge of our *warfare,* the spiritual struggle against the powers of destruction and evil. These three concerns, seen as a whole, demonstrate the comprehensiveness of His care for those who surrender to His Lordship. He pays attention to the most intimate yearning of the heart, the most immediate pressure of circumstance, yet He never loses sight of the ultimate destiny which He has appointed for those whom He names as His own.

He Takes Charge of Our Worth

Every person needs a sense of personal identity or worth. But we live in a time of great confusion and contention over the question of one's worth. Striking workers insist they are worth more pay. Protesting demonstrators insist they are worth a fairer shake in the economic and social scheme of things. Teen-agers insist they are worth more respect and consideration in home and school. Parents feel that they are entitled to more respect. The overall emphasis in much of this is upon one's *rights.* A person has a certain number of rights which he can claim because he's worth something. God begins at a different point. He begins not with our rights, but with our *duties.*

"Humble yourselves under the mighty hand of God." God uses a strong hand in dealing with His own children. Jesus was winsome, convincing and open as He dealt with those who stood far off. But when He dealt with His disciples, He dealt with greater strictness and discipline. The closer you come to Jesus, the mightier becomes His hand upon you.

Often the testimony of new Christians runs something like this: "I became a Christian and my problems were solved; my business improved, my family life improved." Often this is true, but it is not the whole picture. There is the other aspect also: "When I became a Christian, my life got all tangled up. Everything went wrong . . . things I never even thought of before began to be a problem." God's strong hand is upon us. The response to that is, "Humble yourself." Accept His strong hand . . . because He has taken charge.

When God takes charge of us in our families, the first step we take is to humble ourselves under His dealings with us. He begins to show us something about our duty. He doesn't talk to us about our rights. He says, "Humble yourself under My hand. I have a plan for you. I have taken over. I am in charge of the kind of person each one of you is to become, the kind of family, the work you do, and all the different circles in which you move." The human way of demanding rights often ends up in bloodshed, warfare, frustration, and defeat. God's way of beginning first with duty, and humbling ourselves under His mighty hand, ends like this: "In due time he will exalt you." When God takes charge of our worth as persons and families, this promise is imbedded in the very act of taking charge: He will exalt you, in due time (I Peter 5:6).

In a quiet way this conviction must be cultivated in our homes: What we amount to with other people is secondary; the important question is, "What do we amount to *with God?*"

Lars W. Boe, a college president of an earlier generation, said unashamedly, "This college is dedicated to God, with no apologies to men." Why are we so afraid of laying it on the line like this, for ourselves and our families? At one time, in our family devotions, we read the story of an indigenous Christian fellowship in China. Their name, literally translated, meant "The Jesus Family." Somehow that phrase struck us, and we said one day around the breakfast table, "Now isn't that what *we* want to be—a 'Jesus family'?" What do we amount to with Jesus? That's what counts. Let's try to please *Him*, and let Him worry about our status and reputation with other people.

The father who lives by this truth will save himself and his family much fruitless "striving." Suppose you are moving up in the executive structure of a corporation. What a relief to know that God is in charge of your promotion—not the vice-president who sits over you, nor the fellow who is competing for the next step up—but *God*. He is in charge because you have surrendered your life to Him, and your job therefore becomes an avenue for serving *Him*. In a deep and fundamental sense, *you are working for God.* "Whatever your task, work heartily, as serving the Lord and not men" (Colossians 3:23).

Children who are raised with this kind of an ideal may not always find it easy to live by. The standards and status symbols of the world can exert some mean pressures on children. A mother once told us that her teen-age daughter had called up her date for the senior prom and said, "I've heard about some of the things that are being planned for after the prom, and I wanted to give you a chance to break our date while you still have time to get another one, because when I go on a date, Jesus Christ always goes with me." That's about as 'square' as you could get in some circles. The boy took her up on it, and broke the date. She didn't go to the prom. And she cried some because of it. It is not always easy to be a witness for Jesus. Yet He gave her something more lasting and precious than the attentions of a high school boy friend—the sense of worth which comes from *His* approval.

It is inevitable that in order to be approved by God we must sometimes suffer ridicule and rejection by people. This is what it means to be a Christian, and we should never try to sugar-coat it or hide it from our children. Yet in the midst of that ridicule and rejection one can know the quiet joy of an un-broken communion with Him. And beyond lies the promise, 'in due time, He will exalt you.'

What is our reputation, what is our worth?—in the eyes of our neighbors, in the eyes of one another, in the eyes of the community, in the eyes of Daddy's employer, in the eyes of the church, in the eyes of the kids at school, in the eyes of the government, in the eyes of Mother's friends, in the eyes of the town businessmen, in the eyes of society, in the eyes of relatives? Families that turn this whole question over to Jesus are free to enter into each of these relationships as a witness for Him. They are no longer tyrannized by the fear, "What might they think of me, or do to me?" They do not have to worry about their standing, for they have obtained a standing with Him, beside which all human approval or disapproval pales into insignificance.

Tom Skinner, a Negro evangelist who used to be the leader of a teen-age gang in Harlem, offered some level-headed ad-vice when he said: "The Bible tells me that I am seated with Jesus Christ in the heavenly places, which puts me in the highest social level in all the world. Therefore, I do not have to picket, demonstrate, pray-in, sit-in, wait-in to get social acceptability. Why should I break my neck to get into a so-ciety that is inferior to the one to which I already belong . . . I am already loved and accepted. All I ask is the privilege to love you." Mr. Skinner said this in reference to some of the struggles of his own people to achieve fair treatment in our society. Yet it is a word which any Christian family could well take to heart.

He Takes Charge of Our Worries

"Cast all your anxieties on him, for he cares about you" (I Peter 5:7).

A person or a family plagued by worry can hardly be an

effective witness for Jesus. He makes us His witness precisely by delivering us from worry—by taking our anxieties upon Himself.

But how? How does Jesus take charge of our worries? Or, to see it from the other end of the stick, how do we cast our anxieties on Him? This involves more than a mental act. For even though worry is a psychological state, it is related to factors outside one's mind. And God does not invite us to cast merely our mental attitude on Jesus, but to cast on Him that which brings on the mental attitude. Whenever a worry comes up, one must pray for the wisdom to see just how to convey it over to Jesus.

Every family faces situations and choices which can become a breeding ground for worries—little ones and big ones. What about the playmate who seems to have a bad influence on one of the children? What courses should the Tenth Grader sign up for? What should we do on our summer vacation? Should a 16-year-old go steady? Should Mother go to work, to help set aside money for the kids' college education?

One way to convey family worries to Jesus is to practice what might be called "family focus on Jesus." This simply means that the family habitually focuses on Jesus, so that its worries and concerns are always seen in the light of the question, "What does Jesus think about this?"

This is not an emergency measure, but a *habit*. You focus on Jesus as you put the children to bed, and talk with them about a problem in school. You focus on Jesus as you get up and begin to plan your day. You focus on Jesus as one of the teen-agers tries to decide what courses to take in high school. You focus on Jesus as you consider a new job offer. The family is not ashamed to put Jesus at the center of its life, and habitually bring things into focus around Him.

You cannot cast family worries on Jesus if you are trying to arrange your life in all kinds of self-chosen patterns, with Jesus over at the side as a Sunday activity. He will take charge of a worry only when you truly 'cast it upon Him,' which means that He is then free to handle it in His own way.

A young housewife in our congregation once came to me

and said she was thinking of going to work, even though she had two small children. Her husband needed some additional schooling, which would reduce their income for a time. She didn't see how they could make it, unless she were to go to work. We talked about it, and I told her that at this point in life her children needed her more than they needed what that additional money could buy. Half jokingly, I said, "You'd better get used to beans for a while, and stay at home."

That evening her husband came home and said, "I've been thinking about this thing all day, and it just isn't right for you to go to work. We'll have to make out some other way."

"That seemed a clear confirmation of God's will," she said later, "and I accepted it—even though I hate beans!" The worry left. She saw clearly what Jesus had to say about it, and she let Him take charge of it.

A few days later a young widow called to see whether we knew of anyone who could take care of her little boy during the day, while she worked. She had been carting him to a succession of temporary babysitters, which had been quite upsetting for the child. This other young mother came to mind. They got together, and their two separate problems meshed together as if they had been made for each other. Even down to the finances—the amount the young widow could afford to pay was the exact amount which the other woman had said she needed to earn, when she was considering going to work.

What about those worries that are more generalized—a low mood, a sense of frustration or discontent, even outright depression? One might call them emotional worries, worries centered around one's own personality and feelings. Here, too, we must look for the practical steps by which we can convey these worries over to Jesus.

Jesus has provided a way. Your emotions are tied to your whole being. When you become a Christian, you are mystically yet truly related to other Christians in what the Bible calls "the Body of Christ" (Romans 12:5). This is more than an interesting metaphor. It is a mystical reality. Your emotional health depends on what you can receive and give within the Body of Christ. When you are down, some other member of the Body of Christ is going to be up. When someone else is down, you may be up, and able to help him. We depend upon one another. "When one member suffers, all suffer together," says Paul. "When one member rejoices," all rejoice together." (See I Corinthians 12:26). This is the way we convey our emotional worries to Jesus: We live as functioning members of His Body, in which the individual members have a care for one another.

One almost hesitates to mention this, for all too often the Church falls short; people everywhere just do not have available to them the kind of caring, praying, loving, burden-bearing, Spirit-filled fellowship which Christ intends His Body to be. Yet where even a few catch this vision of the Church, and begin to practice it, Jesus will begin to take charge of our emotional worries in a remarkable way. This indeed is but a tiny part of the Church's total function, yet to one burdened with emotional worries, it can be like an oasis in the dehumanizing desert of our present culture.

We have already suggested in an earlier chapter the specific way in which we convey our economic worries to God: We give the first tenth of our income back to Him. That is the simplest answer you'll ever find to economic worries. When you give your tithe to God, it's like planting a seed in the ground. In due time it will yield a harvest. That's exactly what the Bible says. Any father and husband needs to be concerned about his economic circumstances. That's his job, as breadwinner and provider. In order for a father to provide for his family according to God's plan, he takes the first ten percent of his income and gives it to God. He cares about your finances and lets you cast that burden upon Him—in this specific way. Families that cast their worries on Jesus will not have to think up ways to "witness." God *makes* them His witness, by letting them experience His care.

He Takes Charge of Our Warfare

"Be sober, be watchful. Your adversary the devil prowls around like a roaring lion, seeking someone to devour. Resist him, firm in your faith . . . and after you have suffered a little while, God will himself restore, establish, and strengthen you" (I Peter 5:8-10).

Family life today is beset with many conflicts. As you encounter these conflicts under many different circumstances, you begin to see some significant similarities: People are often confused as to just who the real enemy is; they do not know precisely what is expected of them in the conflict; and they do not seem to know where it is all leading.

First of all, then, we do not know the 'enemy.' The conflict in a home may appear to be between a husband and wife, between children and parents, between outside social pressures and family standards. Yet often people make statements like this: "I feel like there's something wrong, but I can't put my finger on it. . . . That house just bugs me—I feel like I have to get out of it, or I'll go nuts. . . . We start out in a good discussion, and the next thing you know, we're yelling at each other, and nobody knows who started it . . . all of a sudden he's afraid, afraid of everything, and we can't figure out why. . . ." It's as though one were plagued by an unseen enemy.

Secondly, we do not know what to do when conflict besets our home. Today we see a confusion of roles in the family. The husband doesn't know what it means to be the head of his home. The wife doesn't know what it means to be a homemaker, living under her husband's protection. The children are confused as to who's what, and just where they fit into the whole scheme of things. We are caught up in conflict, but we don't know what is expected of us.

Thirdly, we do not have a clear vision of just where all this conflict and struggle are leading. We just know we're having trouble. A successful executive once said to me: "I don't know where I'm going. I've done all right, I've battled my way to the top—many would call me successful. But I don't know where I'm going. I feel like I'm stumbling in the dark."

We don't know who our enemy is. We don't know what's expected of us. We don't know where we're going. Into this situation of confusion Jesus comes to take charge of our warfare.

The first thing He shows us is who our enemy really is. "Your adversary the *devil* prowls around like a roaring lion, seeking someone to devour." Behind international conflict, behind social conflict, behind personal and family conflict lurks the Master Agitator, the Master String-Puller—Satan.

Jesus recognized this. In Matthew 16:23, in His close circle of disciples, Peter begins to remonstrate with Jesus, and say, "God forbid, Lord! This shall never happen to you. Go up to Jerusalem and be crucified? This shall never happen to you!" Right away Jesus sees who it is, and says, "Get thee behind me, Satan." He arcs right past Peter and speaks to the power that is agitating Peter at that moment.

Paul knew the same thing. He says in Ephesians 6:12, "We are not wrestling against flesh and blood (human beings), but against principalities, powers, thrones, dominions, the spiritual hosts of wickedness in the 'leavenly places."

You and I are fighting against these same spiritual forces. Those who dismiss such things as superstition, saying that Jesus and His Apostles were 'prisoners of a naive first-century world-view,' display their historical ignorance, and no small bit of intellectual conceit. A thoughtful reading of history will show that the world-view current in Jesus' day, which took seriously the non-physical as well as the physical realm, was held in the West until well into the 13th Century, and in the East has never disappeared. It wasn't until Thomas Aquinas re-discovered Aristotle that the intellectual climate in the West began to change. The great Fathers of the Church, who gave us our Trinitarian Faith, were no intellectual dwarfs. And they all took seriously such things as angels, demons, miracles, revelation—the direct action of the spiritual realm upon the natural realm. This does not mean that they were dreamy-eyed mystics. They simply included ALL of reality in their thinking and consideration—did not limit it to material reality, as we have done in the West.

It is sheer intellectual conceit which supposes that Jesus' knowledge of the spiritual realm was 'naive first-century thinking.' Jesus and His Apostles knew more about spiritual reality than any of our most modern theologians. When they spoke to demons, and cast them out, they were not making a concession to the prejudices and beliefs of their time. They were dealing with spiritual reality with a power and authority which we in the Church today can only wistfully imagine.

The notion that we have advanced in spiritual understanding over the early Christians is based on faulty reasoning. We have advanced in our knowledge of the *material* world, but precisely because of our preoccupation with the material world, we have undoubtedly retrogressed in our comprehension of the spiritual realm. This only makes sense. When you begin to specialize in any particular field, by sheer dint of time-limitation, you are forced to neglect other things. Most adults would flunk a high school math test cold, a few years after graduation. By concentrating on other fields, they inevitably retrogress in their facility with math. What is true of an individual becomes true of a culture. We in the West have absorbed ourselves in the exploration of the realm of physical, material reality—to the neglect of the spiritual realm. Steinmetz, the great electrical wizard, saw this clearly. He said that if we would put the same kind of effort into spiritual research that we have put into scientific research, we would experience greater spiritual advance in the next 200 years than in the past 2000. Far from having progressed beyond the early Church, we have actually retrogressed. We have a less sure understanding of the spiritual realm than Paul and Peter.

Why is it important for Christians to recognize this? What can this possibly have to do with Christian family life? It is this: In the spiritual realm, there is not only God, and good—there is also Satan, and evil. You cannot accept the reality of God unless you also accept the reality of Satan. The Bible speaks of both in identical terminology, as personal beings. When you do not reckon seriously with the power of Satan—when you do not put on Christ's armor! (Ephesians 6:10-18) —then Satan tends to have his way with you. You and your family become a football, which he can kick around more-or-less at will.

When God takes charge of our warfare, He opens our eyes

to see who the real enemy is. You can test this in your own experience. When you find yourself getting unaccountably irritated with a person or impatient with a situation, 'step back.' Let the Lord give you an awareness of the agitating activity of Satan. He may be beaming a thought or an attitude into your mind. (See John 13:2, 27). It's necessary to recognize this. You must step aside and disassociate yourself from that which you accepted as your own feeling. You say: "That's the enemy! Get behind me, Satan!"

It's amazing to see the complexion of the situation change. That person isn't so irritating after all. That impossible situation isn't as impossible as you thought it was. Then you realize that you have been under attack by an exceedingly clever enemy. Surely this does not mean that a person begins to attribute all difficulties to the activity of Satan. Human failure and plain old cussedness still account for their share. What we do mean is that we should not fall into the opposite error, so prevalent in our Western culture, of attributing *nothing* to satanic agency.

Secondly, when Jesus takes charge of our warfare, we learn what is expected of us. "Resist Satan, firm in your faith, knowing that the same experience of suffering is required of your brotherhood throughout the whole world." This is the great theme of embattled Christians: Endure—*endure*—ENDURE. Stick it out. Don't panic. Don't stop until you've reached the end of the race. "I have fought the good fight, I have *finished* the race," Paul could say as he was ready to be martyred (II Timothy 4:7).

Have you and your family finished the battle that God has out you in right now? Or is your call yet to endure for a little while—knowing that the same experience of suffering is required of Christians elsewhere in the world? Jesus Himself was perfected through suffering (Hebrews 2:10). He couldn't run away from it. He had to go straight through it.

This means that a Christian family must learn to say an initial 'yes' to its situation. Every morning when we wake up, we must say, "Yes, Lord . . . yes, to that which you put in my pathway today."

Finally, we know the outcome. The world doesn't know its enemy, it doesn't know what's expected of it, and it doesn't know where it is going. But the Christian knows who the real enemy is. He knows what's expected of him. And he knows the outcome—Victory! "For after you have suffered a little while, the God of all grace (the God whose love is active on your behalf) will himself restore, establish, and strengthen you." This God, who has called you to His eternal glory in Christ, will restore, establish, and strengthen you in His own time.

The Christian family reckons upon a God who is a God of battle, a God who wins victories. When God takes charge of our warfare, then we can reckon upon His promise: In His time He will strengthen and establish us in victory.

Such a family, one in which He has taken charge, will be His witness. As a family, and individuals, they know their worth —they are children of the King. They experience His fatherly care. They abide under the shadow of His strong right arm. Anyone who comes to know them at all will sense that they live under the authority and blessing of a power beyond themselves.

This is what Christian family living is really all about— living by a power beyond ourselves. The kind of things we have considered in this book—teaching, discipline, authority and responsibility, inter-personal relationships, even the life of worship—are mostly mechanics. The mechanics are important. Without them the power has no avenue of expression. But what we need above all is the power itself. Or, let us say, the Power Himself. For the Christian family founds its life and hope upon the faith that the Lord to whom its life and words testify, the Lord whom it awaits with eager longing (Behold, He is coming with the clouds, and every eye will see him! Revelation 1:7), the very God of heaven and earth— this Lord has already taken up His dwelling in the circle of their family, there to manifest beforetime a likeness of His Kingdom, a foretaste of that Day when He will dwell with them, and they shall be His people, and God Himself will be with them (Revelation 21:3).